Curious Unschoolers

Sue Elvis

Susan Elvis

P.O. Box 57, Hill Top

NSW, 2575

Australia

ISBN-13: 978 0 9925588 7 1

For Deb Lewis

Without your love and encouragement, I would never have finished this book.

Contents

Curious Unschoolers

Have you ever thought about the word 'curious'? Depending on how we use it, it could mean:

marked by a desire to investigate and learn

Or it might mean:

exciting attention as strange, novel, or unexpected

So do curious unschoolers have a desire to investigate? Or are they strange, odd or eccentric people who excite attention? Or could both be true?

Part I: An Introduction

Something Important

I've got something very important to share with you.

I want to tell you about unschooling: what it is and how it has changed our family's life and why I think everyone should do it. I'm passionate about unschooling. I hope my words are going to make you feel excited about it too!

If you're already unschooling, maybe you'll relate to my stories. If you're feeling alone in a crowd of people taking the more conventional path, you might be thinking, "Are the critics right? Are we crazy because we unschool?" Will you find it reassuring to hear that we're a bit crazy too? A good kind of crazy. Yes, we're not like everyone else. But that's okay. Actually, I think being different is a good way to be!

And if you haven't yet set out on your unschooling adventure, I hope that when you arrive at the last page of this book, you will say, "Hey, I want my family to be unschoolers too!"

So what am I going to tell you? Will I say, "Unschool and everything will be wonderful"? Will my stories convince you that my family is living a perfect life? No. My kids aren't perfect. I'm not a perfect mother. And life isn't one long and exciting and enjoyable adventure just because we unschool.

Then why am I writing about unschooling if it isn't a perfect way of life? Am I just another voice in the crowd? Are we all shouting about how we've found the best way to live when none of us has? Or is unschooling truly a way of life that is different from everything else?

I believe unschooling is different because it's all about unconditional love. I want to show you how choosing to unschool will result in a love so powerful it will encourage, not only our kids but us as well, to become the people we are all meant to be.

Unconditional love? Surely unschooling is all about giving kids the freedom to learn what they like? How do we get from that to love? It's a long story. Or maybe lots of shorter ones. Stories contained in two books:

Curious Unschoolers

and *Radical Unschool Love*

Curious Unschoolers focuses mainly on the educational side of unschooling. And *Radical Unschool Love* is about the parenting side of unschooling. The two books do overlap a bit because, in real life, parenting and education are woven closely together.

I hope my two books will give you the full unschooling picture!

The Friend Who Comes to Tea

I open my laptop and plug in my mic. After hitting the 'record' button, I say, "Hi, I'm Sue Elvis from the blog Stories of an Unschooling Family. Welcome to my podcast!"

Soon I'm pondering ideas and thoughts as I share my family's stories. And although I might look like I'm all alone, speaking to myself, I'm not. I'm chatting to my listeners who will soon be tuning in to my latest unschooling episode.

My voice travels all around the world while I stay at home in Australia. Isn't that a fascinating thought? And in this way, I'm with people as they run, walk, fold washing, sweep floors, knit, weave, and drive along in their cars. And I'm also in kitchens. At the table, maybe. With tea and biscuits.

I'm the friend who comes to tea and chats about unschooling.

"Sue Elvis comes to my house for tea. Or so I imagine every time I listen to her podcast."*

And I feel honoured to be invited in and welcomed as a friend.

Of course, that's podcasting, and this is a book. And although the situation is different, I'd still like to speak to you as a friend. As you read these pages, perhaps you can imagine us sitting around your kitchen table, mugs in our hands, chatting about unschooling together.

I'm going to share my family and our experiences. We'll ponder ideas and thoughts. Our conversation will go deep and wide. It'll be honest and real. And it'll be flavoured with love and gentleness.

I hope that you're going to get excited about the possibilities. I want my words to encourage you, if you haven't already done so, to set out on an unschooling adventure of your own.

The quoted words come from a podcast review written by Samantha.

Just in Case We're Not Already Friends

Maybe we're already friends. Perhaps we often sit around the kitchen table chatting about unschooling. But just in case we haven't shared tea and conversation, I'll begin by introducing myself.

I'm Sue Elvis, and I'm an Australian unschooling blogger, YouTuber and podcaster at Stories of an Unschooling Family.

I'm married to Andy, who is a loving and supportive husband, an unschooling dad, and a primary school teacher. Andy and I live together with a number of our eight children in a village surrounded by the beautiful Australian bush somewhere south of Sydney.

Our eldest child is Felicity, who was born in 1987. And our youngest is Gemma-Rose who joined our family in 2004. Duncan, Callum, Imogen, Charlotte, Thomas and Sophie fall somewhere in between.

Have our kids ever gone to school? No. Have we always been unschoolers? Unfortunately not. We started as unschoolers, but I got distracted. I led my kids down lots of other pathways before we made our way back to where we began, to the place where we belong.

You'll find out more about my family and me and our unschooling journey as you read this book. I'm going to share lots of our stories.

A Book of Stories

Stories capture the imagination. They create pictures in our minds. As you read my stories, I hope they'll give you a concrete picture of what unschooling can look like in action.

Each story contains a piece of unschooling. Each piece will illustrate some principle or thought or idea. Sometimes the same piece will appear more than once, presented to you from a different angle in a different story. By the time you get to the end of this book, I hope all the pieces fit together, like a completed jigsaw puzzle, to form a good picture of unschooling.

Although I wrote a lot of new stories for this book, I've also included some that I wrote for my Stories of an Unschooling Family blog. I edited and expanded many of these stories. But there are a few that I decided to leave alone. Maybe they'd lose something if I tried to update them: my excitement, worries, joy, whatever I was feeling at the time when I first rushed to my computer and tapped out my thoughts. These stories capture moments in our unschooling life in a way that's impossible to replicate when writing from a distance. I have included the ages of my children in these older stories to give you a rough idea of where our family was on our unschooling journey at the time of writing.

I've arranged my stories according to the subject matter. However, a story may belong to more than one category. Everything overlaps, just like in real life.

How should you read this book? You could start at the beginning and read the stories in order. You could head straight to a topic you'd like to know more about. Or you could dip in here and there, reading stories as their titles catch your attention. Any method is good as long as you read my book!

Part II: An Introduction to Unschooling

What is Unschooling?

Maybe you've heard that unschooling is a method of homeschooling where a child doesn't use a curriculum or a plan put together by a parent. Instead, parents allow their children to learn, in their own way, what interests them. Parents believe that their kids will learn all that they need to know at a time when they need to know it.

That's all true. And that's how I understood unschooling when we first started out many years ago. But since then, I've learnt that unschooling has many layers. Peel off one, and there's another underneath waiting to reveal something else. It's as rich as life itself. Maybe that's because unschooling is about learning from everything we do and experience in life. Life is deep and complicated. So is unschooling.

Here are some other things I've discovered about unschooling:

Unschooling is about fulfilling our missions in life. We're all born with talents. Everyone has passions and interests. They are part of who we are. Unschooling is about having the freedom to develop those talents and follow our interests so that we can contribute to the world.

Unschooling is the way a family lives together. We all learn as we follow our interests and passions. We use and develop our talents. We accept and respect and help each other. We make mistakes, and we forgive. We're growing and developing under the influence of unconditional love into the people we are designed to be. Of course, we're not going to become those people in just a few years. It's a lifelong process.

While we're learning and accepting and helping and forgiving and loving unconditionally, the bonds between us grow strong. Parents and children become closely connected. And this is important because trust is a fruit of connection. We know and trust our kids. They trust us. Trust is essential. It's the foundation of unschooling.

Because unschooling is about learning from everything in life, we shouldn't have to separate education from everything else that we experience. There's no need to think in terms of school subjects. In theory, we can forget about homeschooling. In practice, many of us can't.

Unfortunately, some families, like ours, have to be legally registered as homeschoolers. This means that we have certain legal requirements to fulfil. So in this book, I'm going to be talking about unschooling mainly from an educational point of view.

Why Unschooling Isn't a Method of Homeschooling

Many people think of unschooling as a method of homeschooling. It's one choice among many. We could choose to homeschool our kids in a traditional way and do 'school at home'. Perhaps we might follow the Charlotte Mason method or a classical approach. Maybe we like the idea of notebooking or unit studies.

Or we could choose to unschool.

But is unschooling actually a method of homeschooling? Could it be something very different?

When we first began homeschooling, I didn't think about what method we were going to use. I didn't even realise there were different methods. In those days, there was no Internet and few homeschooling books. I didn't have access to much homeschooling information. But that didn't worry me. I just assumed I'd be able to teach my daughter all she needed to know. Hadn't she already learnt so much with my help in the first five years of her life? It didn't occur to me that I couldn't homeschool my child successfully. I didn't know how we were going to do it, but I had confidence I'd work it out as we went along.

One thing I did know was that we needed some homeschooling friends. I heard about a homeschooling conference and thinking this would be a good place to find like-minded people, we went along. And that's where we heard about unschooling. Suddenly, I realised that there was more to homeschooling than I first imagined. Our approach can make a huge difference. Our attitude towards learning can affect our child's. I started thinking carefully about what I wanted for my children.

At the conference, I heard that unschooling kids can be trusted to learn all they need to know. All we have to do is not interfere with our child's natural learning process. I came home from that conference feeling inspired. We were going to be unschoolers. After soaking up dozens of stories about kids who were doing amazing things, I was sure ours were going to do similar things too.

So we began unschooling our first child, and I couldn't wait to see what she was going to do. But, despite having the freedom to do whatever she liked, nothing much happened. I was very disappointed. How was my daughter ever going to learn all the things essential for a good education if she didn't do anything? Children will learn all they need to know at a time when they need to know it. Is this really true? I began to have doubts.

After a while, my doubts led to 'cheating'. Instead of letting my child discover the world entirely on her own, I began making suggestions about possible things she might like to learn about. I introduced her to such things as poetry and Shakespeare, and I offered to read her my favourite books. And because she responded well, and was obviously learning from this new way of doing things, I decided it was time to stop calling ourselves unschoolers. We had to homeschool in a way that resulted in learning. And that wasn't unschooling. As far as I could see, there was no way unschooling was ever going to work.

Now we might have been okay if we'd stopped right there. We might have discovered that 'cheating' was another word for strewing. And strewing is an integral part of unschooling. But we didn't. I got distracted by other ideas.

I met other homeschoolers who were doing things differently from us. I heard about Charlotte Mason, and classical homeschooling, unit studies, and notebooking. There were many different ways to homeschool. I felt excited! Which one would suit us best? By this time, homeschooling books were becoming more popular. I bought as many as I could. And I pondered lots of questions:

- What are the basics of a good education?

- Are old ideas better than new ones?

- Are the classics important?

- Are some school subjects more important than others?

13

- Do kids pass through different learning stages?

- What books should our kids read?

- Should kids have the ability to listen?

- Is memorisation important?

- Is narration a valuable skill?

- Are short lessons more effective than long ones?

- Is copywork a good learning tool?

- Perhaps making notes helps kids to pick out the main points of a particular subject.

- If they make impressive looking books, does this help them value their knowledge?

- Should learning be fun?

- Should it be challenging?

And while I was pondering, I experimented. My poor children! They were my educational guinea pigs. Yes, we tried all the different homeschooling methods.

I was always full of enthusiasm as I put a method into action. I found the right resources, put the system into place, and then hoped that my kids would soon be producing impressive work, indicating that they were indeed receiving a wonderful education.

And my children did produce some impressive work. They put together interesting lapbooks and beautiful nature journals. They enjoyed hundreds of living books, including many classics. They got excited by music and art. They loved Shakespeare and poetry. But despite these successes, no method lasted very long. We found it hard to keep following the necessary steps: "Do we really have to do this?" Learning soon became a chore, and we'd start battling with each other. I then knew it was time for a change. Perhaps we should try another homeschooling method. Should we return to one we'd already tried? Would it be different this time around? Once again, I'd start reading and researching and thinking.

Homeschooling was turning out to be a lot more complicated than I'd first imagined. With my confidence ebbing away, I faced the fact that none of the homeschooling methods was working. I knew it was time to stop experimenting before my relationship with my kids was damaged beyond repair.

So I gave up trying to follow someone else's ideas and decided to do things my way.

I threw out the things that weren't working for us, one by one. We rejected narration, memorisation, spelling lists, and reading the 'right' books in the 'right' way. I no longer insisted that my kids fulfilled other people's expectations but started listening to them. What were their needs? What was important to them? What were they interested in? Gradually, our homeschooling developed into what I called 'doing our own thing'.

"We read lots of books and follow our interests," I'd say in a vague kind of way whenever anyone asked what method of homeschooling we were using. Of course, by that time, we weren't actually using a method. We'd found our way back to unschooling. The second time around, I understood unschooling better. I realised that not interfering with a child's natural learning process doesn't mean stepping completely back and leaving her to learn entirely on her own. It was quite okay for me to tempt my children with different resources, ideas and experiences. Strewing is an integral part of unschooling.

These days, we're living a rich and interesting life. As a consequence of that, my children are learning. They're learning what's important to them, what they feel they need to know. Their education isn't restricted to what someone else thinks is valuable. They don't need an artificial system imposed on them for learning to take place. My children are learning in a natural way.

When my daughter Sophie was fifteen, she said, "My friend Emma has to finish her school work for the day before she can do all those things she's really interested in. I'm glad we don't have to do that. I'd never have time to do the things that are important to me."

Sophie's words remind me of something I read in an article called *Unschooling 101* by Bridget Bentz Sizer:

Unschooling advocate Sandra Dodd describes a typical 'unschool' day as "the best ever Saturday ... the day people dream about when they are stuck in school."

Deciding not to use a homeschooling method might sound difficult. If you choose to unschool, you won't have a set of steps put together by someone else to follow. Things won't be neat and tidy. You might have to give up your ideas about what a good education looks like and how children learn. All this could be a bit scary.

But if you unschool, you might end up with a week full of the best ever Saturdays. Doesn't that sound good?

Does Unschooling Work?

Living a life full of Saturdays sounds wonderful, doesn't it? But can we afford to let our kids live without the other days of the week? Will they really learn all they need to know to be successful in later life? Or will we jeopardise their futures if we unschool?

I suppose the big question is: does unschooling work?

Perhaps you're wondering how unschooling children turn out. Do they gain the skills that will let them do what they like with their lives? Do they get good grades? Will they be able to compete with school leavers and other homeschoolers, especially the ones who have used a structured curriculum, and go on to study at university? In other words, do they get a good education?

Yes, they do.

If an unschooler wants to go to university, he or she will get there. I have five young adults who've studied at university level without any problems. My eldest son Duncan has a Bachelor of Arts degree in Communications as well as a Master's of Teaching (primary). He's also a qualified chef. Imogen has a Bachelor of Arts degree in Professional Writing and Publishing. And Charlotte is currently finishing a Bachelor of Arts degree majoring in Digital Design. Two of my other young adults completed part of a university degree (with success) before deciding to go along other pathways.

So how did my children get into university? As unschoolers, they followed their passions. Then later, they decided to study these passions at a higher level at university. They knew more than enough about their subjects to pass some preliminary university units and be accepted into the courses of their choice. Their enthusiasm helped too!

But is following passions enough? Will our unschoolers know all they need to succeed in life? Will they have all the basics? I guess it depends on what we mean by basics. What is the essential knowledge that our children should have? There are many different educational curricula, which makes me think that no one can agree on what is essential knowledge and what isn't. We can't make a list of basics that will satisfy everyone.

We could decide for ourselves what is necessary for a good education. Or we could let our kids decide what's important to them by allowing them to follow their interests and their passions. By doing this, they will retain their curiosity and love of learning. I think that's enough to ensure our children will be successful in life.

John Holt said: *Since we can't know what knowledge will be most needed in the future, it is senseless to try to teach it in advance. Instead, we should try to turn out people who love learning so much and learn so well that they will be able to learn whatever needs to be learned.*

The world is changing very fast. In ten years, it will be very different from today's world. How can we prepare our kids for a world we don't know about? We can't. But what we can do is give our children a love of learning. Encourage them to be self-motivated learners. Then when they don't have the knowledge that they need, they'll know how to go about gaining it. They'll have the necessary enthusiasm for chasing that information or skill. Unschoolers won't be at a disadvantage. I think they'll be well ahead!

There's another reason why kids should be allowed to develop their talents. If we let them, they'll use these talents to do important work, work that will affect others. They'll do something that will make a difference to the world.

We also want our children to become people who care about others, who will be full of love and compassion, who know right from wrong. We want to have good relationships with them, feel connected to them, have them want to be part of our lives.

We want our kids to become the people they are meant to be and to fulfil their missions in life. And this is what unschooling is really all about.

So, summing up, if we want our kids to...

- Acquire life skills

- Develop their unique talents
- Be able to get into university if that's what they want to do
- Have a love of learning which will help them cope with an unknown future
- Be their unique selves
- Be happy and confident
- Value family life and have good relationships with us
- Know right from wrong
- Be open to our values and beliefs
- Be able to think for themselves
- Live a purposeful life
- Become the people they are meant to be

...then we can say that unschooling works!

Part III: What Unschooling Looks Like

What Is Unschooling All About?

When we first started homeschooling as unschoolers, I did a lot of standing back. I waited for my children to discover interesting things on their own. I expected the house to fill with impressive projects. But nothing much happened. After a while, I decided that we need to expose our children to the possibilities. I had to surround them with a rich and varied environment. I also had to provide them with an example of learning.

And so I started looking for interesting resources to strew in my children's pathway, though I didn't call it 'strewing'. I'd never heard of that particular word.

I also started sharing learning with my kids, showing them that everyone learns, not just school-aged children. We have to be willing to do everything we'd like our children to do. We can't just say, "Go off and learn something." We have to provide an example of what learning is all about, especially in the early years. Maybe that doesn't sound right. Aren't children born naturally curious and eager to learn?

We play with our babies and surround them with a stimulating environment, and applaud their every little development. But then they get to a certain age, and we stop doing these things. Maybe that's the problem.

I spend a lot of time with my younger girls. I read to them. They read to me. I am willing to help them with any projects they want to do. I share my passions with them. I suggest activities and offer resources. Perhaps a child achieves more if she has an interested person to call upon to share and help when necessary. That person needs to show they value that child's learning. It is real work.

So I am not stepping back and keeping out of my children's way. But this doesn't mean I don't give them space to process what they've learnt, figure out things on their own or just rest. We have to be sensitive and balance our involvement and enthusiasm with our children's needs at any particular moment.

I have noticed that as my children get older, they naturally move away from me. Yes, there comes a time when they are keen to stride ahead on their own pathways without waiting for me. Often they will pause and want to share what they've discovered. Occasionally, they may hit a problem. If they can't solve it for themselves, I can help guide them to a solution. They may just want me to obtain some necessary resources for them or ideas for further investigation. This is where Charlotte (15) is at the moment.

I rarely see Charlotte when she is busy with her learning. She might appear at lunch time eager to share something she is working on. She might want a suggestion for a suitable book to read. She will look at anything I strew, but she won't automatically decide to use it. She has her own ideas about what she wants to do. And I let her learn what she wants, how she wants, and when she wants. I have full confidence that by giving her the freedom to direct her education, she will achieve her goals.

But the younger girls? I am under their control:

"Will you read to us, please, Mum?"

"Can we go to the library, please?"

"Could you show me how to use the sewing machine?"

"Can you explain... ?"

"Do you know how this works?"

"Can we do...?"

They are full of their own ideas:

"I'd like to find out more about the Titanic."

"I want to learn how to draw people more realistically... and cars."

"I'd really like to learn how to play a longer piano piece like the big girls."

So I am here to help my children do what they would like to do.

And they are willing to listen to my suggestions:

"I've found a TV program about the planets. Would you like to watch it?"

"This looks interesting. Do you want to have a look at, listen, watch, try this?"

The girls also go off and do things totally on their own:

"I was reading about Renoir. I made some more jigsaws of his paintings."

"I've been writing. I had a new idea for a story."

"I've been playing some computer games."

"I decided to try and make a mind map."

I know that Sophie (11) and Gemma-Rose (8) will gradually go off more and more by themselves, as they get older. One day I will say, "I haven't seen you all morning. Tell me what you're working on."

I guess I will miss the girls, and I will have to entice them back with such suggestions as, "I feel like watching *Henry V*. Do you want to join me?" And knowing my girls, they will drop whatever they are doing, so they can sit with me on the sofa for an afternoon of Shakespeare. For who can resist sharing a play with fellow enthusiasts?

Or I will say, "Does anyone want to go for a run with me?" Before I know it, the girls will be lacing up their shoes. Despite individual interests, we still have many shared passions.

Spending time together, sharing passions, being interested in each other, learning together, encouraging and helping each other, delighting together as we discover new things, and enjoying being a family. I never imagined this is what unschooling is all about. But it is.

Aren't you glad we don't have to step back from our kids' learning but can get involved instead?

How Unschooling Differs from School Learning

My children are curious people. They ask questions. They ponder. They search for answers. They want to know about all kinds of things such as what happens when a volcano erupts, who was the first person to fly in a plane, and what is it like at the South Pole? A lot of these things are part of a school's syllabus. But that's irrelevant to my children.

Unlike school kids, my children don't think in terms of school subjects. They don't say, "I'm not interested in that because it's history or geography or science." It doesn't matter to them that the education authorities have reduced fascinating topics to required school syllabus subjects. They regard everything in the world as potential sources of wonderful learning experiences.

Gemma-Rose and I are chatting.

"Do you know that there are four different species of kookaburra?"

I don't. I've only ever seen laughing kookaburras. They sit on our backyard fence. Their calls are the sound of our local bush.

Gemma-Rose and I discuss the birds' defining features. We wonder: are kookaburras related to kingfishers? How many species of kookaburra live in Australia? And why haven't I heard about the blue-winged kookaburra before?

I ask Gemma-Rose where she was reading about kookaburras, and she answers, "On the Internet." She had a question (about something else), so she did some googling. One interesting thing led to another, and now she knows more about kookaburras than she used to.

I want to know more too. I want to see a photo of the kookaburra with the blue wings. I'm going to do some googling of my own.

"And, Mum, do you know how cats purr? After I read about kookaburras, I followed another link."

Gemma-Rose tells me about vocal cords and air and vibrations and how cats might purr when they're nervous. "Just like nervous people will sometimes smile."

Classifying birds and vibrating vocal cords are science, but Gemma-Rose isn't thinking, "I'm doing science." She's just satisfying her curiosity. She's learning because she's interested in our fascinating world. Just like me.

So on the surface, unschooling might look similar to school learning. Dig deeper, and you'll find out it is very different!

Is Unschooling Just Living Life?

I once heard an unschooler say, "I live my life. My children live theirs." So is unschooling just living life or is there more to it than that?

At the beginning of the week, we had five empty days stretched ahead of us. There was lots of time to do whatever we wanted. I imagined us pursuing our individual projects as well as doing some things together. Perhaps we could use the new resources I'd recently found.

But the week didn't turn out as I'd expected. We had medical appointments to attend. I had to post some parcels and letters without delay. There were items to buy. Unexpected things happened. I found myself in the car going to and from town. I also walked to the village a few times. And so I haven't been able to stay home and spend time with my girls doing all the things I had anticipated.

The other day, as we were walking back from the village after having done some errands, I said to Gemma-Rose, "It's just as well you don't go to school because we don't have time for it." It's also just as well my girls don't do structured homeschooling because we don't have time for that either. Life would be getting in the way of school. It's just as well we learn from everything that happens in our lives.

You might have heard that unschooled kids learn just by living life. But is it really that simple?

Do we just get up each day and see what the day offers and learn from it? We could, but I think there's a bit more to unschooling than that. Yes, there's always something we can learn from whatever is happening around us. But sometimes life does get too quiet. And I can see that there are times when my girls yearn for more excitement. They need bigger learning experiences. Sometimes, so do I. We might feel we're in a bit of a rut. Everyday life isn't enough. Our minds want more. At these times, we can strew. We can enrich our children's and our own lives by looking for some new experiences and resources. So I search for things that we can watch, read or play together. I suggest a few outings. I also share thoughts and ideas, which usually lead to some interesting discussions. Strewing can put a spark back into life.

But, of course, there are times in our lives when we don't need to strew. Life is exciting enough on its own. Occasionally, it's too exciting. Maybe we'd rather life were more ordinary. There could be a crisis in the family or our immediate environment that we have to deal with like a bushfire burning on our doorstep.

A few years ago, a fire started a few kilometres down the road from our village and then spread over thousands of hectares of land. It lapped the bush at the end of our road. For several weeks, we had firefighters on our street, and we were on alert for evacuation. It took many weeks for the fire to be contained and put out.

During the height of the fire, we spent our days at home keeping up with the fire reports. Our thoughts were focused on the emergency in which we found ourselves. It was difficult to turn our minds to ordinary things like the books we were reading or the videos we were watching. Instead of doing our usual things together, my head was constantly in my computer, keeping up with the latest news on the crisis.

But even though I wasn't spending much time with my girls, I could see that they were still learning. The bushfire presented them with lots of learning experiences, including bushfire safety, the regeneration of the bush after a fire, and safety within our home. The girls talked to firefighters and watched water-bombing helicopters. All these things encouraged discussion and research about all kinds of fire-related topics. We didn't learn much about anything other than the fire, but that was okay. So I didn't do any strewing. I didn't go looking for learning experiences. I didn't have to. Life was (too) exciting as it was. My girls were learning. And I had lots to record in my homeschooling records book!

When life is rich and exciting, I don't think we need to worry at all about education. Of course, bushfires aren't the only potential learning opportunities. Life is also very full when we're looking after babies, dealing with medical issues, moving house, enjoying the company of friends, catching up with housework and shopping, or filming a music video for a sister. At these times, we don't need to enrich our children's lives. They are rich enough already.

So is unschooling just about living our life? Yes, when life is full and interesting!

The Curriculum of Life

Of course, even without strewing, our days contain many learning experiences. If we look carefully, we might discover all kinds of interesting questions to ponder.

What curriculum are you using this year? The girls and I are going to be using the curriculum of life.

Surely day-to-day life doesn't provide many learning experiences? Most days are the same, aren't they? And perhaps this is true unless we regain our sense of awe and wonder about life, and keep alert.

How often do we wander from day to day without asking any questions? I am sure we miss many opportunities to muse and ponder and take delight in what's around us.

On Friday, the repairman came to fix our washing machine. After hand washing our clothes for nearly three weeks, I certainly took great delight in a washing machine restored to perfect working order. And the delight may have ended there except Sophie (13) said, "We won't have to hang dripping clothes on the line any more. No more soggy clothes! I wonder how the machine makes them so dry."

We found ourselves talking about centrifugal forces, which led to other forces such as gravity. We mentally visited a playground and an amusement park. We rode the roller coaster and slipped over on an iced-over lake. Then the best bit of all: I told the girls an old story of when I used to work in a research lab in a university. (They love hearing stories of my life before children!) I described how I used a centrifuge to separate the contents of my test tubes.

Later that same day, Sophie and I were making yoghurt, and we did some more wondering. It started when Sophie wondered if her batch of yoghurt would be a success. Perhaps it would end up runny like a few of our recent yoghurt making attempts. Could the yoghurt culture be alive? Is it similar to yeast?

What is it exactly? After we'd determined that yoghurt culture is bacteria and is indeed alive, we then talked about how we have microbes living within us. I won't describe how we moved onto worms. That was rather an icky story!

We are having a solar hot water system installed in a few days' time. Andy is busy putting down some paving stones for the water tank to stand on. "It's a big tank. Lots of hot water and we won't have to pay for it!" Soon we were discussing the advantages of solar hot water. We compared clean, renewable energy sources to that generated by electricity power stations. Someone even remembered the wind power farm we saw near Canberra. The discussion went all over the place. Oh my! I'm sure we covered a huge part of the school curriculum in one conversation, without even trying. But we could have done even better.

Andy and I did the initial research when we were trying to decide which solar hot water system to buy. Perhaps we should have included our children in the discussion. We could have shared the maths too when we were working out the bills and wondering if we should use some of our 'extra' mortgage payments to buy the system.

Electricity came up again when someone noticed that some appliances have a two-pronged plug while others are three-pronged. Why? I had another old story to tell: "When I was a teenager we lived in England for a while. The appliances there were sold without plugs. We'd have to buy one and fit it before we could use whatever we'd bought." I then described the wires inside the cords and how they are attached to the plug. The girls were very interested because it's very different from their own experiences.

This morning, on the way home from Mass, we were discussing some statistics that had been published in our parish bulletin. They had been taken from the last census and described the Catholic population in our two local parishes. We found ourselves comparing numbers. We tried to work out why some figures were higher for one parish than the other. We talked about percentages and made some predictions about our growing Catholic community. We did some real life maths while we travelled home from the church.

There are learning experiences everywhere.

I bet there's a whole wealth of them in our supermarket trolley. Sophie asked me the other day if I read labels. Do I read labels? Oh yes! All the time!

The girls are sewing dolls. I bet there are lots of things to discuss there. Gemma-Rose asked me to buy her a piece of black felt so she could make her doll's eyes. But does she know what felt is exactly? And how does the synthetic variety differ from the real stuff? And how does a ball of wool end up multi-coloured? (I would like to know the answer to that question!) And when we look at a paper dressmaking pattern, what exactly do the imperial measurements, the ones we usually ignore, mean?

Do you think anyone could learn anything while doing the housework? How about the action of bleaches and disinfectants? And stain removers. Then there's static electricity and dusting. How do vacuum cleaners work? Oh dear! If we muse too long, we'll never get the cleaning finished.

Musing too long? Turning everything into a lesson could be overwhelming. Asking questions that we expect our children to answer might dampen their curiosity: "Oh no! Mum's asking questions again." I could easily have ruined a great trip to the animal sanctuary on Gemma-Rose's birthday by turning the outing into an excursion: "Now Mum's giving us a lecture!"

And I wouldn't want to force my children to listen when they'd rather learn about something else.

But idly pondering on an equal basis can be very enjoyable. Taking the time to talk together about anything and everything and telling stories. I reckon stories are a wonderful way to share. They fix things into our memories without any effort at all. And the best stories – according to my children – are the ones I tell about my own experiences, especially if they belong to another time and place.

I think I will get out my homeschool records book, and jot down all the things I have just mentioned. I'm sure we covered a lot of the school syllabus without even meaning to (which is rather useful as we have to fulfil certain homeschooling registration requirements). Why make complicated lesson plans? All I need to do is share all the experiences that happen every day around us – just in case my children are interested – and be willing to answer all the questions they are always asking, and then write it all down in my book at the end of the day.

And, of course, if the day does look like it's going to be rather ordinary and boring, and no one has any ideas of their own about what to do, there's always strewing. That's good too!

I'm saying good night to Sophie and Gemma-Rose. Before I turn out their bedroom light, Sophie smiles and says, "I really enjoyed talking to you today, Mum! Didn't we have some interesting conversations?"

"We certainly did!"

A Typical Unschooling Day

Years ago, after I'd finished reading an unschooling book, I'd think, "Yes, I can see you trust your kids will learn all they need to know, but what do they DO each day!" I couldn't imagine unschooling in action. So that's why I'm including some typical unschooling day stories in this book. You'll find them sprinkled in among the other ones.

Is there really such a thing as a typical unschooling day? Well, unschooling does look different in different families. And even within one family, unschooling can look different on different days. But I think these stories are representative of our family's unschooling life. As time passes, and my children grow, and their needs change, our days gradually assume a different appearance. My typical unschooling day stories reflect this dynamic nature of unschooling.

I wrote A Typical Unschooling Day *at a time when my children were learning maths in a formal way. I convinced myself that my girls loved doing maths. They chose to work on their online courses. I didn't want to face the fact that this might not be the true situation because how would we fulfil the maths requirements for homeschooling registration if we didn't have any worksheets or online course results to present to the education department? Sometimes we look at situations through half-closed eyes, not wanting to see things clearly. However, I did eventually examine the 'maths problem', and we made changes. I will share more details in my unschooling maths section!*

We started our day with prayers at 8 am. We like gathering together as a family before we all go our separate ways. It gives us, not only a chance to pray together and read the Bible but also an opportunity to talk over everyone's plans for the coming day: who's going where and when, who needs a lift where and when, who's home for dinner. And to find answers to important questions like, "What shall we have for dinner tonight?"

It's very cold here today. After prayers, the girls and I headed to the family room and the gas heater and some maths. After doing some maths problems, Sophie (10) wrote some emails. Then she pondered spelling. She said, "I don't think I need to know how to spell the word 'thong'? It's a word I'm never going to use. I hate thongs. I can't walk in them."

This started a discussion about thongs (the footwear and not the underwear!), and I told a story of my younger days. My grandmother gave me a pair of Indian leather thongs, and I very foolishly took them with me on a university field trip to Spain. One sunny morning, I decided the thongs would be the ideal footwear for the beautiful weather. A few hours later, I'd changed my mind. I was totally fed up with trying to keep the thongs on my feet while walking along as if I didn't have a care in the world. I really could have thrust the thongs into the nearest garbage bin and walked barefoot.

So we decided that the big question was: why can some people walk in thongs, but we can't? Are Elvis feet different from everyone else's? Not having any other people around to do some experiments on, we moved on to reading.

The girls love listening while I read. They snuggle up under blankets, together with the cats, and enjoy. At the moment, we're reading *Ballet Shoes* and *Ramona the Pest* (they saw the movie recently) and a historical fiction book about the Eureka Stockade.

Morning tea time, check-our-emails-time, time for a bit of blogging.

Imogen (16) said, "Now you're an ex-ex blogger, Mum - I'd been considering deleting all my blogs, but I changed my mind - you need to write a blog post. We want to write posts as well." So for the next hour and a half, we typed away, each at our own computers. We found our cameras, downloaded and compressed photos and added them to our blog posts. Then everyone sat back for a short, restful and satisfying moment before returning to our computers to check out each other's blog stories. Lots of compliments and a few tactful suggestions later, I suddenly noticed it was lunch time.

We prepared sandwiches to the accompaniment of all the funny bits out of the movie *Singin' in the Rain* (which we'd watched together on Monday evening). "Do you want cheese?" "No. No. No." "Or would you rather have peanut butter?" "Yes. Yes. Yes." And then some amusing tongue twister thing about noses and roses. It's amazing how easily my kids pick up and remember things from movies.

After a quick lunch and clean up, we gathered our library books and headed into town. Imogen had a two-hour house cleaning job, and while she was busy, I took the other girls to a library two towns away that we rarely visit. A whole library of fresh books: we were in paradise. We staggered back to the van with twenty books each and then it was time for the afternoon tea we'd packed in our basket. We discovered a playground where I could park the van alongside the equipment. This allowed the sensible soft people - Charlotte (13) and I - to stay in the van and read our newly borrowed library books while the tougher ones - Sophie and Gemma-Rose (7) - ventured out into the wind to play on the swings and get some exercise. We collected Imogen (who had newly earned money to add to her growing buy-my-own-car fund) and headed home.

Walking through the door, the delicious smell of a red wine and beef casserole greeted us, which I omitted to say, the older girls prepared first thing this morning. Imogen and Charlotte cooked some polenta and vegetables in between practising the piano and completing musicianship exercises. The rest of us did a quick tidy up. Andy arrived home from school, and the whole family gathered around the table for dinner.

This evening, everyone has dispersed. I am writing. Andy is preparing lessons for his class for tomorrow. Some of the girls are reading, and some are drawing. And what the boys are doing is anyone's guess.

And that is our day. I omitted all the less impressive things like how the ironing is still not done and how I still haven't sorted out some household paperwork or organised dental appointments or haircuts...

Part IV: Starting Unschooling

When A Spouse is Reluctant to Unschool

Maybe you've read about unschooling. You've spent a lot of time pondering it. It all makes sense, and you can't wait for your family to become unschoolers. There's just one problem: your spouse doesn't share your enthusiasm. He or she is reluctant to unschool.

What does my husband Andy think of unschooling? Was he always in favour of it? Or did I have to convince him that unschooling is the right thing to do? Parents frequently ask me these questions, especially when their spouses or partners are reluctant to unschool.

When we began homeschooling, Andy and I went to a couple of unschooling conferences together. The information we received was all positive. When we got home, we were both excited about what we'd heard. We couldn't wait to unschool. Of course, neither of us understood unschooling properly even though we thought we did. And eventually, we moved away from this way of life.

A few years later, when we returned to unschooling, Andy didn't know we were unschooling. I didn't either. We had arrived in a gradual and natural way, and the word 'unschooling' was never mentioned. As far as we were concerned, we were just 'doing our own thing.' We lived like this for a long time before it occurred to us that we are unschoolers, that we'd come full circle. What we were doing looked and felt different from our initial attempt to unschool. But even if we'd had some reservations about unschooling, it wouldn't have made any difference. We could see what we were doing, suited our family perfectly.

But most people don't arrive at unschooling in an accidental kind of way. Many families make a conscious decision to unschool. One spouse might hear about unschooling and then, after doing a lot of research, decides that this way of life is perfect for their family. But her husband or his wife might not agree. Maybe they've heard some negative things about unschooling. Perhaps it just doesn't make much sense. Yes, unschooling is definitely different. Could it also be irresponsible? Surely it won't work? It's something that needs a lot of time and thought before it can be understood and accepted. One person might have been pondering unschooling for a while and worked their way through all the various issues. It's not so easy for the person who isn't so familiar with unschooling. He or she might need more time.

Talking about unschooling may help. One spouse might share what he or she has been reading, and this could spark some productive discussions. But what if the conversation can't even begin? The word 'unschooling' could conjure up a rather negative image. It can put people off. Close them off from the possibilities.

So how about leaving the word unschooling out of the discussion? Instead, it might be better to talk about what's working and what's not, what we want for our kids and what we want to avoid, our children's hopes and dreams and how we can help them achieve them, and what is important for our family.

Having such conversations might be more profitable than announcing a desire to unschool. Unschooling can sound like a weird idea, can't it? But there's certainly nothing wrong with nurturing our kids' talents, being a good example ourselves, enjoying learning, being curious, accepting and loving our kids unconditionally, and becoming the people we are meant to be.

Despite discussing all the issues and addressing any concerns, one spouse still might not be on board with the idea of unschooling. The other person will probably feel very disappointed. Unschooling is important. Their family has to unschool. It's the answer to everything. Nothing else will do. So what can be done? Well, we could keep nagging in the hope that eventually, our spouse will back down. Or we could respect our spouse's point of view. Respect is more important than getting our own way even when we're talking about something as life-changing as unschooling.

I know all about ignoring my spouse's concerns, not with unschooling, but with another issue. Many years ago, I was convinced that moving to a tiny rundown cottage two hours' drive from my husband's workplace was the right thing to do. Of course, it wasn't. It was a crazy idea. But I didn't see that because I'd already made up my mind. Maybe if I'd been willing to listen to my husband, we could have spoken together about what we wanted for our family. We could have come up with an alternate and more feasible plan that would have satisfied both of us.

If we're not on the same wave-length with our spouse, perhaps we could think about how we're communicating with each other. Are we as connected as we should be? Could we spend more time listening rather than talking? Instead of taking every opportunity to put in a word for unschooling, we could try and see things with our spouse's eyes. We might learn something unexpected. The bonds between us might grow stronger. Trust will build up.

Trust is an integral part of unschooling. We're always talking about how we need to trust our kids. And sometimes we chat about how our kids need to be able to trust us. But do we think enough about how spouses need to be able to trust each other?

When we trust each other, we trust each other's judgement. We don't need to question the choices the other person makes.

I'm very fortunate. Andy trusts me. He never questions what I'm doing with our children. He also knows I make mistakes. But then again, so does he. That's just part of life. But Andy knows that I have our children's best interests at heart. If I'd said to him, "I've been reading about unschooling, and I think we should give it a go," he'd have said, "Okay. Sounds good." And then he would have supported and helped me. Just like he did when I tried Charlotte Mason and classical homeschooling and unit studies and notebooking.

Because of trust, I wouldn't have had to convince Andy that unschooling is the right thing to do.

So maybe we have to think about trust first. Hopefully, unschooling will come next!

Time to Unschool

Sometimes we have to reach crisis point before we realise that it's time to stop worrying about other people's expectations and start listening to our children.

Gemma-Rose (7) had a loose front tooth. Every spare moment, she put her fingers in her mouth and wiggled and twisted and turned that little tooth. Soon it was hanging by a thread. At lunchtime, two days ago, it finally fell out after one bite of her sandwich, much to my youngest daughter's delight and relief. She presented it to me on the palm of her hand as if it were a trophy, as if she'd achieved something tremendous. And, of course, we all congratulated her and shared in her happy moment.

"You can write a blog post about your tooth," Imogen suggested.

"You'll need some photos," Sophie added.

"I'll get the camera."

Gemma-Rose obligingly opened her mouth wide in a huge grin. Snap! Snap! We captured this childhood milestone forever.

Gemma-Rose looks so cute. My mother's heart goes soft and gooey looking at her. I just want to pick her up and hug and kiss her.

So what has all this got to do with unschooling?

We have been homeschooling since 1992. That sounds like a long time, doesn't it? However, it doesn't feel that way. It seems like only yesterday that we began homeschooling our first child. And soon, perhaps the day after tomorrow, the adventure will be over. Before we know it, our youngest child Gemma-Rose will be all grown up and setting off into the wide world to live a life of her own.

41

Our daughter Felicity sometimes describes herself as the guinea pig child. I know what she means. I was the oldest child in my family too. Yes, her upbringing and the way we homeschooled her was a bit of an experiment.

I remember the day we brought Felicity home from the hospital. I gathered her in my arms, that tiny tightly wrapped bundle of newborn baby, and I walked out through the hospital doors rather hesitantly, expecting to be stopped at any moment: "Excuse me, Madam, but we can't just let you walk out of here with that baby. Where's your experience? Do you know how to bring up a baby? She's too precious to be given to just anyone." But, of course, no one stopped me. Felicity belonged to us, and it was our job to discover the best way of raising her.

We did our best, and she survived the first five years, despite our rather bumbling style of parenting. And then the day arrived when we had to consider her education. We decided not to send our daughter to school. Surely we could teach her at home? Of course, in the beginning, we didn't know much about homeschooling. Like parenting, we had to learn about it on the go.

I think about those up and down years as we tried to gain experience and confidence and find the best way to educate our children. It wasn't easy. Quite often, I felt so stressed out trying to do what was right for my children. I had to be not only the best mother but the best homeschooling mother too. And I didn't really know how I was to achieve that. At times, I felt such a sense of responsibility. I felt as if I were carrying a huge burden.

There were days when I'd crack: "If you don't do your school work, if you don't learn this or that, if you don't try, I will send you to school. I can't take any more." I'd rush out the back door and sit on the garden wall, my head pounding, my heart racing. I'd kept my children home so we could enjoy each other so that I could give the best to them. And some days we didn't enjoy anything at all: the baby would cry, the toddler was demanding, and I didn't seem to have the energy to encourage the older ones along, to make them do the work I thought they should be doing. I didn't enjoy feeling so tired and helpless and frustrated. I felt I was failing both as a mother and a homeschooling parent. Was it worth it? Should I just carry out my threat and send my children to school? But I couldn't quite do it. I knew this job of raising and educating my children was mine alone, and I had to find a way that worked.

After some time sitting on my sun-drenched wall trying to calm down, with my children peering anxiously out the window at their 'dragon' mother, I'd return and force a smile on my face saying, "Grab the picnic basket and make some sandwiches. We're going bushwalking." Worried expressions would instantly disappear, and everyone would fly around the kitchen, gathering the necessary supplies. Part of me would think, "You should make them return to the work they didn't complete. What kind of lesson are you teaching them?" But most of me didn't care. I just wanted to forget all the problems, leave them behind at home and set out on an adventure.

Soon we'd be tramping down the bush tracks, taking turns carrying the baby and swinging the toddler along. And I would look at my kids with love, and think, *This is what it's all about.* Joy had returned to the day. I'd come home thinking, *I want to homeschool my children, but I don't want to fight with them. They won't learn anything in an atmosphere of conflict, and our relationships will be ruined. We are a family. And a family should be a place of love, joy, encouragement, support and peace, as well as a place of growth and learning.*

Gradually, I was discovering what was important. And bit by bit, I rejected anything that led us away from that close and happy relationship that I knew was the most valuable thing in the world.

I realised that a lot of what was causing our conflict was other people's expectations and timetables: my children had to do this, that, and the other, not because it fulfilled their needs, but because someone (not very important) expected them to achieve this or that. Worse, sometimes this or that had to be achieved by a particular age. And sometimes I brought trouble upon myself: I simply wanted my children to do certain things to impress certain (not very important) people.

Also, our homeschooling routine didn't take into account the needs of our little people. Either I taught the older children, or I looked after the younger ones. I couldn't seem to do both at the same time.

But we learn with prayer and time and experience. Eventually, I let go of all those expectations imposed on us from outside. I learnt to listen to my children. And trust. Our children are learning but not at the expense of our family relationships.

And so here we are, many years later, our last child seven years old. And my problem these days isn't finding a method that works for our family. No, our problem is time, time that passes so quickly. The day after tomorrow will arrive very soon and my homeschooling days will be over. So I have to make every moment count. I have to live for today and enjoy every minute.

And how I wish I could have had the confidence to do that with our first child.

"What shall we do this morning?" I ask my younger two girls. They look longingly at the book that's lying on the coffee table.

"Could you start *Ballet Shoes*, Mum?"

I remember this old childhood friend and settle on the sofa with my youngest daughters snuggled up to me.

Soon we are absorbed in the tale with me reading and an occasional question from Gemma-Rose: "What's a fossil, Mum?"

I come to the end of the first chapter. "Ohhh! Couldn't you read just a bit more, Mum? Please!"

Both girls have pleading looks on their faces. Who could resist?

Later, my throat dry and my voice scratchy, I finally close the book. And Gemma-Rose smiles. She opens her mouth wide, and I see the gap where once she had a tooth. She looks so cute. I just want to hug her and kiss her. I think about time and how it passes so quickly. Soon I won't have a little girl.

And I reach out, and I pull Gemma-Rose onto my lap and close my eyes, and I enjoy.

The Different Approaches to Unschooling

Years ago, whenever I decided to try a new homeschooling method, I knew what I needed to do. When we adopted the Charlotte Mason way of homeschooling, for example, I found a supply of living books. I bought a few nature journals. I wrote a schedule for each day based around the idea of short lessons. Once I had the basics in place, I then used the techniques of reading aloud and memorisation and narration to teach my children.

Starting unschooling is different. There are no step-by-step instructions to follow. So what do we do? How do we actually begin unschooling?

Maybe before we do anything, we have to decide whether we're going to jump feet first into unschooling or take things more gradually.

Yes, there are a few ways we can approach unschooling.

We could try and fit our family into the unschooling framework. We're going to unschool, so this is what we have to do. Even though there are no step-by-step instructions to follow, unschooling is based on recognisable principles that can be adopted.

Maybe this approach is perfect if our family has had enough of what we've been doing. Nothing is working. Everyone is ready to leave the old life behind and do something new. Unschooling might be the answer. We've done our research, and now we're ready to dive straight in.

Or instead of starting with unschooling, we could start with the family. Think about all the things that are preventing us from living a close, happy, and productive life together. Then, over a period of time, make changes, eliminating the things that aren't working, one by one. Stop doing all the things that are causing conflict and getting in the way of everyone becoming the people we are meant to be. By doing this, we will arrive at unschooling in a natural way.

If we want to take things more gradually, this approach might suit us. Perhaps we're not completely comfortable with unschooling. We like the sound of some things but are unsure about others. We might need time to do more research and ponder and adjust our ideas. We're happy to go slowly.

Or we could adopt a gradual approach without even thinking about unschooling. Just do what we feel is right for our families and arrive at unschooling accidentally. Of course, this is how we became unschoolers.

So we can dive into unschooling with both feet. Or we can take a gradual approach. Or we can arrive without meaning to! Which approach is the best? Perhaps the perfect way to start unschooling is the one that works for our family. In the end, it doesn't matter how we get here, as long as we arrive!

A Gradual Approach to Unschooling

Sometimes people will say, "You're either unschooling, or you're not. There's no such thing as partial unschooling. You have to commit." This might be true because we either trust, or we don't. Nothing else makes sense.

But what if you are just not ready to adopt the principles of unschooling fully? Some ideas, such as unlimited screen time might make you feel uncomfortable. Should you ignore your fears and jump straight in? Or is it okay to take things slowly and adopt a gradual approach to unschooling?

Maybe you've been reading about unschooling, and you like the thought of it. Yes, it sounds good. But you're not sure you can do it. It will take a lot of trust. You'll have to think about things in a new way. Maybe you'll need to make a lot of changes. It could feel very uncomfortable.

"What if my child wants to sit in front of the computer all day?" you ask.

"Yes, he might want to do that at first," someone says. "He'll be catching up. Later, when he realises you're not going to restrict his computer time, he'll relax and move onto other things."

But what if he doesn't? What if he sits there for hours and hours? He might not go outside and get any exercise. He could miss out on all kinds of other experiences.

"Perhaps computers are his thing. Shouldn't kids be allowed to spend as much time as they need on their interests? No one tells adults how long they can spend working on their passions. Why should it be any different for children?"

This is all very true. I imagine being deep in my creative writing world. The words are flowing, and then someone comes along and says, "That's enough writing for one day. It's time you did something else. You need a balanced life. And exercise. Go outside." How frustrating to have to return to the normal world when we're deeply immersed in our work.

Despite our concerns, we gather up our courage and say to our kids, "Yes, you can use the computer," and then we stand back determined not to limit their time. Even if they spend all day there. Which they do. And they're still there the next day and the one after that. Deep down, we're not happy about this, and we get anxious. Do our kids notice? Do they know we're not really comfortable with the whole idea of letting go of control? Maybe they're waiting for the moment when we grab back the reins. In the meantime, they might as well spend as long as possible on the computer while they've got the chance.

Even though we might be doing our best to let go and unschool, maybe we don't really trust our kids, and so they don't trust us. No one is happy. And eventually, we decide we won't unschool after all.

But what if we only let go as far as we're comfortable? What if we approach unschooling in tiny steps? Let ourselves get used to it bit by bit? Not jump in the deep end but instead, adopt a gradual approach?

You know what? I reckon this is the best way to move to an unschooling way of life.

Yes, we can listen to people who have more unschooling experience than us. Ponder what they have to say. Maybe push ourselves a little bit out of our comfort zones. But we shouldn't do things that we're not happy with just because others have told us that this is the way to go if we want to unschool properly. If we do, maybe we'll end up rejecting unschooling altogether.

And who knows where a step-by-step approach to unschooling will lead? If someone had told me a few years ago that we'd become radical unschoolers, I would have protested loudly, "Oh no, I could never let go to that extent. I'm not even sure I should. It doesn't feel right." But here we are living the life I said we would never live.

:d to change our way of life overnight. Perhaps we onder and absorb and work things out for ourselves. , our motivation for change will come from deep within us and not from other people. We'll want to unschool because we truly believe, right to our cores, that this is the best way to live.

Diving into Unschooling

I didn't get up one morning and say to my children, "Today we're going to start unschooling, and this is what we're going to do." But I have heard that this is exactly what some parents do. They're not happy with their current method of homeschooling or schooling, so they research unschooling by reading books and blogs and talking to other parents. Then they decide that they're going to give unschooling a go. And they want to dive straight in. So how do they go about it?

Do parents say to their children, "From now on you're going to follow your interests? That's what your work is going to be. You can choose whatever you want to do." Perhaps they imagine their children immediately grabbing their pencils, turning on their computers, diving into their books, asking a lot of questions, and getting very excited because they are now going to be unschooled. But what if that doesn't happen? What if their children give them blank looks and don't start rattling off long lists of things that they'd like to do? Will parents feel disappointed if their kids don't start doing amazing things like the unschooled children they've read about in blogs and books?

Unschooling sounds like a wonderful opportunity, doesn't it? No more having to fulfil other people's expectations. No more doing things we don't enjoy. Not all parents give their kids their freedom and let them loose to do whatever they like. So why wouldn't our kids feel excited when they hear they're going to be unschoolers?

I wonder if asking our children what they would like to learn about is too confrontational. It might sound like we're applying pressure: "Come on, you've got to learn something." Also, I wonder what a child would think if a parent said, "You can do whatever you want." Whatever you want. Anything in the whole world. It seems to me that that's rather an overwhelming thing to think about, especially if children are used to being told what to do. Suddenly, they have to make their own decisions.

I know all about that disappointed feeling. I remember when we were first unschooling when we started out on our homeschooling journey all those years ago. I expected my children to rush off and start producing amazing things. I'd read about other unschoolers, and their children seemed to be very excited about everything. They were doing a lot of wonderful work, asking questions, doing fantastic things that no one would expect them to be doing. And my children weren't doing anything of the kind. I wondered why my children weren't excited about learning. Why didn't they dive in and fill the walls of our house with diagrams and pictures? Why weren't they making things like the children I read about? Why wasn't unschooling working for us?

Later, I discovered that parents have to get excited about learning if we want our kids to feel the same way. We have to get involved, provide an example of learning for them, enrich our children's environments and tempt them with learning experiences. I don't think my children could see the possibilities. I had to share that vision with them. And maybe it's the same when children start unschooling at a later age. The whole world is out there waiting for them, and it's too much. They need some help, some guidance, some possibilities until they find their own way.

Unschooling is a whole new way of looking at things, and it affects the way we live our lives. It's a big step, and I think it does take time for parents and children to adjust. Maybe parents have to trust that given time their children will start following their interests. With a little bit of encouragement, they will want to follow their particular pathways. In the meantime, it can be very difficult for parents to have that trust, to say, "Well, it's going to happen; all I have to do is wait."

Yes, starting unschooling takes time. Time to recover from past experiences. Time for relationships to heal. Time for trust to build up between parent and child.

My relationships with my family were suffering when we were doing structured homeschooling. I often put other people's expectations ahead of my children, which resulted in a lot of hurt. Maybe one of the first things we can do is to work on those relationships so that we build up trust with our children.

Some people suggest treating the early days of unschooling as a holiday. Have lots of slow days relaxing together. Sleep in late.

Have plenty of rest. Talk about past experiences. Share hopes for the future. Talk about anything and everything. Get to know each other again. Do all those things you were always planning to do together but never actually found time for.

The early days of unschooling are also a good time to continue reading about unschooling, to continue pondering ideas. Maybe make contact with unschooling support groups. Find some new friends.

With time and encouragement, children will start following their interests. They will rediscover their love of learning. They'll get excited about the possibilities. But what if it doesn't happen as quickly as you'd like? Keep trusting. There's no hurry.

Of course, even after settling into unschooling, our kids might not want to go off and learn entirely by themselves. They might prefer to learn with us. This doesn't mean that they're not capable of learning independently. They could just enjoy our company. Even after years of unschooling, my younger daughters love learning with me by their side, not because they need my help but because they enjoy sharing the learning experience.

Maybe if you do get anxious because your kids don't appear to be doing much, you could start jotting down all their learning experiences. Think about how you could translate everything into familiar educational language. You just might be surprised by how much your kids are doing and learning without you even realising. Of course, they might not be doing what they used to do. Their learning won't look like it did before. They might even be doing things that you consider not very educational. Like spending lots of time playing computer games or watching TV. If that's the case, maybe we have to change our ideas about what learning is and how it happens. We have to unlearn what we've learnt about education.

Unlearning What We've Learnt about Education

I've had times in my life when other people have presented me with new ideas, and I haven't wanted to know about them. I hear what they're saying, but I don't want to consider the ideas too deeply. Why would I do that? Isn't it good to be challenged, to learn and to grow?

Sometimes being challenged makes us feel very uncomfortable. What if we decide our beliefs or our actions are wrong? We might have to change. Change pushes us out there into the unknown. We lose our place of security. Of course, we might find something a whole lot better, but that doesn't always make the first step any easier.

As well as losing our security, accepting new ideas might involve admitting we've made mistakes. If these mistakes are associated with our children, it's even harder. We might not be able to bear the thought that we haven't done as well as we could.

So what do we do? Do we refuse to engage in any challenging discussions? Do we close our eyes and continue on as normal?

I have found that with time, the challenging ideas begin to nag at me, regardless of my refusal to consider them. I find them creeping into my thoughts at inconvenient moments. And then one day, I'm ready to listen. So maybe it's quite okay to go slowly. We don't have to accept new ideas all at once. We can continue to ponder for as long as it takes.

Here are some of the questions I pondered that led me to change my ideas about education:

Is it necessary to force kids to learn? Or are kids naturally curious people?

Is it even possible to force kids to learn? We may be able to persuade them to learn using bribes or rewards or shame or punishments, but is this real learning? Will children retain knowledge gained in this way? If they feel what they've learnt is irrelevant or uninteresting, will they let go of it as soon as they can: when the exam is over, when they've written the essay, when they've turned the page of the workbook? Is forcing kids to learn a waste of time?

Do children need to be taught? Or is education more about learning rather than teaching?

Does a school or parent-written curriculum really contain all the knowledge that our children will need to set them up for life? Or do our children have a better idea of what is important to them?

Maybe what's important to kids is irrelevant because parents have more life experience than children? Are parents in the best position to see The Big Picture and therefore know what a child will need for his future?

But with the world changing so fast, how can we know what skills and knowledge our kids will need when they get to the stage where they're looking for employment? Surely if a child loves learning, they'll be able to keep up with a changing world and learn new skills as they are needed?

Is it essential that children use and develop their talents? Do we all have a mission or something special to accomplish in life? Could our talents be wrapped up with our missions? Are our passions and interests part of who we are? Do they make us unique? Does following our interests and passions and using our talents make us fully alive?

Does learning take place outside of school hours? Do children learn from all experiences in their lives or only from the ones that we think of as being 'educational'?

Do children have to do things they don't like so that they are prepared for the 'real' world? Perhaps kids should be forced to learn things they're not interested in, even if they don't retain the knowledge because it's good for them? Or do children decide for themselves to do things they don't particularly like? Could they actually be capable of working hard at difficult tasks that aren't necessarily pleasant?

Should we push our kids to learn? Or should motivation to learn come from within a child? Do we want our kids to do what we ask, or is it better that they choose to do what is right?

Does learning continue throughout our lives? Does it matter if we don't all learn on the same timetable? Is it better to learn when we are ready? Do kids really 'get behind'? Or do they learn at the perfect time for them? Is it never too late to learn something?

We might not have enjoyed our own school days, but we survived. Is this a good enough reason to impose a similar learning system, to the one we endured, on our children? Or do we want something better for them?

There is no doubt that our kids will learn if only they are given the freedom to do so. The success of unschooling doesn't depend on the child. It depends on the parent. We might have to change our ideas about what education is and how children learn. Unlearn what we were taught.

Does that sound impossible? Give it time. And keep reading. We're going to explore the many questions I asked. I hope by the time you reach the end of this book, you'll feel much more comfortable about these uncomfortable ideas!

Part V: How Children Learn

How to Get Children to Do Their 'School Work'

I often hear parents chatting together about how they can't get their kids to do their school work. What do they do? Keep pushing their kids because that's what parents are expected to do? Is this part of their duty? Or maybe they could change their ideas about how kids learn.

I'm at a dinner party. A woman sitting next to me says, "I'm Irene," and then she asks, "What do you do?"

"I homeschool my children," I answer.

Irene's eyebrows rise as she says, "Oh! Sounds interesting, but how do you make your children do their work?"

Over the years, I have been asked this question many times. So what is the answer?

I chain my kids to the table until they've completed everything I want them to do.

I threaten them with some dire punishment.

I tell them I'll send them to school unless...

Or perhaps I don't actually expect them to do anything. They only have to do the things they want to do.

While we were eating lunch the other day, I discussed this question with my daughters. "If I said, 'How do I make you do your work?' what would you say?"

"Make us do our work?" Charlotte (15) was indignant. "We want to learn. You don't have to make us do anything."

I think about that: wanting to learn. That was one of our original reasons for homeschooling our children. I wanted to raise children who love learning, who view learning as an essential and enjoyable part of life.

I have to admit that I didn't get off to a great start. Well, maybe we began okay, but I kept getting side-tracked. I looked at what other families were doing, or what the experts recommended, or I caught a glimpse of a fantastic looking curriculum or philosophy of education, and my confidence would start to subside. I felt a great sense of responsibility, and sometimes, I felt inadequate. Was I homeschooling my children in the right way? We did a lot of chopping and changing as I tried things out, and along the way somewhere, I stopped listening to my children. They no longer enjoyed their work and started rebelling, and I began saying such things as:

"You have to do this! This is important."

"You can do what you want to do after you have done what I want you to do."

"If you won't do this work for me, you'll have to go to school." (I didn't mean it.)

Sad.

I think about what is different these days. Why are my children happy to learn? Why don't I have to prod them along?

I think I gave my first couple of children the impression that education is something that children do. I'd completed my education. Now it was their turn to work (and their turn to suffer). It was me against them, a real battle at times.

Now we view education as a family affair. It's just something everyone does. It's as natural as eating and sleeping, an essential part of life. I really believe in leading by example. Children see us doing something, and they want to copy us. If they see us learning, they want to learn. They know what is important to us, and that becomes important to them.

When I was fighting with my children over education, I can see they might have been thinking, "Why do we have to do this? You don't!"

"Because I told you to."

58

"Because you are the child, and I am the mother."

"Because I know more than you."

We can use our authority as parents to force our children to work. But is there a better way? A gentle way?

Yes, I think I found one that works for us. These days, I trust my children will learn what they need to know without me forcing them. I try and provide them with new experiences. I help and encourage them. I show them I love learning too. I spend lots of time sharing and learning with them.

Instead of saying, "You have to do this!" I am saying:

"That looks interesting. Would you like me to help you find out more?"

"I've bought a new book. Would you like to read it?"

"I've just read your blog post. I enjoyed it! Would you like to read mine?"

"Where shall we go for our Wednesday adventure?"

"Yes, I'll listen if you want to read to me."

"Did you enjoy that story? Would you like to tell me about it? What are you going to read next?"

"Does anyone want to watch a Shakespeare play with me?"

"Look what I drew!"

"Can I tell you what I learnt?"

"Of course, you can have a go."

"What would you like to do today?"

"What a great day! I love spending time with you."

Our days are full and enjoyable. My children are certainly learning. But are they only doing things they like? Maybe I should force them to do things they'd rather not do. Wouldn't that be good for their self-discipline? Perhaps they need to learn how to stay with an unpleasant task until the job is done.

I have come to the conclusion that there are plenty of opportunities for my children to put aside their selfish tendencies and practice self-discipline: getting out of bed each morning at 6 am to go running, fulfilling their share of the household tasks, taking time to pray and learn about their faith and go to Mass, giving up their time to help each other, and committing themselves to outside lessons and music practices, all of which they do willingly.

"How do I make my children do their school work?" I repeat to Irene. "I don't use threats or bribes or punishments or force. I use love."

Irene looks puzzled, but it would take far too long for me to explain. I can see she is already losing interest. And anyway, would she understand? I doubt it. Some things need to be lived.

How Children Learn According to Sophie

I've been pondering how children learn. So has Sophie.

Sophie (11): If you want to learn something you have to be interested in it, like the elephants I was reading about today. That was really interesting, and I remember so much.

Sue: What happens if you're not interested?

Sophie: Then it all goes straight out the door. You don't absorb it.

Sue: Can you learn something like times tables even if it's not interesting?

Sophie: Yes, because you can use those.

Sue: So you can learn things that are needed?

Sophie: Yes. I use my time tables all the time. They're really useful for telling the time - the five times tables, you know. Then I use them for calculating money. Did you know you can use multiplication to do additions? And you can multiply back to front. Actually, times tables are very interesting.

Sue: Interesting and needed?

Sophie: Yes. I never used to think they were interesting. It depends on how you learn them. There are some really boring ways of learning maths like workbooks.

I guess Sophie and I came to the same conclusion:

Children will learn what they need to know or what they find interesting, and sometimes what they need to know actually turns out to be far more interesting than they first thought. I never pointed out the advantages of learning times tables to Sophie. She discovered these for herself. She's been doing a lot of thinking...

... just like me. And I'm thinking that I can read all the books about education I like, but I'll probably discover far more about how children learn by observing and listening to mine.

What Do Children Need to Learn?

Gemma-Rose thrust her feet towards me and said, "Please can you lace up my shoes for me, Mum?"

I was busy tying my own laces, so I replied, "Can't you do up your own shoes?"

Gemma-Rose shook her head, and I was aghast. My youngest daughter is eight years old, and somehow, I forgot to teach her how to tie shoelaces. And then I remembered something: these were new shoes, her first pair of lace-up ones. She's always had the Velcro-fastening kind before.

We were in a hurry to get out the door and down to the playing fields, so I didn't stop and demonstrate lace tying. Instead, I did them up for her myself.

And apparently, Imogen did them up for Gemma-Rose the next day and the next and the next.

Then last Monday, as we were preparing for our morning run, I said, "Come over here if you want me to help you with those shoes."

"It's okay, Mum. I can tie them myself."

"But I didn't show you how. How did you learn?"

"I asked Charlotte to tie my shoes for me after swimming on Saturday, and she didn't really want to, so she just showed me how to do it myself."

Three weeks ago, Gemma-Rose had no lace tying need: she didn't own shoes with laces. Last week she had no need: she had willing helpers to do the job for her. This week because of a need, she is a now a fully qualified shoe-lacer-upper.

Having a need is obviously the best mo·· learning.

So Gemma-Rose can now tie laces. But what else have I forgotten to teach her that she should already know? And what are the 'essentials' she needs to learn before her homeschooling education is over? How will I make sure I have everything covered?

John Holt said :

Since we can't know what knowledge will be most needed in the future, it is senseless to try to teach it in advance. Instead, we should try to turn out people who love learning so much and learn so well that they will be able to learn whatever needs to be learned.

I think about this. How can I possibly know what sort of world Gemma-Rose will be moving into when she is grown up? The world is changing so quickly that I have no idea what it will be like in a few years' time.

After graduating from university, my husband Andy worked in the same industry for 25 years and then his job disappeared. He had the opportunity to do a post-graduate degree and study for a whole new career. And although Andy was excited at the prospect, he was a little nervous too.

"The world has changed so much since I last attended uni," he confided to me. "We didn't even use computers when I did my last degree. Will I be able to cope? All the other students will be young, and they'll be familiar with the modern way of learning."

I assured Andy he'd have no problems at all. He'd soon pick up all he needed to know. And he did. He graduated in the top 2% of his year and received a Dean's medal. I was a delighted and very proud wife. But Andy had difficulty believing his achievement until the medal was actually placed in his hand, which was rather silly. Andy loves to learn, and so he had no trouble learning what he needed to know.

But back to Gemma-Rose. With such an unpredictable future, should I try and stuff as much knowledge into her as possible, just in case?

Or should I just encourage her love of learning, and then trust she will learn everything she needs to know?

How Children Learn When They Have a Need

My blog needs a new template. My daughter Sophie says, "I'll help you find one, Mum." So we spend hours with our eyes glued to our computer screens searching template websites.

"What about this one, Mum?" says Sophie, turning her computer screen to face me.

"That might work," I reply.

Soon Sophie has installed the template on my blog.

"What do you think?"

I take a look and then say, "I don't like how all the photos of a blog post are tiled together to make one preview thumbnail."

"No problem," says Sophie. "I'll look for something else."

Hours later, our heads are aching, and we're no nearer finding the perfect template. "I'm really sorry for wasting your time," I say to Sophie. "Let's give up. I can just leave my blog as it is for now."

"No, this is important. I'll find something suitable if I keep looking."

So the big perfect template search continues.

Eventually, I point to a design. "This one will do. It's almost perfect. It doesn't have a footer column, but I'll have to do without one."

So Sophie installs the template on my blog. And then she says, "I think I could adjust this template. I might be able to make a footer column for you." She dives into the HTML code, and a few minutes later, she says, "Look! I did it!"

I now have an attractive new blog design that includes a footer column. I'm happy. I move all my tags - there are a lot of them - into the newly created footer space. Perfect!

I then look at my welcome message. It's in my sidebar, taking up a lot of room. I move it into the main part of my blog and place it above my recent blog posts. I like what I've done. Until I discover a problem.

"My welcome message is showing up on every single page of my blog," I tell Sophie. "I'll have to move it back to the sidebar."

"No, don't do that, Mum. I can fix it for you. I just need to add a bit of code."

A couple of minutes later, my welcome message is only visible on the home page of my blog.

If Sophie can create footer columns and restrict welcome messages to my home page, perhaps she can make other changes to my template. I tell her what I want, and she gets to work. It's not long before my blog template is exactly what I'd been looking for. It's perfect.

"When did you learn how to adjust blog templates?" I ask. "How did you know what to do?"

"Don't you remember that coding course I did, Mum?" says Sophie. "It's good to know about coding if you're a blogger. That's why I learnt it. I need to know how to change the HTML code on my photography blog."

I'm a blogger, and I'm fussy about my blog's design. Perhaps I need to know HTML coding too. I should finish that HTML course I started a long time ago. But I won't. You see, I don't really have a need. I have Sophie. She helps me. But if she wasn't here, I just might be motivated to learn something that I'm not passionate about.

Children will learn when they have a need. And that's just what Sophie did.

Making Children Learn What They Don't Want to Know

My children follow their interests when it comes to learning. This sounds rather indulgent, doesn't it? Why should I let them direct their own learning? Hey, they're only kids. How do they know what they need to know?

I stop and think about these questions for a moment, and then I remember something my youngest daughter Gemma-Rose said to me a while ago:

"You can't make me learn anything I don't want to learn."

These weren't the words of a defiant child. They were the observation of a rather astute eight-year-old.

"You can't make me learn anything I don't want to learn." These words remind me very much of trying to make children eat. We can't forcibly feed a child something she hasn't a desire for, however hard we try. In the same way, we can't really stuff knowledge into a child's head if she isn't interested, though it might appear we can. For, of course, children learn things they don't want to learn all the time. Anyone who's been to school is very aware of this.

For years, I was subjected to bribes or punishments, or even shame, to ensure I learnt many things that I had no interest in. Gold stars, and reports full of compliments, and high grades encouraged me to do my best. The threat of my parents receiving a bad report of my academic work, and the fear of failing the numerous tests and exams (which were apparently essential for a successful and happy future), pushed me to study when I didn't really want to. The thought of being at the bottom of the class and labelled 'stupid' shamed me into trying harder.

But those methods of getting me to work were worth it, weren't they? I ended up with a great education, didn't I? I received high enough marks. That cannot be denied. But a great education? On the day I finished my formal schooling, I said with great relief, "No one can make me learn anything ever again," and then I promptly forgot most of what had been forced into me over the preceding years.

Albert Einstein said:

Education is what is left after you've forgotten everything you've learned.

I didn't end up with much of an education.

But our children don't go to school. Surely homeschooled children are in a different situation? Many years ago, I was absolutely sure there were certain things my children needed to learn. They didn't agree. The battle was on, and I was determined to win. I was the mother, and I knew better than my children. Or did I?

Even if I am convinced I know best, how am I going to get past the problem Gemma-Rose stated so clearly: "You can't make me learn anything I don't want to learn"? Like the schools, I could bribe and punish and shame my children into studying what's in my homeschool plan. But I don't believe knowledge gained this way is very valuable. I want my children to have a better education than the one I received, and for that to happen, the motivation for learning must come from within, and not from outside a child. That internal motivator is love which every child seems to have until forced learning chases it away.

But just because my children follow their interests, doesn't mean I can't suggest new experiences and ideas they might like to learn about. Like anyone with a healthy attitude towards food, they try this and that and often discover something new which they develop a real taste for. So frequently my children, motivated by their love of learning, end up learning things I would like to share with them, without me insisting.

John Holt said in his book *Teach Your Own*:

Of course, a child may not know what he may need to know in ten years (who does?), but he knows, and much better than anyone else, what he wants and needs to know right now, what his mind is ready and hungry for. If we help him, or just allow him, to learn that, he will remember it, use it, build on it. If we try to make him learn something else, that we think is more important, the chances are that he won't learn it, or will learn very little of it, that he will soon forget most of what he learned, and what is worst of all, will before long lose most of his appetite for learning anything.

Doesn't that quote sum up everything perfectly?

My daughter Imogen walks by, and I say, "Listen to this: 'You can't make me learn anything I don't want to learn.' True or false?"

"True," she replies. "And even when children do learn something they're not interested in, they only learn just enough to satisfy whoever wants them to learn it. They don't retain that type of learning."

"Do you have an example?" I ask.

"I'm thinking about music exams," Imogen replies. "I'm not interested in all the general knowledge, but it's part of the exam. I just remember as much as is needed until the exam is over, and then I promptly forget it."

Then Imogen adds, "But playing the music, of course, I never forget how to do that. That's the bit I love!"

Preparing Our Kids for an Unknown Future: Can We Do It?

The other day I bumped into Jane Fonda after not having seen her for many years. There she was in my Facebook feed, 70-something-years old and still looking rather good.

Jane and I are old friends though, of course, she's not aware of this. She doesn't know she spent many a sweaty hour with me, years ago, as I worked my leotard-clad body hard. I'd stretch and bounce and breathe fast, as I listened carefully to her aerobic instructions.

"Make it burn!" Jane would yell at me at regular intervals. And I made sure I did. Afterwards, I'd press the 'stop' button on my cassette player before collapsing on the floor in an exhausted untidy burning heap.

I threw out my Jane Fonda aerobic workout cassettes a very long time ago. There seemed no point keeping them as I didn't have anything to play them on. Technology had moved on, and I'd replaced my cassette player with a CD player.

Jane Fonda also moved with the times. Her cassette workouts were replaced with video workouts. Sound and pictures! Oh my! It was no longer necessary to listen quite so carefully to her instructions. We could see what we were supposed to be doing. We could also see what we'd look like if we 'made it burn'. At least, I assume women hoped they'd look like Jane. I never actually bought a Jane Fonda video. I'd discovered the gym by that time.

If I ever have the urge to revisit the past, I could buy a Jane Fonda workout, not on video, but on DVD because, of course, videos have gone the way of cassettes. And if I want to do a workout RIGHT NOW without buying a DVD, I could go to YouTube and follow along with a direct streaming video. (There are lots of choices.) Yes, that's another thing we didn't have in the 'old days': the Internet.

70

Life has changed a lot since I was in my twenties. All this new technology. As an adult, I've had to learn a lot.

I've learnt how to use a mobile phone, a TV that has a remote control, a T-box which has now been replaced by a Telstra TV, and DVD and CD players. I've learnt how to use a computer, send emails, navigate Google, sign up for accounts and create passwords. I've become familiar with software programs and downloading and using them. I can now make and edit videos, record and edit soundtracks, make podcasts, and edit photos. That reminds me: I've also taught myself how to use a digital camera, even a DSLR one on manual mode. I've even worked out how to write, format and self-publish a book. I am sure these are only a few of the things I've learnt as an adult.

School didn't prepare me at all for life as a 21st-century woman. How could it have? No one knew what the future was going to be like. This makes me wonder what life will be like in another 5, 10, 20, 30 years. What will it be like when my daughters Sophie and Gemma-Rose leave home? And what kind of work will they be doing? I'm sure, with the advances in technology, there will be many job opportunities we can't, at this present time, imagine.

The big question is: how will I ensure my children know all they need to know for their independent adult lives? Maybe I can't because I don't know what their future needs will be. But that's okay. I think sharing a love of learning with our children is far more important than making sure they know particular things.

Once again, I want to return to these words from John Holt's book *Teach Your Own*:

Since we can't know what knowledge will be most needed in the future, it is senseless to try to teach it in advance. Instead, we should try to turn out people who love learning so much and learn so well that they will be able to learn whatever needs to be learned.

I guess my girls will continue learning what they need to know when they need to know it. They'll keep up with the changing world, I'm sure.

Learning from My Children

My children are always eager to learn.

"Wow! That looks wonderful. Will you teach me to crochet too? Do you think I could make a blanket like yours?"

They always seem willing to have a go. They don't worry about the possibility of failing.

But me?

I'm an adult, and I've learnt a few unfortunate adult habits. I do like to learn new things, and I attempt to gain new skills all the time. But sometimes, if someone is watching, and there's the possibility I could fail and make a fool of myself, well, maybe I don't even try.

"Can you serve in tennis, Mum? Will you show us how?"

"I could serve as a child," I say as I take the racquet, throw the ball into the air, and miss by a mile. One more attempt and I give up. Was anyone watching? I creep back home, deciding tennis isn't for me. My children remain on the court and keep throwing balls and keep swinging racquets. Soon they'll be able to serve, and I guess I never will.

I wonder why I'm so afraid of failing, why I'm not as willing as my kids to give new things a go. Could it have something to do with my childhood experiences? Do I still remember what happened when I failed as a child? Do I still hear voices taunting and shaming and making fun of me because I didn't succeed?

For months I've been watching my children draw. I haven't passed on any artistic talents to them. I didn't teach them. They just decided they'd like to draw so I supplied materials and encouragement and they went off and experimented. My children haven't worried about the results. If they don't like how their drawings turn out, they just do another one. With time and persistence, they have become quite skilful. I'm rather envious.

Secretly I harbour a desire to draw. I don't have any lofty ambitions. I don't yearn to be a portrait artist like my sister Vicky. I just want to have fun experimenting with shapes and colours, solely for my own pleasure and relaxation. But I have told everyone I can't draw. I have told myself I can't draw. Really, I have been too afraid to try.

Then the other day, I was thinking about how my children learn, how they try without worrying about the results. So I thought perhaps I could do the same.

I gathered together some watercolour paper, some pencils, paints, an eraser, a Sharpie permanent marker - the girls all say a Sharpie marker is essential - and decided to draw, just like my children. Draw? Perhaps doodle is a better word.

I doodled some flowers with a pencil and then inked them with my trusty Sharpie marker, just like I've seen my children doing. I coloured them in with some watercolour pencils. Next, I took a water-laden brush and swiped it over my doodle, and I got so excited when the colours started to flow and blend. I couldn't wait to try another doodle. I then wondered what would happen if I used watercolour paint instead of pencils. Should I paint first or ink the doodles first? I was having a great time and the results, though not works of art, were good enough to produce a very satisfying feeling: flowers looked like flowers; I liked the combinations of colour in my pictures; I worked out a few watercolour tricks. Soon I dared to show my children.

"Wow! Mum, did you draw that? I love the colours! Did you use paints or watercolour pencils?"

My drawings weren't very good, but my children were very generous with their encouragement. If they'd said, "What is it supposed to be?" or "I wouldn't have done it that way, Mum," and had started giving me drawing advice, I would probably have never drawn another picture again. But I returned to my desk and paints with a big smile on my face, thinking, "Hey! I can do this! The kids like my pictures!" Since then, I have been enjoying doodling. With time and repeated effort, my doodles may even one day turn into something worth sharing.

Other people's words can have an important effect, especially on our inclination to learn.

"Do you think I should post some of my doodles on my blog?"

"Of course, you should, Mum!"

Yes, perhaps, I will. I shall be like my children. I shall say with great excitement and confidence, "Hey! Look at my pictures! I had great fun doodling them." I won't think about failure or looking foolish or negative comments.

I haven't got time for that. I'm far too busy thinking, "Now, what shall I draw next?"

Encouraging Our Kids to Become Independent Learners

Many years ago, at a homeschooling picnic, I met a family who had a baby a little less than a year old. I watched her as we sat on a picnic rug together, eating our sandwiches. The little girl reached for a knife. It was rather big and sharp. I looked at the mother and father, expecting them to take it off their child. But they didn't make a move. I felt obliged to do something, so I smiled at the baby and offered her a safe cup to hold while retrieving the dangerous knife. The father noticed what I had done and said, "We don't take knives off our children."

I guess the idea behind the father's attitude is that a child will learn the right way to deal with a knife by watching our example, and by being allowed to handle one. As long as we don't act with fear, she will be quite safe. A child will become afraid if she thinks we are afraid, and that's when accidents happen.

I have been thinking about this incident.

Do we place too many restrictions on what our children can and cannot do? Do we underestimate their capabilities?

Leonie, a fellow blogger, reminded me of something I hadn't thought about for a long time. She wrote:

Independence for my teen sons has begun, not in the teenage years, but in the toddler years. When they want to sit on a 'big chair' and not in their high chair or on mummy's lap for meals... I let them. When they push the chair to the toaster to try to make their own toast for breakfast... I encourage them and show them how.

Toast for breakfast? I smiled as I remembered three-year-old Gemma-Rose making her own breakfast. Actually, she might have been only two. I forget exactly. Anyway, she was a tiny little thing, but she could reach the oven griller. She knew how to press the gas pilot button and turn the dial to light it. She knew how to pull out the tray and lay her bread on it. She was quite capable of making her own toast. And she never burnt herself once.

So Gemma-Rose made her own breakfast because she was capable, and because she was shown how, and because I let her.

She still thinks she is capable of doing everything her older siblings can do.

Gemma-Rose's head is inside the washing machine. Her legs are dangling over the side. She emerges and throws a handful of wet clothes down to the basket, resting on the floor. Then she disappears once again. By the time I discover her, the basket is almost full.

I carry the basket outside to the clothesline. Gemma-Rose grabs a pair of socks and a couple of pegs and hops up onto a chair. Up and down, up and down. She works by my side, and soon, the washing is all pegged out. I thank her, and she smiles.

The other afternoon, Gemma-Rose came running to me and said, "Are we leaving the washing on the line overnight?"

I replied, "I think it will be dry by now, so we'll bring it in."

Gemma-Rose ran off. A few minutes later, I followed and discovered she was standing on a chair unpegging the washing. I started to help. And before long, Imogen, Charlotte and Sophie appeared too. It didn't take long for the word to go around: there was a washing party going on in the back garden, and everyone wanted to come along and be involved.

I thought Gemma-Rose would be happy with all the help, but she was scowling. "*I* was going to bring in the washing," she said. "I can do it all by myself."

When it came time to carry in the three baskets of washing, Gemma-Rose went to pick one up, and I said, "That's too heavy for you. Let one of the bigger girls carry it." Then I realised what I'd done. I had underestimated her capabilities. I wasn't giving her an opportunity to demonstrate what she was able to do. I was treating her like a baby and wasn't encouraging her towards growth and independence.

How many times do we hold our children back? And why do we? Sometimes I think we are just careless with our words. We have our stock sentences that we say without considering their truth: "You're too young. You're too little. It's too heavy. It's too difficult." And maybe we just want to avoid the work that comes with letting our children become independent workers. Often it is easier and faster for me to do a task than it is to take the time to show Gemma-Rose how to do it, and then wait for her to carry it out.

I remember discussing the question: how can we encourage our high schoolers to become independent learners? It all begins when our children are very young. It's about letting them make toast and allowing them to carry a heavy washing basket. These things may not seem to have anything to do with academic learning. But one forms the foundation for the other. Children are capable and will become independent as long as we give them the necessary opportunities.

But I'm still not sure about letting babies play with big sharp knives. What if there was an accident? (Parents sometimes unexpectedly cut themselves.) Do I need more time to consider this idea? Or maybe not? What do you think?

Everything is Educational Even Disney Princesses

I've been thinking:

Are some things more educational than others? And what makes something educational anyway? Can Disney princesses be educational? Or are some things only fun things?

The other evening I discovered my teenage daughters, Imogen and Charlotte, in the family room deep in conversation. One had a white-board. The other was typing furiously on her computer.

"What are you girls doing?"

"We're planning a new novel," Charlotte told me. "We've brainstormed ideas on the white-board. Now Imogen is making detailed notes on the computer."

"Who's writing the novel?"

"We both are."

How can two people write one novel? Apparently, they are writing alternate chapters.

"We have two main characters," said Imogen. "I'm going to write my chapters from the viewpoint of one, and Charlotte the other."

"What's the novel going to be about?"

"It's going to be a fairy tale, an old tale rewritten."

And then I understood. We'd all been to see the latest Disney movie *Frozen* only a couple of days before. It's a rewritten fairy tale.

"We might make our fairy tale a modern day story."

I remembered Regina Doman's stories. These are all rewritten modern fairy tales for teens and young adults. When I told the girls about these books, they sounded interested, so I'm going to buy one.

"We might rewrite *Sleeping Beauty*," said Charlotte.

"Another time, how about choosing a more obscure fairy tale to rewrite?" I suggested. We then talked about *The Book of a Thousand Days* by Shannon Hale. It's based on the lesser-known Brothers Grimm fairy tale, *Maid Maleen,*

Charlotte remembered a Grimms fairy tale book we have on our shelf. It could contain loads of novel writing ideas.

Then we started talking about how Shakespeare used other people's stories for his plays. We've got a book called *Shakespeare's Story Book* which contains seven tales that inspired Shakespeare.

"I'm going to draw the characters of our novel," added Charlotte. "This will help us visualise them while we're writing."

It all sounded good to me. So for the past week or more, the older girls have been planning and writing and drawing. Their fairy tale is coming alive.

Yesterday, Charlotte wrote a blog post called *In My Disney Place*. It's about how she and Imogen are writing their novel. She posted pictures of the two main characters.

I read the post: "It's full of magic, has a couple of curses and a dragon...," and then I said, "I thought you were writing a modern fairy tale."

"We changed our minds!"

So the girls went to see an animated movie. Now they are writing a novel. They've discussed other novels and plays, and authors and playwrights along the way. Charlotte has been drawing and has written a blog post. Would you call that educational? Do you think they are learning? Or perhaps they're just having fun.

"What are you doing girls? Are you doing something educational? Or are you just having fun?"

"Everything's educational, Mum!"

Even Disney princesses.

"And we're also having fun."

I go into Sophie and Gemma-Rose's room to say goodnight. They are deep in conversation. Gemma-Rose is making notes. Sophie has a white-board. "What are you two girls doing?" I ask.

"We're writing notes for a novel."

Let me guess. They're doing something educational? They're having fun?

They're writing a fairy tale too!

A Doctor's Waiting Room Education

We are sitting in the doctor's waiting room. In the corner, a TV is blaring. Sound and images come hurtling towards us. It's impossible to ignore them, and soon we are staring at the screen watching *The Morning Show*.

"What's that for, Mum?" asks Gemma-Rose pointing at a machine on the television screen.

"Hair removal."

"Hair removal?"

"You use it to get rid of unwanted hair like... if you have hairy legs," I whisper.

"Hairy legs!" Gemma-Rose shouts. She screws up her face in disgust and then remembers something. "We have a lot of unwanted hair at home. The cats leave it everywhere."

For a moment, I sit there thinking about the electrolysis hair removal machine and our long-haired cats. Would it work? Surely they'd complain? My wicked lips start to curl into a smile as I imagine three bald cats. "I think the cats would protest and we can't use that machine on carpets," I explain to Gemma-Rose.

"Oh..."

Now Larry is introducing a fashion expert. Christmas is a very stressful time of year. There's all the shopping to do and then all those parties to attend. Poor us. The last thing we want to be worried about is choosing the right clothes for the right occasion. So true. So Trevor has come on the show to help us with some fashion tips. Thank you, Trevor.

"A man can't be a fashion expert," protests Gemma-Rose indignantly. I glance around to see who's listening.

A lot of people are not sure what to wear when the invitation says smart casual. Yes, we've been worrying about that. Zoe has put together the perfect outfit. A model wiggles her way down the red carpet.

"Skinny red jeans and high heels! I wouldn't wear those," declares Gemma-Rose screwing up her nose again. "Look at those high glitter shoes! We saw some of those in the shop the other day. Could you walk in those, Mum?" I don't think I could. Gemma-Rose and I smile at the thought of me tottering along.

Now an earnest lady is telling us about Mothers' Rescue, a multi-vitamin for exhausted mothers. The woman looks very concerned. She wants to help. I'm a tired mother. I haven't enough energy. Perhaps I need this miraculous pill. But Gemma-Rose has other ideas. She's decided that I don't need Mother's Rescue. It's not for me.

"You don't need anything in a bottle to make you feel less tired, Mum. You have us. We help you with all the work." Is that lady sitting opposite us smiling?

Gemma-Rose is probably right, and by now we have moved onto Zumba DVDs. We sit mesmerised as all these super-fit people keep time with the strong beat. They are all working hard and sweating profusely. They are full of energy. They probably eat Mothers' Rescue by the handful. They all look like they are enjoying themselves immensely.

"You will burn up 1000 calories from one hour of Zumba," promises a lithe and toned woman. I mentally compare that to the calories I burn up on the exercise bike. Zumba? It's starting to sound good. I start to wonder how much the DVD set costs to buy.

"You couldn't do that, Mum! Look at all those bare tummies. You couldn't wear those clothes." Yes, the clothes are rather skimpy, revealing smooth, tanned, toned bodies. Perhaps the hair removal people should get together with the Zumba DVD people

"Couldn't we do Zumba in our normal exercise clothes?" I ask Gemma-Rose. I forget to whisper.

Gemma-Rose is no longer listening to me. She's staring with wide eyes at the Baywatch Babes bouncing their way across the beach towards the camera. And then Charlie's Angels slink across the screen. She opens her mouth. What will she say? Then Maxwell Smart appears. Relief! He asks, "Don't you think we should use the cone of silence, Boss?" Cone of silence? How about a cone of no vision? We're watching a segment about unsuccessful remakes of popular TV series. If they were such a flop, why are we hearing about them again?

Then perfectly-styled-and-immaculately-made-up Kylie tells us who is getting married to whom, and who is expecting (how did everyone miss that baby bump?). What an education we're getting in the doctor's waiting room. How have we survived up to now without *The Morning Show*?

But eventually, our heads start to ache: all those flashing pictures and loud music and repetitive ads. "When's it our turn?" asks Gemma-Rose, starting to fidget. "The doctor's taking an awfully long time." She's lost interest in the TV.

Finally, the doctor calls Gemma-Rose's name and ushers us into his surgery. We learn Gemma-Rose has a bad case of eczema on her face. We also learn the doctor has yet to learn what is causing it.

We walk home. We are exhausted. We were at the doctor's a long time. But it was worth it. We are clutching a tube of magic eczema fixing cream. Soon Gemma-Rose will no longer have an itchy face.

I think about that hour we spent in the waiting room. Chatting to an opinionative seven-year-old, with a loud voice and expressive features, can cause people to prick up their ears. They listen and stare. Do I care? No! Gemma-Rose and I had fun discussing all that nonsense from *The Morning Show*. Yes, we laughed and talked and pulled silly faces together as we learnt lots of useless stuff. Or was it useless? Was all that time in the waiting room a total waste? Or did we receive an unexpected education?

We now know that the $2,800 electrolysis machine won't solve our unwanted cat hair problem.

I learnt that if I didn't have so many children, I would have to rely on Mothers' Rescue multi-vitamin tablets to get me through each day.

Thanks to Trevor, we have become fashion experts. And we are now hoping we won't get invited to any smart casual Christmas parties because none of us has tight, skinny, red jeans.

And the Zumba? Sounds like fun. But will I need Mothers' Rescue to give me the necessary energy or will it be easy because I have lots of children?

Yes, everything in life is a potential learning experience, even *The Morning Show* in a crowded doctor's waiting room on a Tuesday morning.

How Younger Siblings Learn by Listening In

On Sunday, Father S began his homily: "In *Hamlet*, it says, 'To thine own self be true'."

Gemma-Rose dug me in the side and whispered loudly, her eyes wide with excitement, "Hamlet!" We are halfway through reading this Shakespeare play, and Gemma-Rose couldn't believe Father knew about *Hamlet* too.

Later around the table, while we ate our Sunday cereal and crumpets, we had a good discussion:

"Which character said, 'To thine own self be true'?"

"Polonius!"

"I wouldn't agree with anything Polonius said. I don't think he was very wise at all."

"Father wasn't agreeing with the words."

"He was saying that's what the world thinks. But we have to be true to God."

And so the discussion continued.

The other day, I overheard the following conversation:

Sophie: "What are you reading, Gemma-Rose?"

Gemma-Rose with a gleam in her eye: "Words, words, words." She looked so pleased with herself.

Sophie recognising this quote from *Hamlet* replied: "What is the matter, my lord?"

Me (joining in): "Between who?"

Sophie: "I mean the matter you read, my lord."

Gemma-Rose: "That's Polonius' speech. You know, Ophelia's father. He's talking to Hamlet."

Imogen, Charlotte, Sophie and I are reading *Hamlet* out loud together, at the girls' request. They love taking parts and pretending. We sit in our family room, but we're not really there at all. We're in a castle at Elsinore.

I hadn't planned to involve Gemma-Rose. At eight, her reading isn't quite up to the task of reading Shakespeare's complex speeches quickly. I had this vague idea of reading her a children's version instead. But it seems I don't need to. Gemma-Rose sits in the same room as us, playing or drawing. And listening. She's also transported into that other world at Elsinore. Occasionally, I notice she puts down her pencil or her toy. She's thinking about something she's heard. Sometimes she even has her say when we're discussing the play. And when we turn on the DVD to find out how the experts act out Shakespeare's words, Gemma-Rose makes sure she gets a good seat. She is just as eager to watch as any of us. She doesn't want to go off and play by herself. This is all much too interesting.

We have already read *Hamlet* a number of times, and I guess we'll keep returning to it. Each time we visit the play again, we all understand just a bit more than we did last time. There is always something new to discuss, a new DVD version to watch, another Shakespeare book we have found to share. What we can learn from Shakespeare's plays seems to be endless.

I guess when Gemma-Rose's turn comes to read *Hamlet* for the first time, she will already have a huge head-start. She will open her script with great anticipation as if she were about to meet up again with an old friend. She will be eager to get to know him better. And she won't be disappointed.

I think about Gemma-Rose's excitement when she realised Father was talking about *Hamlet*. I can understand that. We all get very excited when we recognise Shakespearean quotes. They turn up in the most unexpected places like in a homily or a novel or someone else's movie.

Someone is jumping up and down with excitement: "Did you hear that? That was Shakespeare!"

"What play is that from?"

"*Macbeth*?"

"No."

"It was from *Othello*!"

And the person who works out the correct play feels so very clever.

"It was Iago who said that!" adds someone else, eager for extra points.

Soon, I think Gemma-Rose is going to be competing with us older Shakespeare fans. We're going to have to be quick if we want to get the correct answer before she does.

I'd like to claim I have this brilliant daughter who is barely eight. I want to tell you I am using this fabulous curriculum to teach her Shakespeare at a tender age. But the truth is I'm not teaching her at all. All I'm doing is sharing one of my passions with the older girls. And all Gemma-Rose is doing is listening while she plays. Isn't that a great way to learn?

Is it Really Okay if Kids Play All Day?

Parents value play when children are very young. But should older kids still be allowed to play as much as they would like?

When children reach an age when they could go to school, play is often pushed to one side. It no longer holds the centre position in kids' lives. It's now time for more serious things like learning about maths and how to read. Parents may no longer feel happy letting their children play all day. And perhaps, even if they are willing to let them continue playing, they are still a little worried. Maybe they keep pushing certain thoughts to the backs of their minds: *Are my children really doing anything of value? Are they learning? Should I direct them to more structured learning experiences?* Perhaps children should do a few of the more 'important' things first and then play afterwards. Do some reading. Manipulate a few numbers. And then be allowed to go and play.

Or perhaps play should come first. It's something of great value.

When kids play, they get an opportunity to let off steam. Play, especially the physical kind, relieves stress. It helps develop the imagination and creative thinking. While playing, kids try and make sense of the world by exploring different ideas and situations. Sometimes play can be a safe way to explore ideas that might be a bit scary.

Children discover interests and passions through their play. They try things out to see if they want to go further with them. One day, they might start to follow those interests and passions differently: perhaps they'll read books, explore websites, watch videos and make things associated with their play. Play may eventually develop into something that looks a lot like what most people would call 'education'.

I think we'd be very surprised if we could see all the positive things that result from our children's play.

I once spoke to my young adult daughter Imogen about play. She told me that play is a very important part of her life. Playing helped develop her imagination and creative thinking skills. (It still does.) The games she used to play when she was a child influenced her writing, music, and all the other things she is passionate about.

When my children were younger, they had lots and lots of free time to play. Most days, at morning tea time, all my girls would disappear out the back door with mugs of hot chocolate in their hands, chatting about the game they intended to play together. Hours later, distracted by hunger, someone would return to the house for food supplies. Then after munching sandwiches, they'd continue their game until dark.

Sometimes I used to wonder if I should be more involved in my children's days. Was it really okay if I didn't see them from one end of the day to the next? But looking back, I can see that having space to play away from any adult influence was just what my children needed. Kids don't need us hanging over them, making suggestions, judging their games, or trying to direct them in a certain way.

My children often talk about their childhood games.

Imogen says, "Do you remember that baby bath we had, Mum? Do you remember how we all used to climb inside? We'd try and push it over the ground using sticks. It was our boat." Yes, we had a baby bath, but we never used it for the purpose it was designed for. The bath was a prop for imaginative play. Some days it was a pirate ship. Other days it was something completely different. (In case you're wondering, I used to bath the baby in the laundry sink!)

"Do you remember the big tricycle we had, the one with the seat at the back?" asks Imogen. She once told this story as a blog post:

We used to live in a house with a steep hill on one side of it. The hill swooped down, down, down, before curving around the back of the house, and around a tree. It was a perfect hill for a billy-cart.

Not that we had a billy-cart. But what we did have was a tricycle. It was yellow and green and had two seats. And it was the perfect vehicle for flying down the hill on. Two girls would sit on the seats, the smallest girls, of course, because the seats were the safest position. And we two older girls hung one on each side.

Up to the top of that very steep hill, we pushed that tricycle. At the very top, we'd stop and arrange ourselves. Then, 'One. Two. Three!' We pushed ourselves off the top of the hill and went flying down the side.

Faster and faster, the tricycle went. Faster and faster, and all the time, we shrieked and shouted with glee. And faster and faster, the tree at the bottom of the hill came closer. Would we make it this time? Would we get around the curve without spilling over or hitting the tree? Most often not. But sometimes, just sometimes, we'd go swooping around that corner and sail on down the garden.

Finally, we'd coast to a stop, unclench white-knuckled fingers, and push the tricycle back up to the top. Over and over again, we flew down that hill. Until at last, one day, four girls were just too many, and the front half of the tricycle parted ways with the back half, ending our fun on the hill.

I suppose the tricycle game was a bit risky. The bike wasn't designed for four children. The girls used to fall off. A serious accident could have happened. But even though I knew I might have to deal with scratches and cuts and bruises and broken bones, I still let my kids play their rather wild game. We have to let our kids be daring and risk a few spills and thrills. They have to test their boundaries. Learn what their bodies are capable of and how to control them. Be adventurous. If children don't do all this, they could grow into the kind of people who will always choose the safe path, too afraid to do anything. Or they might go in the opposite direction and deliberately head out into extreme danger, to fulfil the need that was denied them as children.

Play has had a tremendous effect on my children's lives. It has taught them a lot. It has helped turn them into creative and imaginative people. But even if play hadn't influenced their learning in these positive ways, I would still have done things the same way. I'm glad I let my kids play for hours and hours just because of the happiness it gave them.

Whenever my children share stories of their play, their eyes light up. Joy flows from them as they remember. The older ones tell me that they had a fantastic childhood. (The younger two are still experiencing happy childhood days!) And isn't that what we want to give our children? We want them to grow up and then look back and say, "I really enjoyed being a child. My childhood was wonderful!"

I could have turned my children away from play, thinking that there were more important things for them to be doing. Serious things like academic studies, additional classes, and structured camps during holiday breaks. I could have filled up my children's time with what most people call important activities. I might have put lots of pressure on them, hoping that one day all that activity would lead to an excellent education and eventually a good career.

But I could never have deprived my kids of their free play time. Why not? Because before children become adults, they have to be children. They have a right to enjoy their childhoods and should be allowed to play. That's what children are designed for. That's how they learn. That's what they need to do.

Is it really okay if children play all day? I know some people might disagree if I voice my opinion, but I'm going to say it anyway. Yes!

Why I'm Not a Good Homeschooling Teacher

Everyone thinks I homeschool my fourteen-year-old daughter, Charlotte. I don't. She homeschools herself.

I try to help her: "Charlotte, I have a new book we're just about to start reading. What you like to join us?"

"No thanks, Mum. I have something else planned."

"Charlotte, we're going to watch this DVD. Do you want to watch too?"

"Not right now, thank you, Mum. I'm in the middle of something else."

So Sophie, Gemma-Rose and I settle on the sofa together and enjoy learning without her. Charlotte disappears into her bedroom, her mind busy with her own activities.

We meet up again at lunchtime. "What did you do this morning?" I ask.

My middle daughter puts down her mug of tea. Her face lights up as she shares some of her morning's discoveries.

"Don't you ever get fed up working on your own?" I ask.

"No," Charlotte replies. "I've got too many interesting things to do to get bored and fed up."

After lunch, I pull out the records book I am required to keep for our homeschooling registration. "You'd better tell me again exactly what you did this morning, Charlotte. I need to record everything in my book."

"I watched a video on Germanium. Did you know...?"

A few minutes later, she moves onto the next item. "Then there's maths. I beat Imogen's score on that Pinata game." Charlotte grins with delight. Obviously, there's some sisterly rivalry going on.

"I'm reading about Catholicism and the New World. Did you know...? And I read some more of *Through Shakespeare's Eyes*. I'm also reading_*Villette*. Then I did some Latin. I had a problem, but I sorted it out. I've nearly finished the course! Oh yes, I'm planning another chemistry lesson for the girls."

I am scribbling at a furious rate. Then I have a brilliant idea. Why didn't I think of it sooner? I grab a new exercise book from the shelf and thrust it at Charlotte. "It will be much easier if you keep your own records book. You know exactly what you're doing. Just write it all down."

"Okay!" Charlotte seems to like this idea. I like it too. It will be easier. But is it good that I have less to do? Soon Charlotte won't need me at all.

I think of the fun we used to have learning together. Times have changed. Charlotte and Imogen have charged off on their own learning adventures without me. Yes, they still like to join the younger girls and me when we are doing something that sounds particularly exciting like watching a Shakespeare play or driving to the lake or going for a run. But really, they are independent. They have their own ideas and don't need me anymore.

"You don't need your mother any longer," I tell Charlotte with a sigh.

She puts her arms around me and hugs me close. "I *do* need you, Mum. Actually, I need some new suggestions. I've read all those books you found for me. I want to know more about..."

Yes, Charlotte does need me. She needs me to search for all those wonderful books and other resources which keep her enquiring mind satisfied. I open the computer and start looking.

"Look at your Kindle," I shout a while later. "I've found some great books. And I discovered a wonderful website about history and Shakespeare. I'll email you the link."

Charlotte appears with a grin. She can't wait to look at what I've found.

Am I a good homeschool teacher? No. I don't really teach. I just find interesting things to engage my girls' interest and step out of the way. They do the rest.

But is that enough?

I guess we all have doubts at some time. Are our children learning all they need to know? Will they really be prepared, when it's time to move on from homeschooling to tertiary level study (if that's what they'd like to do)? Just to be sure, shouldn't I structure my children's curriculum in the last year or so? Perhaps I should insist Charlotte and Imogen need me to direct them.

Sadly, I am aware my girls don't need such help from me. Sadly? I'm not really sad. That's just the mother in me talking. Instead, I am very excited. Children really do learn what they need to know. They *can* be trusted.

"So what are you going to do this afternoon?" I ask Charlotte.

"I will practice the piano. Then I'm going to bake some muffins. After that, I'm going to work on my Camp NaNoWriMo (National Novel Writing Month) novel."

It looks like Charlotte has it all planned out. Imogen is busy too, and Sophie and Gemma-Rose have just disappeared out the door into the garden. It seems no one needs me this afternoon. Sad? No, I am happy. I have a couple of hours all to myself.

I think I will write. I think I will write about why I am not a good homeschooling teacher.

Part VI: Encouragement

Encouraging Kids' Ideas

Most afternoons, Sophie (14) and I head down to the bush tracks with our dog, Nora. As we walk along in the shade of the gum trees, we share our ideas. Sophie has lots of them. Enthusiasm bubbles from her as she tells me about her latest one. She asks me what I think. Is this a good idea?

Should we encourage kids to follow their ideas? Maybe we think some of them are rather silly and not practical at all. We're sure they won't come to anything. So should we tell our children this? Or should we let them find out for themselves?

Parents can discourage children all too easily. We can squash their ideas before they've even had a chance to tell us about them properly. Who knows? An idea might actually lead to something exciting. But what if it doesn't? Well, a child will still learn a lot by investigating it and trying it out. She'll learn a lot about herself as well.

So I always listen to Sophie's ideas. I encourage her to think them through. I ask her, "What will you need to do this? Should you do some research? Have you got the necessary skills? If not, can you learn them?" And then when we've examined the idea from all angles, I say, "Perhaps you ought to go and try it out."

But is it right to encourage a child to go out there and attempt whatever they'd like to do? Some people would say we shouldn't tell children that they can do anything they want. That's unrealistic because there are things some kids are just not designed for.

However, I don't think it's necessary for a parent to point out the things a child does not have the skills to do. She'll find that out for herself. Also, how many children start off in life wanting to be an astronaut or a ballerina? And how many children really want to do that later on? It's good to dream. And there is always the chance our children will surprise us. Too many children have their ideas squashed. A few words from a parent and their dreams float away.

Some people say that kids can't do whatever they want because that might not be what God wants them to do, and I agree with this. But that doesn't mean we can't follow our dreams; we can't use our talents. Because maybe those talents have been given to us for a particular reason and we're meant to use them.

Sometimes I have great ideas. Well, I think they're great ideas for a while, and then as I mull them over, I change my mind. Perhaps people will think my idea is silly, and so I hold back, and I don't put it into action. And I wonder whether I think it's a silly idea because I can hear in my head an echo of someone putting down my ideas.

Going through the school system, we're not always encouraged to follow our dreams. No one wants to listen to our ideas. Maybe someone has said to us, "You've got to be sensible. You have to earn money. You must be practical. This is a much better idea. Yours is a silly one."

But what if I refuse to listen to that voice in my head? What if I tried anyway, refusing to worry about what other people might think? Amazing things could happen. And if they don't, if I fail, it doesn't really matter because we all learn from everything we do. And maybe my first idea will lead to another one. It's okay to learn and to modify and to keep on trying. I never know where I might end up.

And the same is true for our children. They need us to listen to them, to take their ideas seriously, to encourage them to try things out. And if we do all of this, perhaps unlike us, our kids won't be afraid of failing. They won't be influenced by other people's opinions. They'll have confidence. They will go out into the world and use the talents they have to do something good.

We just never know where an idea will lead.

Crushed by a Label

When I was a child, I loved to sing. I was so excited when our school music teacher announced that we would be performing Gilbert and Sullivan's *HMS Pinafore*. I knew that I'd have no chance of being given one of the main roles. However, I was quite content to be part of the chorus, and so I took my place as a sailor. I learnt all the words and loved all the rehearsals.

One day, the singing teacher came up onto the stage while we were singing. She moved slowly around, listening carefully to everyone's voices. Then she stopped in front of me. After a few moments, she quietly told me that I was tone deaf so I wouldn't be able to sing with the chorus. I felt crushed. I couldn't be in the production? After another moment's thought, the teacher said if I mimed the words and didn't actually make a sound, I could still be a sailor. And although I was deeply hurt, I was also grateful not to be thrown out of the group. I would still be on that stage when the curtain went up on the opening night.

And so I grew up believing I had no musical ability whatsoever.

My eldest daughter, Felicity, also loved to sing when she was small. We knew a very musical family who was involved in choirs and musical productions, and Felicity dreamt of performing too. When she was eight years old, we heard about a city children's choir, and we were told that it was very easy for a child to get accepted. "They're not looking for exceptional ability. If she can sing in tune, they'll accept her," I was assured.

The day of the audition rolled around. We knew Felicity would have to sing the national anthem and she'd been practising with the aid of a CD for days. I had a baby in arms as well as two other children who needed looking after, so Felicity bravely entered the audition room on her own. After some minutes, she reappeared together with the choirmaster. "I'm afraid I can't take your daughter. She isn't hitting the notes. I don't think she can sing in tune."

Felicity was disappointed, and so was I, but I accepted the decision. I thought, "It seems she has inherited my inability to sing."

About a year later, we moved house and parish. At the new church, we chose to sit in the very back pew in front of the organ. I reasoned that by seating there our baby's noise would be drowned out by the music and no one would hear her.

A few months went by, and then after Mass one Sunday, Marion, the organist, stopped us on our way out of the church. "Would the children be interested in singing something special for Easter?"

"But my children can't sing."

"I've been listening. They have delightful voices."

I couldn't believe what I was hearing. I thought the organist was just being kind. But apparently not. Marion spent time with the children, sharing her talents with them. That Easter, Felicity, nine years old, stood at the front of the church and sang several solos. She was confident, and she sang beautifully. I then realised she could sing.

I am very grateful to Marion. She encouraged my children to sing and play the piano and the clarinet. She even arranged bagpipe lessons for them. And eventually, Felicity also learnt to play the organ.

Music is now a family passion. Andy is a singer too, and he performs with the older children in two different choirs.

I listen as they gather around the piano. Imogen plays each person's part in turn. Then everyone tries the piece together. Someone makes a mistake, and there are sounds of laughter, and they begin again. Then it all comes together. The hymn sounds beautiful: two basses, an alto and a soprano. The last note is sung, and there are huge smiles.

"Wow! That sounded good!"

"That was much better."

"I think we've got it."

"Could you sing it again? I really enjoyed listening."

And my children and husband repeat the hymn, and I stand listening with wonder. Is this my family who are making such a magnificent sound?

Yes, I still have trouble believing I have a musical family. What happened to the tone-deaf genes?

Actually, I no longer believe I am tone deaf. I think that I could sing if I were encouraged by the right person. Imogen tells me that I need to have better control over my breathing. It is hard to breathe properly when I am so embarrassed by my voice. My throat tends to choke up as I try not to be heard. And although Imogen has a very high soprano voice, I think my voice is a lot lower, and I strain to reach many of the notes when I am trying to sing with her.

I think about my childhood music teacher and how she crushed me with her words. I labelled myself a non-singer based on her declaration that I was tone deaf. And then I was prepared to give that label to my daughter.

And I think about our dear organist Marion who listened carefully and encouraged my children. She uncovered their talents and nurtured and developed their skills while giving them confidence.

As an unschooling mother, I now encourage my children in their interests. I no longer tell them they are aiming too high, that they don't have the necessary talents. I arrange opportunities and offer encouragement, and we see where it leads. And if it leads nowhere? Well, our kids might not end up where they expected, but they will end up somewhere. One thing leads to another. Nothing is ever wasted.

Focusing on What We Can Do

Yesterday, I came home from my plod around the playing fields with a huge smile on my face: I'd kept up with the third week of my intervals running program. In fact, it was the second time I'd run/walked the whole distance properly without giving up during the running segments. But I have to admit I didn't do it easily. I had to keep chanting, "I can do it! I can do it!" while wondering if I was going to collapse on the field and have to be carried home. Well, maybe I'm exaggerating just a tiny bit.

I can now run the two 90 second segments and the two 3 minute segments that are sprinkled in amongst the walking bits. That doesn't sound a lot, does it? But it certainly feels like a long way to me.

Last night, I had an important decision to make: should I remain on this level until it comes easily to me or should I push on to the next challenge?

I had a look at the run schedule for week 4 of the program. There are four running segments, two lasting 3 minutes each and two lasting 5 minutes each. My heart sank, and I thought, "How can I go from 3 to 5 minutes? I'll never keep moving for that long." The challenge seemed too big.

I mulled my problem over with my husband Andy who reminded me, "Sue, two and a half weeks ago, you weren't running *any* distance. You weren't even sure you could run. Now you're running almost all the way around the playing field in one go."

Almost all the way around the playing field? That's nearly 500 metres or half a kilometre if that sounds more.

Andy added, "Don't focus on what you *can't* do at the moment. Think about what you *can* do!"

I know he is right. If I spend too much time thinking that I can't run for a 5-minute stretch, then I will get discouraged. I will give up, and I will never do it.

I think about how my children learn:

Gemma-Rose is eager to show me a story she has written. She thrusts it into my hand and stands back, feeling very pleased with herself. I start to read and soon realise she has made a lot of spelling mistakes. Do I say, "You'll have to work on your spelling," and then watch her face drop? Maybe she'll never want to write another story again. Or do I ignore what she can't do and focus on her achievements? "That was a really great story. I liked how you managed to rescue the mermaid from the cave. I didn't think she was going to escape!"

Spelling? Running? It's all the same. I have to focus on what I can do and not on what I can't. And if I get stuck at week 3 or week 4 for a long time, does it really matter? I can go at my own pace. I'll get there in the end just like Gemma-Rose will with her spelling.

So this morning, as we were walking down to the park, I decided to stick with the week 3 program. I fiddled with my mp3 player, and soon, a steady beat was pounding in my ears, and a full-of-energy voice boomed out: "Hi, welcome to week 4 of the interval series." Week 4? I wanted week 3! I didn't have time to change the music because Andy was already striding ahead of me so I shrugged my shoulders and decided if I couldn't keep up, I wouldn't worry about it.

So what happened? I did the 3 minute runs easily and took a short walking break halfway through each of the 5-minute segments. Did you hear that? I did the 3 minute runs easily! That makes me smile.

And tomorrow morning? I'm going out there, and I'm going to do it again!

Note: I didn't give up. I finished the whole running program. Now I can run 5 km and even further. Thank you, Andy, for your encouragement.

Should We Push Our Kids?

This morning, Nora didn't want to come for a run with me. She dug her heels in and refused to move. I pulled on her leash without success. Then I walked around her and pushed her from behind. I cried, "Come on, Nora! You'll enjoy a run through the bush. It's a beautiful morning."

To my relief, our dog suddenly gave in. She followed me through the garden gate. Moments later, we were running down the road to the bush tracks.

I can understand Nora's reluctance to run. She probably had other ideas about how she wanted to spend her time. I suppose, after filling her tummy with breakfast, she planned to snooze in the early morning sun. I'm often reluctant to exercise too. I have to force myself to change into my shorts and lace up my running shoes. Some days, I can think of a hundred other things I'd rather be doing. But usually, I head out the door despite not wanting to.

I tell myself, "Sue, you only have to run down to the park, and along one bush track, and then you can come straight back home." That's only about 1 km. Not far at all. So on days when I'd rather stay at home, I set off for what I've promised myself will be a quick, easy run. But it never turns out to be quick and easy. Once I'm sailing along the track that winds through the gum trees, I start to enjoy myself. After a kilometre or so, I don't head for home. I say, "Now I'm here, I might as well do a proper run after all." I've tricked myself into doing some real exercise. It works every time.

This morning, Nora and I had a good run, our first before-breakfast-run of the season. It's spring here in Australia, and it's getting light enough and warm enough to exercise first thing in the morning. I enjoyed pounding up and down the bush tracks breathing in the fresh air, jumping over rocks, glancing at the wildflowers as they rushed past me.

I haven't always been a runner. I was a runner in my twenties, and then children happened, and running didn't. But for years, a thought was lodged at the back of my mind: can I run again? Should I give it a go? I knew getting aerobically fit was going to be hard work, so it took me a long time to turn thoughts into action. And when I did, I wished I hadn't. It hurt. A lot. But I persevered because my girls were so encouraging. They thought I was wonderful taking up running. I liked feeling wonderful. And then when they decided to join me and run too, I certainly couldn't give up. We became the Team, and I began to believe I could do anything.

The Team has been running together for a few years. Increasing our fitness has been good, but the Team has achieved something even better than that. Running together with my daughters has drawn us close together, strengthening the bonds between all of us. We spend lots of time with each other, working hard as we challenge ourselves, and then we enjoy those precious moments as we link arms and plod home feeling exhausted but satisfied.

Running has become part of our life. So is everything perfect? Unfortunately not. For quite some time, another thought has been living in the back of my mind. It's been jumping up and down trying to get my full attention. And this morning it succeeded.

My daughter Sophie has been doing an eight-week exercise program. Five days a week, she has been stretching, jumping, lunging, lifting and bending. And after every workout, I've been admiring her capacity for hard work and perseverance. At the same time, I've been thinking, "I'm never doing workouts like that. They look far too hard."

But this morning: "I found a new program, Mum. Do you want to see it?"

Have you ever noticed how people love sharing their interests? If we ask a question or two, their faces light up. They are delighted when someone wants to know about a passion that's important to them. Sophie smiled widely as I said, "Oh yes! Show me!"

Sophie opened her computer, and soon, we were discussing the merits of the various available workout programs.

"I'm happy about my level of fitness, but I don't feel strong," I said. "Well, my legs are strong, but my core and arms are rather pathetic. I really should tone them up. What would you recommend?"

It didn't take Sophie long to find me an eight-week program called Maintenance/Cross Training. There are only three workouts per week, perfect for fitting in between my usual runs. So I'm going to follow Sophie's example, be brave, take the plunge and do the program. I know my arms and middle are going to hurt for a while. I'm not going to enjoy the first week at all. But eight weeks down the track, I'm going to feel so good.

It's now lunchtime. Nora is lying in the sun, fast asleep. She can enjoy her leisure. She's earned it. She didn't choose to run 5.5 km this morning. I made her come with me. Of course, I don't make my children run with me. They run because they want to.

I suppose Nora did want to run really. She looked happy enough once we started. And she came home grinning. Now, this has led me to a new thought: should we sometimes pull our kids along a little, encourage them to give something a go? Invite them to join us and do it together? Perhaps they'll enjoy it once they get started. Yes, a gentle tug might be all that's needed.

But if that nudge fails, I don't think we should walk around our children and push them firmly from behind. That's definitely for dogs only!

A final thought: if our kids aren't interested, perhaps we should set off on our own. Who knows what will happen? Sometimes our example is the most powerful motivator of all.

Encouragement from a Super-Hero Sister

Sophie is the seventh child of eight and the fourth daughter of our family, and she mistakenly believes she is the only one without any special talents.

"I can't draw as well as Charlotte."

"I can't play the piano like Imogen."

"Callum and Imogen and Charlotte can sing and I can't."

"I can't run as well as Gemma-Rose."

Sophie doesn't see that she can do all these things, and will excel at them, like her siblings, if only she perseveres. She gets discouraged when she thinks she doesn't measure up and gives up trying.

Most mornings of the week, the girls and I go running together along the bush tracks close to home. Usually, when we run as a pack, Charlotte and Gemma-Rose will be out there in front setting the pace. Sophie will be bringing up the rear. But yesterday, I noticed something very interesting.

On our way down the main fire trail, Gemma-Rose stumbled over a rock and fell, grazing a hand and a knee. She shed a few tears, and I decided to take her back to the 'pits', where we leave our water bottles. I told Charlotte and Sophie to go on without us. So they continued down the track, side by side.

Later, when they reappeared, Sophie had a huge grin on her face. "As we were running along, Charlotte told me all about muscles and how they tear and heal and grow bigger with use. I like talking to Charlotte."

Sophie ended up running further than normal, and she ran at her older sister's faster pace. And she obviously enjoyed herself.

Today Gemma-Rose was back in front, and Sophie was lagging behind the pack again.

"I'm tired."

"My knee hurts."

"I feel sick in the stomach."

It seemed Sophie had one problem after another that was preventing her from running well.

"Do you want to go home?" I asked.

"Yes, please."

I almost took Sophie home but instead said, "You could run with Charlotte."

"Yes, run with me," Charlotte encouraged.

Sophie instantly forgot about her sick stomach and headed down the track, in the lead, for our final lap. Charlotte chatted to Sophie as they ran. Gemma-Rose and I stayed out of the way. And Sophie did a wonderful run. She had a huge grin on her face when we got back to the pits. She even looked like she was prepared to head out for another lap.

"Wow! Good work, Team!" I said. "We worked hard today." Sweat was dripping off us. "Great run, Sophie! You ran up that hill fast. I couldn't keep up. Are you glad you ran that final lap with us?"

Sophie nodded, that huge smile still on her face.

Tiredness, sore knees, sick stomachs? I think the real problem was discouragement and a lack of confidence.

I thanked Charlotte for taking an interest in Sophie, for encouraging her along. "You're her hero, you know." Charlotte smiled but looked a bit doubtful.

Later, I took Sophie to town to buy her some new running shoes (and have some one-on-one time), and we chatted while I drove.

"A lot of people think you have to be tall to be beautiful," said Sophie, "but that's not true. Charlotte is my idea of a beautiful person." (My third daughter is very much on the short side.) Yes, Charlotte is definitely Sophie's hero. Sophie doesn't realise she is actually a very beautiful person herself.

"It's a pity it's a rest day tomorrow," sighs Sophie.

"You want to try out your new shoes?" I ask.

Sophie nods.

"I bet you'll run like the wind in those shoes."

I imagine Sophie flying along the track, out there in front, leading the pack.

When a girl receives some encouragement from a mother or a super-hero sister, she can achieve anything. Sophie is smiling. Perhaps she is starting to believe this too.

Helping a Child Get to Where She Wants to Go

Not so long ago, we had a big running week. Day after day, we rolled out of bed early and hurried down to the bush tracks at the end of our road for a 5 or 6 km run.

Then one morning, my husband Andy groaned when I woke him up. "I'm tired. Do we have to run this morning?"

"No, you stay there," I said. "I'm only doing a short run today anyway."

"A short run?" Andy opened his eyes. "Perhaps I could manage a short run. How far are you going?"

"Six laps."

"I can manage six laps."

So a few minutes later, Andy and the girls and I were strolling down the road, water bottles in hand.

After six laps, Andy slowed to a halt and stopped. He'd finished. But I sailed on past.

"Hey!" he shouted. "Only six laps!"

"I always make myself run one more lap than I want to," I yelled over my shoulder, as I disappeared back down the track.

A lap later, I'd run far enough. I was just reaching for my water bottle when Sophie appeared.

"Finished?"

"One more lap," she panted as she ran by. I could see determination in her eyes, but I noticed tiredness as well. Would she make it around the track one more time? Perhaps I should help her. I ignored my tired legs and rejoined Sophie on the track. She smiled as I caught up with her.

"Where are you going?" asked Andy as we disappeared between the trees.

"One more lap," I yelled back.

A few minutes later, the finish line was again in sight, and I was relieved. But Sophie didn't stop.

"I think I could run one more lap," she said.

I breathed deeply and continued running. Sophie and I headed back down the path. But we weren't alone. Andy, Imogen, Charlotte and Gemma-Rose had joined us. We all wanted to encourage Sophie to keep running.

Except it wasn't one more lap. Sophie headed out for yet another loop of our circuit, followed by all her supporters.

Then to our combined relief, she finally slowed down and stopped. Her face was red, her breathing was fast and noisy, but she was beaming with delight. "I ran ten laps. That's 6 km. I haven't done that in a long time!"

"Great work, Team!" I puffed. "You did so well, Sophie! We all did." We high-fived. We grinned at each other. And then we plodded slowly home.

"I thought you were only going to do a short run today, Mum," said Imogen.

"When I made that plan," I replied, "I didn't know Sophie wanted to run so far."

"You didn't have to run with her."

"Oh, yes, I did."

"Why?"

"Because I'm her mother."

Imogen looked confused.

"Sophie wanted to run 6 km, and I had to help her. It's a mother's job to help her children get to where they want to go."

Later, I thought about those words. A mother has to encourage, help and support her children. She has to run alongside if necessary, sharing the experience, enjoying the journey, striving forward constantly and taking delight in any achievement. She has to provide an example. And she has to do all this even if she's tired.

That sort of sums up what mothers do every unschooling day. What do you think?

Igniting a Child's Love of Learning

Do you wake up each morning with a delicious feeling of anticipation? Do you swing your legs out of bed quickly, anxious to get dressed and move onto the business of the day? Another day of learning with your children stretches ahead. Do you feel excited?

Once upon a time, I used to drag myself out of bed and reluctantly face the day. Homeschooling seemed like a chore, a duty I had to fulfil. I wasn't full of joy, and my children's love of learning was under threat. I knew I had to do something. I made a lot of changes. Eventually, we became unschoolers.

I like this quote from Suzie Andres' book, *A Little Way of Homeschooling*:

God will give each of us the time that we need to learn everything He wants us to know; this applies to both ourselves and our children. Why do we expect we must teach it all to our children in our homeschool? And why do we automatically assume that this burden of prospective learning will be painful for them, arduous for us? There is a less frightening way...

Learning doesn't have to be painful for our children or arduous for us. Homeschooling can be enjoyable, fun, full of delight. Being realistic, I know some days are just not fun at all. I've experienced dark days when I haven't been able to smile, even darker days when I haven't wanted to live. But on an ordinary day, I don't want to make homeschooling into an unnecessary burden. Why add to life's sufferings when we don't have to? I want to enjoy my children, storing away happy memories as we learn together. Unschooling has made it possible for us to live this kind of life.

Have you ever noticed how a feeling of delight is contagious? When I am excited about the day and all we will learn, my children pick up on my mood. They can't wait for us to finish the morning chores so that we can all dive into the real 'work' of the day. Maybe homeschooling is more successful, and certainly more enjoyable, if a mother is as full of the love of learning as she wants her children to be.

It seems to me that if we greet each day with a smile and a feeling of anticipation, our delight can't fail to ignite a child's love of learning.

My youngest daughter, Gemma-Rose, comes to visit me while I'm still in bed.

"I've come to give you a hug," she announces, as she climbs under the quilt next to me.

"You're up early," I observe.

"There's so much I want to do today," Gemma-Rose says, a big smile on her face. "I can't waste time lying in bed."

"I'd better get up too," I say, disentangling myself from my daughter's arms. "I've got lots I want to do as well."

We smile. A whole day stretches before us. What will we both learn today?

How do we ignite a child's love of learning? Perhaps we need to ignite ours first.

The Ingredients of a Typical Unschooling Day

Is there really any such thing as a typical unschooling day? Each day can be so different from the one before; each day is a new adventure; each unschooling day has its own delights. That's one of the wonderful things about living an unschooling life. So perhaps my last 'typical' unschooling day wasn't really typical at all. Perhaps I should tell you about another day.

Yesterday, the day did start in the same way with 8 am family prayers, but then when we asked the who's-going-where-and-when questions, I discovered both the boys were going to be working away from home all day. This meant that I didn't have any sister-sitters. There was no one to look after the younger girls while I took the older ones into town for piano lessons. So at 9 am, I was climbing into the van with all four girls. Sophie (10) and Gemma-Rose (7) didn't mind coming along. They had plans of their own, plans they'd been waiting for an opportunity to put into action.

"Can we go to the shops while we're in town, Mum? We want to buy wheels for our shoes."

Wheels for shoes? I had no idea what Sophie was talking about, but I agreed we'd go and have a look while we were at the shops. While Imogen (16) and Charlotte (13) are having their piano and musicianship lessons, I usually take the opportunity to do some shopping. I have learnt that I have to make the most of every trip to town.

We found the wheels. I never knew they existed, but Sophie led me straight to the right aisle of the department store. She knew exactly what she wanted. She checked the price and consulted with Gemma-Rose. They decided the wheels were worth buying and after fumbling in their bags for their money, they paid for them themselves.

Don't you hate coming home to find wet clothes still in the washing machine? I have a wonderful son who never fails to hang out the washing. I can always rely on him. Except for yesterday. Duncan didn't have time to do this job before he left for his day's work. I must admit I considered turning a blind eye and leaving the clothes hidden in the machine. I could quite easily have moved straight on to a cup of reviving coffee. But my better side won out. Imogen, Charlotte and I very bravely headed out into the icy wind with the overflowing basket of wet clothes. We instructed the younger girls to have hot drinks ready for when we returned.

Of course, we had to take some time out for morning tea. It had been a hard morning of music and shopping (and hanging out clothes), and we needed a break. Then, of course, it would have been unkind not to have assembled the shoe wheels for the younger girls. They were eager to see how they fitted onto their sneakers. And naturally, I had to let Sophie and Gemma-Rose try them out. And as it was a new activity, it took them a while to get the hang of balancing on their heels. Not that I noticed how fast the minutes were passing. I was in a different timeless world. I was out there in the blogosphere catching up with all the news. The older girls also had their computers on their knees. We answered emails, did a bit of blogging and, before we knew it, lunchtime had arrived.

"Lunchtime already?"

Someone broke into a Disney song, and there was music and laughter as the girls prepared the sandwiches. Then we gathered around the table and Charlotte brought up the topic of Troy.

"Do you think Helen was still beautiful by the end of the ten years of war, Mum?"

"Perhaps the Trojans wanted to hand her back: 'Here's Helen. We don't want her anymore. She's no longer worth fighting over. Take her away'."

"They couldn't have done that. That might have looked like they were giving in. They had to fight to the end whether they wanted to or not."

We continued talking about the Trojan War before discussing the problems of being beautiful. Then I had to rush out the door. I had a rare invitation for afternoon tea with a fellow parishioner. An invitation just for me. I left the girls washing dishes knowing they'd find plenty to keep themselves busy for a few hours.

What did they do? They practised the piano and prepared for a singing lesson, baked a celebration cake for a father who'd just been awarded a Dean's medal, cooked a brand new recipe for dinner (spicy meatballs), read their library books, and drew some dragons and horses using an art book as a guide. When I returned, the house was tidy, and the dinner was almost ready to eat.

When we were sitting around the dinner table, Andy told us all about his day at school. Then he said, "What did you do today?"

"Nothing," Charlotte replied.

I frowned, and Imogen hurriedly said, "Charlotte! We did heaps. We had piano and musicianship lessons, and we practised again when we got home. Mum and the other girls did the shopping. I learnt how to assemble wheels for shoes. We read, and we wrote and brushed up on our computer skills. We did domestic science and household management and art and Greek mythology and exercise, and we prayed and read the Bible and talked and sang..."

And all that adds up to much more than 'nothing'. That was yesterday. What about today? Our adventures today included maths, Australian history, Mozart, first-aid, electricity, teeth, reading and more reading, writing and more writing, cooking and exercising and praying and...

So back to the question: is there any such thing as a typical unschooling day? I think there is.

A typical unschooling day contains lots of enjoyable opportunities for children to learn and to grow. There's enough time for us to sit and chat and mull over interesting questions or have lively discussions or just enjoy being together. We might share mugs of hot chocolate and eat meals together. We'll fill the house with music and laughter. We'll do real work like writing for blogs or emailing or cooking dinners or performing in concerts or doing a St John Ambulance duty. And we'll pursue individual or family passions and interests like drawing dragons or writing stories or crocheting fingerless gloves. We might go out into the community to have piano or singing or swimming lessons or do the shopping. We'll read books and watch movies and play games. We'll exercise by bouncing on a trampoline or playing indoor soccer or some other physical activity such as scooting or rolling along on flashing wheels. We'll help and listen and share and learn.

Most importantly, a typical unschooling day will be filled with love and trust and peace and real joy.

Part VII: Strewing

Creating a Rich Learning Environment

Many years ago, when Felicity was five, we went to our first homeschooling conference. Our speaker was Jill, an experienced unschooling mum, and she was pure enthusiasm. She walked around and around the room talking at speed, flinging her arms this way and that in emphasis. Jill told us how children are eager to learn; they love learning; they don't need to be taught. A parent's role is not to be a teacher but a facilitator. She illustrated her point with an example from her own family.

"One of my children loves frogs, so I took her to a talk at the museum. The speaker was an international expert in the frog field. He was passionate about his subject. My daughter came home. She borrowed every library book about frogs she could find. She wrote, and she drew. She covered the walls with pictures of every kind of frog. So many frogs. I didn't know that many existed. Wow! She's now a frog expert. She knows far more than me, far more than most adults, and all I did was drive her to the talk."

I soaked it all up. I went home dreaming. Would my children be frog experts? What projects would cover our tables? Perhaps there'd be hundreds of different butterflies adorning our walls. It didn't matter what Felicity took an interest in. I was sure she'd be an expert at something.

I waited. And I waited. I waited some more. Felicity didn't seem inclined to research anything. She didn't ask me to take her anywhere. She didn't draw dozens of pictures of frogs or butterflies or anything else. She didn't set up any experiments. In fact, she seemed inclined to do nothing interesting at all. She didn't appear to know what she wanted to learn about. How could I be a facilitator if she didn't let me know what she was passionate about? I didn't understand how unschooling could possibly work. Perhaps my children weren't of the right personality type. Perhaps Felicity was the sort of child that had to be pushed to do anything.

Looking back, I can see that I missed something important: children need a rich environment in order to learn. We need to be actively involved with them. We can't just step back and leave them to learn entirely on their own.

When my children were babies, I read a lot of parenting books, and so I knew all the latest ideas and research. I discovered I had to provide a stimulating environment to maximise my child's development. So I drew human faces and hung them where my babies could see them. I sat each baby in a chair in front of a frame. Every day I searched the house for new and interesting things to tie to that frame, things that they could touch and suck and feel: soft socks, cold spoons, a bristly toothbrush, a long ribbon. I took my babies swimming, sat them in the sandpit, sang to them, read to them in an animated voice, showed them bright pictures, danced with them, played peekaboo and a dozen other games, told them the names of everything we saw, carried them around and included them in the real world.

And then when they got to the age of five, I thought it was all up to them. I stopped providing new experiences for my children. I no longer looked for ways to enrich their environments. Perhaps that was my mistake.

Eventually, I decided that I had to help Felicity find some interests, so I enrolled her in a few different lessons, and she experienced swimming, gymnastics, physical education, music, and Brownies. Maybe I went overboard a bit at first. I don't know if she really needed all these different classes. However, Felicity discovered a lot of things she had no interest in whatsoever, and a few things, such as music, that she loved.

I took Felicity to the library, and we borrowed dozens of books, both her choices and my suggestions, and we read together. And soon she wanted to learn to read.

Occasionally, I organised an outing to a museum, the beach, the bush, to friends' houses, the shopping centre, or the park.

I made sure we had a good supply of art and craft materials. Sometimes we tried a specific craft project, but mostly Felicity experimented with all the supplies. She drew fairy after fairy after fairy and then, for a change, she decided to paint fairies instead. She made covers for the little books she enjoyed creating. And she wrote little stories (about fairies).

Besides childhood music education lessons, I bought a range of CDs, and we listened to music and danced and sang.

Felicity wanted to write. She made up poems, told stories, wrote letters. And I didn't worry about the spelling.

She spent lots of time playing.

And we talked. We talked about anything and everything.

Sometimes it looked like I was 'steering' Felicity's education by pointing her in directions she hadn't realised existed, but she was, at the same time, discovering passions of her own. Our walls did not fill up with pictures of frogs or butterflies or anything else, but soon we had dozens of books filled with poems and stories. We had a daughter who loved music and reading and who asked questions about everything and was eager to learn.

There was only one problem. Because I was exposing my daughter to all kinds of experiences, I thought we'd left unschooling behind. Don't unschooling parents have to step back and not influence a child's learning? Of course, I didn't understand unschooling very well. What I was doing was just what I should have been doing. I was strewing.

I found this little article Felicity wrote for a homeschooling newsletter when she was nine:

Hi, my name is Felicity Kate Elvis, and I am 9 years old. I have two brothers, Duncan (7) and Callum (4) and a baby sister Imogen (1 ½). I have always learnt at home. I would like to tell you about how we home school in our family.

One reason we home school is that we think learning should be fun. We also like spending time with each other and being able to learn in our own way.

Mum doesn't make any plans for each day. We don't have a timetable. We just have a fresh new day to fill with reading, writing, learning and doing.

I usually start the day by writing a poem because all our thoughts are fresh in our heads when we get up. When Imogen wakes up, I do my clarinet practice. Then we do our maths because Mum thinks it's important. We spend the rest of the day learning whatever we want like drawing, writing, reading, doing experiments, and making things.

I especially like reading. In the evenings, Daddy reads us a few chapters of a book. Dad makes different voices for each character and brings the story alive.

I do lots of cooking, and Dad's a great cook. Mum is good at handicrafts and sewing, and she shares all these skills with us.

There is still plenty of time left each day to play, watch TV, visit friends and do whatever else we want to do.

We love homeschooling!!!!

Note: My children no longer learn maths "because Mum thinks it's important." Instead, I look for resources that might capture my children's interest in this subject. They learn maths because they have a need or a desire to learn, rather than because I insist. Unschooling is a continual learning experience for me as well as for my kids!

Time for Some Strewing

Sometimes life provides my children with more than enough learning experiences without any help from me. A bushfire might be burning on our doorstep, giving everyone a unique learning opportunity. At other times, ordinary life provides one question after another for us to answer: we might discuss the problem of a broken washing machine, or we could be anticipating the installation of a hot water system. Maybe we're engrossed with a huge pile of books. Or we could have dozens of projects we're working on. There's a lot going on. We are discussing and reading and learning a great deal without any trouble at all.

Then one day, we wake up, and the day feels very flat.

"I don't know what to do!"

"I've finished that project. I don't know what to do next."

"I'm fed up with learning about this. I feel like doing something different."

"I read that book. What shall I read next?"

Time for some strewing!

So what is strewing? It's enriching our children's environment with interesting resources or experiences. We scatter or strew things in front of our children, hoping they might capture their interest, and inspire them to set out on some exciting and enjoyable learning adventures.

So what can we strew?

We can strew anything: websites, books, ebooks, DVDs, online videos, podcasts, CDs or MP3 files, computer software programs, suggestions for places we can visit, art and craft and handicraft materials, cameras, food, maps, science kits, pictures and paintings, games, online classes such as art classes... Strewing resources don't have to be big or expensive. I could strew a simple shell or a leaflet about solar heating or some used stamps or a magnet or a set of Sharpies or a new notebook or a photo.

I am always on the look-out for things to strew. Some I buy. Others I bookmark. Some I gather. A number of them even appear from my mind!

And then when I see my children are at a loose end, looking for something to get involved with, I start strewing.

Like most people, we have lots of resources scattered about our house that no one seems to take much notice of. There are games stacked on top of our bookshelves that we don't often use. We have dozens of DVDs we've never watched. There are books and more books and drawers full of CDs and bags of fabric. Now and then, I walk around the house pulling out a few things from here and there that look interesting. I scatter them on the coffee table. I don't worry about making a mess. Everything needs to be under our noses where we can see it, where it can wait to be discovered.

Sometimes, instead of placing things in a visible spot and then waiting for someone to take an interest in them, I might strew in a more direct manner. I issue invitations to share particular resources.

"I read this book. Would you like to read it too?"

"Does anyone want to watch this DVD with me?"

"I found a version of *Swan Lake* on YouTube. Shall we watch it?"

"Would you like to go to the lake for a picnic? We could take our pencils, scooters, running shoes, and cameras."

"How about we visit the garden centre?"

I often strew electronically.

"I've bought some new books. Take a look at your Kindles, girls!"

"I found some good websites. I'll send you an email with the links."

And then there's my Evernote unplanning notebook. I'm constantly adding strewing resources to this digital folder.

Can thoughts and ideas be strewed? Can they be dropped into a conversation?

"I was thinking about..."

"What do you think of this idea?"

"I was reading about..."

"Did you hear about...?"

If I watch and listen carefully, I get lots of possible strewing ideas.

"If you enjoyed that book, you might like this one."

"I bookmarked a podcast on that topic. Shall I send you the link?"

"After we were talking about that painting the other day, I found a YouTube video about it. Do you want to have a look?"

Of course, I haven't got time to get involved with every resource I strew so the girls will try out things for themselves. Or I could get them going and then leave them to it. This is what happened when I strewed a coding website.

"Hey, look what I found, girls! We could make our own animations using code. Shall we give it a go?"

Gemma-Rose and Sophie were interested. Charlotte wasn't. Soon the younger girls and I were coding. Since then, they have returned to their projects many times even though I have moved onto other things.

Sometimes I strew my own interests and passions. I set myself up where the girls can see me and start work.

"What are you making, Mum? Can I try that?"

"You're drawing! What book are you using? I could do that."

"What are you watching, Mum? Can I join you?"

Occasionally, I deliberately strew something I'd like my children to know about. I might offer them my favourite poems, a DVD of a Shakespeare play, or a novel I enjoyed.

But what if my children aren't interested in what I have strewed? What if they reject my strewing? Then that's quite okay. The world is full of interesting things to learn about. If my children don't pick up on some of the resources and experiences I put before them, then I go looking for other things to capture their attention.

I think I might go and do a bit of strewing right now. Earlier today, I noticed a science board game a friend gave us several months ago. We've never played it. Do you think if I stand on a chair and reach for it, the girls will say, "What are you doing, Mum?"? When I wipe the dust off the box, will they say, "What's that game about Mum?"? And when I start to pull everything out and set up the board, will they say, "Can we play too?"?

I hope so!

And if not, I'll just place the game on the coffee table. It might capture someone's attention another day.

What to Do When Our Strewing Is Rejected

Sometimes we can get very excited about the things we're strewing. It can be hard to remember that our kids have to be free to accept or reject whatever it is we want to share with them.

I found all kinds of things to strew in front of Charlotte.

I came across a website and DVD series that has an episode about a man who settled on the uninhabited Cocos Islands, later making himself king over the workers of his coconut plantation. His family ruled for 150 years before Australia brought that rule to an end. Doesn't that sound interesting?

I discovered a TV program about *Mao's Last Dancer*, Li Cunxin, and told Charlotte about it. I remembered we owned the book. I thought she would love to read it. And then there's the movie version.

I subscribed to a website that's full of maths and science gizmos and imagined all the fun Charlotte would have playing with them.

I found a chemistry book, full of experiments that we could perform with materials bought from our local shops. I thought it would be perfect for Charlotte, who has a passion for chemistry.

And what about the computer science tutorials I found?

There were other things too.

Don't you think all these resources sound very interesting? If I were a teenage unschooler, I would be very excited by what I'd found. I'd want to start watching, reading, and clicking straight away. So why did Charlotte screw up her nose and ignore my suggestions?

What shall I do? Shall I keep nagging her to take a look at my strewing? I think for a moment, and the answer comes loud and clear:

Leave Charlotte to learn what she wants and use the resources myself. Because when it comes down to it, it's me who's excited by what I've found, not Charlotte.

So I am using the computer science tutorials. I'm trying to work out how to translate and rotate my drawing using Javascript. I watched the TV program about *Mao's Last Dancer*. I might re-read the book. I'm about to order a copy of the movie (for myself). I'm going to watch that DVD about the man who ruled the Cocos Islands.

I guess there's always the possibility that when Charlotte sees how involved I am with my DVD, tutorial, and book she might suddenly become interested. She might settle down next to me and want to take a look after all. But if she doesn't, that's perfectly okay.

We are all different. We don't have to learn the same things. There are so many interesting things to investigate; it doesn't matter at all if Charlotte rejects some of my strewing.

So what do I do when my strewing is rejected? I keep looking for other resources for my children, and I use the rejected ones myself.

How to Have a Great Art Conversation

A few years ago, I had a new strewing idea. I tried it out, and it was a huge success. Don't you love it when that happens?

So what did I strew? I printed off a copy of a famous painting, using a high-resolution file downloaded from the Internet. I then displayed the image at my children's eye-level in a high traffic area of our home. I hoped my kids would walk past, see the painting, stop and look, and then want to talk about it. Well, they did all of that, and now we are having some great discussions!

I began with *Young Woman with a Water Pitcher*, a painting by Vermeer, the Dutch artist, because I love his work. I hoped my girls would love it too. I framed a copy of the picture, hung it on the wall, added a label with the artist's and painting's names, and then waited.

"I like that picture."

"What nationality is Vermeer?"

"He's Dutch? That means he lived in Holland, doesn't it?"

"*The Winged Watchman* (a novel) is also set in Holland."

Next, I printed off a copy of Vermeer's *Young Woman with a Pearl Necklace*.

"You've changed the painting!"

"Look! Vermeer has painted another woman standing in the corner of a room. There's a window on the left-hand side in this picture too."

I found a book about Vermeer on our bookshelf. The girls were eager to find out more details about the paintings.

"Vermeer composed many of his paintings in the same way: a window to the left with sunlight pouring in, a table and a chair or two, a woman in the corner..."

At dinner last night, the younger girls wanted to share their knowledge with their older sisters.

"Can you see the yellow jacket that woman is wearing in *Young Woman with a Pearl Necklace*? It's made of yellow satin and edged with ermine. It's Vermeer's wife's jacket."

"Do you think Vermeer's wife minded her husband borrowing the jacket so his models could wear it?"

"Do you think she ever said, "Johannes, I want to wear my jacket on Sunday. Please make sure your model returns it by then.""

Everyone giggled.

"The yellow jacket appears in a number of Vermeer's paintings," I added.

"Do you think that jacket was one of his props? Photographers have props."

Then someone wanted to know what ermine is. Charlotte's guess was ferret. Imogen hurried off to get her tablet so that she could do some instant research.

"Ermine is the pelt of the stoat which belongs to the weasel family. The stoat is similar to a ferret."

We know all about ferrets. A few years ago, I gave my son Callum one as a pet. That was a big mistake.

"Weren't there some bad weasels in *The Wind in the Willows* books?" I asked. The girls nodded. "Do we have those books?"

It seems we do. We have the original story by Kenneth Grahame. We also have the sequels written by William Horwood. Now Sophie wants to read them all.

I hung a painting on the wall. My children noticed. They started talking and asking questions. We did some research and began discussing. One thing led to another. I think that was a very successful strewing operation, don't you?

Part VIII: Passions and Interests

Passions, Careers and Time

There seems to be a minority of people in the world who can say, "I'm really lucky. I get to do what I enjoy most each day. And I get paid for it too!" Everyone else goes to 'work', and passions and interests have to fit into the leftover hours of the working week.

Wouldn't you love your children to be in that minority, and end up in a career that they are absolutely passionate about?

How does a child know what to do after school? When someone asked me that question when I was in my final year of school, I answered, "I don't know." I had no real idea of what I was interested in. I ended up studying for a Bachelor of Science degree, not because I loved science, but because I was told science would be a good career choice.

After I graduated, I worked in a research department of a university. Although the work was quite interesting, I didn't wake up each day thinking, "Wow, another day!" I didn't jump out of bed saying, "What will I discover today? I can't wait to find out." No, most mornings, I thought, "Is it Friday yet?"

What was I passionate about in my high schooling days? It's hard to remember. I went to school all day and did mountains of homework during the other hours. Andy and I played squash every now and then, (we went to school together), I dabbled a bit with handicrafts, I read novels, and that's all I can recall. That's probably all I could fit into my schooling week. I didn't have enough free time to experiment and try new things out, to see what I enjoyed, and discover what I was good at. I didn't have time for passions because I was too busy doing what I was told.

A year or so ago, I asked Imogen if she had any ideas about a possible career, and she replied, "Well, I like music, but medicine sounds good too, and then there's writing." Imogen actually had too many passions, and it was a tough decision narrowing down her choice.

132

Imogen used to be very involved with St John Ambulance (as were most of my children). Administering first-aid to injured people at sporting and other public events nurtured her interest in medicine. Surrounded by St John's officers and nurses and doctors, she got to experience what it would be like to work in a medical field. Being a homeschooler, she was able to accept many extra duties during official school hours.

But Imogen has always been surrounded by music too. Music is as natural as breathing in our house.

"Who's singing the psalm on Sunday?"

"How did your practice go?"

"Can we get together and run through Sunday's music?"

"Are you going to choir practice tonight?"

"Would you like to come and see me perform?"

"What time are our piano lessons?"

And then there's writing. We all spend hours experimenting with words and sharing the results.

Medicine, music, or writing? Imogen could pursue any of these. There are many things she could do as a career. She has lots of big passions (and lots of smaller ones too).

How do we nurture our children's passions? I think time is a very important part of the answer. Here, unschoolers are at an advantage. Our children have loads of time to be themselves, to explore the world, to experience anything and everything, to decide what they like and what they don't, and to determine where their talents and strengths lie. Time to do what they want to do. All this helps when someone asks, "What would you like to do as a career?"

"I think I'd like to be a writer, Mum," says Imogen. "But I want to continue with my music."

I smile. I am sure Imogen will end up doing something she enjoys very much. She will love her work and therefore excel at it. And she'll even get paid for doing it. Unless of course, she ends up writing for the sheer joy of it. For when you really enjoy working, money doesn't seem to matter at all.

But time does matter. For without time, how do our children ever discover who they are and what they are good at? How do they discover their passions?

Helping a Child Discover Her Talents

If a child has a talent, won't it just appear without any encouragement? If you're meant to be an artist, it will be very evident. The same with being a writer or a musician or even a fireman. Surely, a talent can't stay hidden? Or maybe it can.

When I was growing up, I didn't think I had any talents. I thought I was an unremarkable, rather ordinary child. I used to dream about being someone special without realising that, like all kids, I already was special. I just didn't know it.

As an adult, I have discovered I do, indeed, have many talents. So why didn't I find this out as a child? Perhaps I didn't experience the right conditions for my talents to become obvious.

Sir Ken Robinson once said: "Talent is often buried. You have to go looking for it, and create the conditions for it."

He tells the story of how the Beatles and Elvis Presley went through the school system without anyone discovering their musical abilities. Elvis Presley was actually refused entry into a singing group. That sounds unbelievable, doesn't it?

So why did Elvis and the Beatles and I never discover our talents? Perhaps we were all too busy fulfilling other people's expectations and requirements. We were all forced to do things other people thought were important.

"I had a few interests when I was at school," I say to my daughter Imogen, "like writing, but I had to squeeze them into the 'leftover time' of my week. I didn't have time to explore them properly. I didn't have the opportunity to find out whether I was good at them."

I remember my daughter Sophie saying, "I'm glad I can do the things I enjoy at any hour of the day." Yes, she doesn't have to wait until the afternoon or the weekend arrives to interests. She doesn't have to wait until she has done else before she can dive into the things she loves doing.

When we have to squeeze our interests and passions into the 'leftover time' of the day, we feel that no one else values them.

"Everything that a child is interested in should be considered as valuable," says Imogen." It doesn't matter whether it's advanced maths or computer games."

Sophie said that the things she's interested in are the things she wants to base her career on, so shouldn't those be the things she's working on right now? But what if Sophie's interests change which is quite possible because children's passions can come and go. It's a natural process. Throughout our lifetimes, we will continue to grow and change, and this will be reflected in our passions.

"People expect kids to know what they want to do for the rest of their lives very early," says Imogen. Everyone says, 'What are you going to be when you grow up?' Children need time to explore what they're interested in. They should be allowed to work on their passions, and if their ideas change, that's okay."

Maybe some parents hope some passions do change. For example, they might feel their kids are too interested in computer games. Perhaps they'll move onto something else, something that sounds safer and more secure. But maybe they won't.

Part of creating the right conditions for children to discover their passions is accepting that what children are interested in might change over time and probably will. So there's no point in trying to prepare them too early for a future career. We shouldn't be in a rush to tie them down.

Imogen changed her ideas about her career. Up until the point of enrolling in a university degree, she thought she wanted to study medicine. She'd spent the previous year studying the prerequisites for the course, which included both science and advanced mathematics. But while she was preparing herself for a possible degree in medicine, she continued working on her other passions of writing and music. In the end, she rejected medicine. Writing won out, and Imogen went on to do a Bachelor of Arts degree majoring in Professional Writing and Publishing.

"When I told everyone I was thinking about applying to study medicine, they thought it was a great idea," says Imogen.

"They said, 'We need more doctors. You'll make lots of money.' They thought medicine was a safe thing to do. But when I said I was going to do writing instead, all that changed. Everyone said, 'But there's no money in writing. You can't make a living out of that.'"

"When I was at school, no one encouraged me to write even though I liked writing," I say. "If I had said I wanted to be a writer, probably everyone would have said that wasn't a sensible idea. Very few people get published. But I should have been allowed to have that chance to try. I might have been one of the few who did get published. How was anyone to know?"

Yes, someone must have the right talents to be a successful writer or artist or astronaut or whatever. How do we know that we're not the person who will be successful? We've got to be allowed to go out there and try.

Imagine if Elvis or the Beatles had said they wanted to make a career out of music while they were at school. They'd have been told, "It's too hard. You won't be successful. You haven't got enough talent. Not many people make money out of music."

As an adult, I have discovered I do have some talents. These days, I do lots of things, including writing. And I publish books because I can. Yes, the development in technology has opened up the possibilities. No one can say to me, "You'll never get your work published." The whole writing world has changed.

"Parents might push their kids towards safe careers," says Imogen. "But those jobs might disappear in the future. And other opportunities will open up." Yes, how do we know what's ahead of our kids? Can we really say, "You won't be able to make a career out of your interest"?

"Do you think it's important that a child knows exactly what he or she wants to do by the age of 18?" I ask.

"No," says Imogen. "If they do know that's great. But if not, that's okay too. People have the idea that children have to know certain things by certain ages. They have to be grown up by a certain age. They have to be ready to leave home and know what they want to do next. We all grow up at different rates. We all have different ideas at different points. If a child doesn't know what he or she wants to do at 18, it's not the end of the world. Maybe they need more time."

Parents can feel pressured to prepare their kids to go out into the world at 18. Society expects this. As kids get closer and closer to this age, parents get worried if they look like they don't know where they want to go. This kind of pressure can cause conflict with teens.

"You reach your teens, and people expect you to know what you want to do," says Imogen. "You're expected to be responsible, grown up, and independent. All of a sudden, you've gone from being a child to being an adult. Being a teenager, you're not always ready for all this. Teenagers need time and space to learn and grow as people. They shouldn't be expected to be ready to go at 18."

"Did you feel you were under pressure or did you have the space to be who you are and take it in your own time?" I ask.

"The only time I felt pressured was when people from outside the family questioned me: 'What are you going to study at uni? What do you want to be when you grow up?'" There was no pressure within the family.

"So how do we encourage our kids' talents to become visible?" I ask. "How do we create the right environment?"

"Kids need time to explore. And parents have to value any talents that do appear," says Imogen.

They have to trust their kids are going in the right direction and not hold them back even if they can't visualise where their talents might lead. We don't know what opportunities will develop. We can't predict what will happen. Surround kids with a rich environment, spend time together, take the pressure off. Give kids time to grow without any expectations. Play, do enjoyable things together. Interests will appear.

So what do people say when they hear you've published a novel?" I ask Imogen.

"Oh, wow!" She smiles. "They want to know if I've sold any copies." Which she has.

You know what? I think people are very surprised. Could they be a little envious too?

Chatting About Passions

Don't you love watching kids involved with their passions?

Sophie (13) has a new passion. She has just created her own YouTube channel. She wants to be a vlogger. We've been experimenting with different video cameras together. Sophie downloaded some new video editing software to try out. And now she has made and uploaded her first public video.

After Sophie had uploaded her video to YouTube, she had a big grin on her face. "You did very well," I said. Then I added, "Isn't it satisfying learning a new skill?" Sophie was so excited. I know how she felt. I've made a few videos too recently. The best bit is doing something I didn't think I had the courage to do. A few weeks ago, I thought I wasn't brave enough to appear in one of my own videos. But I was. That feels good.

I've been thinking about how passions can change. At one time Charlotte's passion was chemistry. I bought a lot of living chemistry books for her, and she watched every video on a periodic table website. It looked like she was heading towards a career in chemistry.

The other day, Sophie discovered those chemistry books on her Kindle and announced she was going to read them. I remembered Charlotte had a couple of paperback chemistry books too, and a periodic table jigsaw. She was happy to pass them onto her younger sister. She's finished with them. Yes, Charlotte's chemistry passion is over.

Callum and Imogen were passionate about medicine at one time. They were both St John Ambulance volunteers. Callum actually completed a year or more of a Bachelor of Nursing degree, and Imogen was talking about applying to do medicine at university. But they both changed their minds. Callum's passions at the moment involve cars and mechanics and welding. Imogen is doing a Bachelor of Arts degree: Professional Writing and Publishing.

And what about Charlotte? She moved from chemistry to art. She loves graphic art and has been using the graphics pad and Photoshop. When I think about Charlotte, I think about art school. I imagine her illustrating books. But who knows? She may change her mind too.

I don't think changing passions is necessarily a bad thing. I guess a parent might even be relieved when certain passions come to an end: "You could never have made a career out of that interest!" Except she might have done. I have learnt not to crush dreams however unrealistic they seem (to me). We all need to be allowed to follow our passions. They will lead somewhere, probably somewhere totally unexpected and maybe very exciting.

Perhaps there are times when we don't need to be passionate about anything. Charlotte is having a quiet time at the moment. This was worrying me. "What are you interested in, Charlotte? What makes you feel excited?" She shrugged her shoulders and didn't seem excited about anything in particular. "But what about your art? How's that going? Remember how you used to love chemistry? Perhaps you need to explore new areas?" Oh, the pressure we can put on our kids! I have decided to be sensible and back off. Perhaps we all need these quiet times. No doubt new inspiration will hit when least expected. That's what happens to me.

I am very much involved with a new passion at the moment: video making. I've even become passionate about homeschool record keeping, which seems rather miraculous. I'd never have predicted that one. Recently, so many of my thoughts have been occupied with Evernote. Actually, I had another Evernote idea last night. It appeared out of the blue while we were watching a movie. I had to turn on my computer again and try it out. Then, of course, I got to bed later than I planned because I wanted to work on this idea. And when I did get to bed, I couldn't sleep because I was thinking about it. Passions do that to a person.

Anyway, what's this fabulous idea of mine? It's an idea for 'planning' unschooling. The words unschooling and planning don't really belong in the same sentence. Unfortunately, educational authorities don't seem to understand how unschooling works, and they ask us for our educational plans when registration time rolls around. How can we give them what they want without putting

141

together plans we will never use? Yes, I have an idea that might satisfy us and the authorities.

Could I put together an Evernote unplanning strewing notebook? I could fill it with resources associated with the school syllabus topics, including links to videos, websites, music, books, and articles. My girls might enjoy dipping into these notes whenever they're looking for something new to investigate. I might enjoy dipping into them too.

After I'd mulled my idea over for a while, I thought, "I must make another Evernote video about this idea!" My second thought was, "But everyone must be sick of my Evernote videos. I've already made four of them.

"Write a blog post instead, about something other than Evernote," I told myself. So I'm writing a blog post. But what I really want to do is make the video. I don't suppose it matters whether anyone wants to share it. That's the way it is with passions. We want to do them just for their own sake.

Talking of videos, one of my blogging friends has recently made a few interview type videos. After watching the latest one, I'm now wondering: could I learn to make one of those? Who would I interview or chat with?

"Imogen, would you like to chat with me? Could I interview you for a video?" I ask.

"Okay. What would we talk about?"

Talk about? I have no idea but, no doubt, one will appear if I think long enough. So I'm going to learn a new skill. Another one. I'm feeling excited. Again.

"Do you know where I got the idea to become a vlogger from, Mum?" asks Sophie. "It was you. I saw you doing it and thought I might be able to do that as well."

Do our kids watch us? Do they see our excitement for learning? Are they inspired by our example?

You know what? I think parents need to follow their passions too. We shouldn't just help our kids with theirs. We should spend time doing what we love. It's important. It's essential. For us. And for our kids.

Do Our Passions Complete Us as People?

I wrote this story the day after Gemma-Rose competed in her first 5 km run. I wanted to explore a new thought about passions and interests that had occurred to me as I stood on the sidelines, cheering my daughter on.

Yesterday, I saw Gemma-Rose engrossed in her passion for running. Something extra appeared while she was racing. It was as if she became fully alive.

Is it possible that our passions complete us as people? Can they make us more fully who we are meant to be? As Gemma-Rose flew along the track, surrounded by runners of all ages, confidence, skill and joy oozed from her. Her eyes were alight. A huge smile lit up her face. She looked strong and capable. Gemma-Rose's passion for running had pushed her into a happy zone.

Do we allow our kids to be more fully who they are? Do they deserve to feel the joy that results from being involved with their passions? Is it our role to ensure that this happens? Or do we believe deep down that nobody deserves to be that happy? Life is tough. It's better if our kids get used to this idea.

Following interests doesn't necessarily mean an easy and lazy life. We might think children will work harder if we insist that they learn what we feel is important rather than what they like. But pursuing passions can sometimes be frustrating. It's not all pleasure. A lot of effort, perseverance and commitment are involved. Like training for a 5 km race. Or writing an unschooling book. Maybe the joy we feel from doing the things that we are passionately interested in comes from the satisfaction of knowing we are working hard, overcoming the difficulties, and developing our talents as we try to achieve something new.

Of course, our children's interests may change. They might move from one to another. But this is all part of the process of self-discovery. Children should be allowed to discover who they are. If they don't do this while they are young, they'll flounder when they leave the security of the family. As my daughter Sophie said, when young people don't know who they are, they might go out into the bigger world and copy the people around them, adopting their values and lifestyle. But when our children know themselves, they are confident, they like who they are, and the opinions of others won't sway them.

Sophie has many passions and interests. She doesn't have time for all the things parents worry about: alcohol and late night parties, bad company, smoking and other habits that injure the health. "You're boring!" someone recently told her when he found out she isn't a party animal. Sophie just grinned. Later, she said to me, "How can I be boring? I have so many interests. They are all part of who I am."

So when children are exploring their interests, are they discovering who they are? Do they become confident and skilful? And happy?

Are our kids' passions and interests part of who they are?

How I Removed an Engine from a Car

Callum arrives home from town. He stops by my bedroom to say hello. I glance up from my computer and say, "Callum! You could have changed your clothes before going out!"

Callum grins. His long shorts are streaked with grease. His fingers are black. He has a smudge on his face.

"What will people think?" I am smiling. I don't really care what people think.

"You're a reflection of your family," I tease my son. "Everyone will say, 'Didn't Callum's mother teach him anything?'"

"You taught me how to get an engine out of a car."

I don't remember giving Callum any car mechanic lessons, so I say, "Huh? What do you mean?"

"You taught me all that maths and how to develop my fine motor skills." He thinks for a moment because this isn't really what I taught him and what he wants to say. "You taught me to be a self-directed learner."

Yes, that's better. I didn't actually teach Callum much at all. I just encouraged him to follow his interests, and he taught himself.

Callum is a classic example of an unschooler. He has passions. His biggest passion is cars. Over the past several years, he has bought himself three old cars and has taught himself car mechanics. He's had lots of opportunities to work on many different types of problem. His cars are old. What could go wrong does go wrong. As he fixes one problem, something else breaks. It's never-ending. It's a never-ending learning experience.

Callum hasn't done any mechanics courses, but he has read books, joined online discussion forums, and most importantly, he gets his hands dirty (very dirty!) while he tries things out.

The doorbell rings. It's the postman. "Parcel for Callum Elvis." I sigh. The mail is never for me. Heavy parcels, small parcels, odd-shaped parcels: it's all for Callum. It's always spare car parts.

"Hey, Mum! Look at this." Callum shows me a piece of metal and rubber. "Doesn't that look good?"

"Oh, yes!" I agree. I have no idea what I'm looking at, but Callum's enthusiasm is infectious.

"What do you like best, my camshaft or this?"

"Definitely the camshaft," I say. "Poetry in motion." We both smile. I think Callum likes how I take the time to look and listen even though I haven't much idea about things to do with cars. I'm always exclaiming over the beauty of some part or other. (Have you ever noticed the excellent design and engineering that goes into every single piece of a car?) It's our bit of fun, but it's serious too. We share a lot. Callum is always talking over his plans, his dreams and his ideas with me.

Callum has been working full time as a trainee manager at a local big chain supermarket for the last few years. It's a good job. It's well paying. It's a job with prospects. But it no longer excites him. He has bigger and better ideas.

"I've found out about that welding course," Callum announces one day. "I can fit it in around my work shifts." His eyes are glowing. "When I can weld, I can..."

Yes, one day, Callum hopes to restore and modify cars. Welding, spray painting, mechanics, engineering, a business of his own. Yes, he has plans.

I love watching Callum involved with his interest. He's always encountering problems, but he works doggedly away at them until he has solved them. It's hard work. Sometimes it's frustrating. But it's also satisfying. It's what he loves doing.

There's only one downside to having a child (even an adult one) with a huge passion: the mess.

"The engine is out of my ute," grins Callum. He's replacing it with a new one. "Do you want to see?" So I go outside, and

147

there's this huge engine attached to an engine crane, sitting on our driveway.

"Where are you going to put that?" I ask. I already know the answer. Soon it'll be a feature of our garden, together with his other spare engine and all the extra bits and pieces scattered here and there. I remind myself: no one learns unless they make a mess.

"You got that engine out of the car, Mum."

"I did?"

"Yes, if it weren't for you, I never would have learnt the skills to do it."

Isn't that nice? Isn't that encouraging? I didn't have to teach Callum a single thing about car mechanics.

"You got that engine out of the car, Mum."

You didn't know I can remove car engines, did you?

Engines, Muscles and Spending Time with Dad

I remove the engine from Callum's old ute. It's no longer needed. "I'm going to fit a bigger, more powerful one," my second son tells me.

So Callum goes on a search and finds just the engine he's looking for. "It needs a bit of work, Mum, but it's going to be fantastic!"

The new engine sits on our driveway for a few weeks, and then one day, Callum says, "You want to help me work on my engine, Dad?"

"Go on," I encourage. "You two men will enjoy working together."

Andy and Callum spend a day outside in the sun, tinkering and chatting. Late afternoon, they reappear with huge grins on their faces. (They're a bit sunburnt too.)

"It's in great working order," announces Andy.

"You should see it, Mum!"

So I go outside to admire the engine.

"That's *our* engine, Mum," says Callum proudly. "That's Dad's and my engine."

"*Our* engine?" I ask.

"Well, Dad did just as much work on it as me. He's pretty good at mechanics."

"Dad has been working on cars for a long time..."

Just before dinner, Callum says to Andy, "Do you want to come to the gym with me, Dad?"

Andy looks a bit unsure, so I say, "Go on! You'll enjoy working out together."

So the men put on their workout gear and head off to the gym. They return a couple of hours later with huge grins on their faces.

"You should have seen Dad," says Callum. "You should have seen the weights he was lifting."

"Well, I'm not an old man yet!" says Andy.

"Nah! There are lots of older and less fit men at the gym than you, Dad!" Then he adds, "I'll get you a copy of my training program. We should work out together all the time."

"Okay," agrees Andy, "but I'm not going to drink your protein shakes." He grimaces. "They taste awful."

Later that night, Andy groans. His muscles feel sore. He gingerly lifts his arms. "I have muscles I didn't realise I had. All that work on the engine and then the gym."

Callum grins. "You don't have to use those muscles tomorrow, Dad. Tomorrow's lower body day."

"You'll come home from the gym with sore legs instead," I predict.

"Silly idea working on engines and going to the gym!" Andy moans. "I'm too old for all that."

But it wasn't a silly idea at all. Kids, even adult ones, love doing things with their parents.

"Hey, Dad! Now our engine's in working order, when shall we put it into the ute?"

"Can't you do that bit?" asks Andy.

"Well, it is *our* engine, Dad!"

Don't you love watching fathers and sons spending time together, sharing their skills and enjoying each other's company? I do.

Part IX: Trust

One of the biggest obstacles to unschooling for some people is the requirement to trust: "I could never let go far enough. I find it hard to trust." So what is trust? And how do we gain it?

Unschooling and Trust

Do we truly believe our kids will learn what they need to know in their own time, without us interfering? Do we trust our kids? Or deep down, do we still have certain expectations? Perhaps if our children aren't fulfilling them, we will start to doubt what we're doing.

So what can we do? How do we learn to trust our children and let go completely?

Perhaps we have to be convinced unschooling actually 'works', though I hate the word 'works'. To me, unschooling isn't about giving a child the best educational advantage we can. It's not about getting high grades and being accepted into university. It's not just an alternative to the various homeschooling methods. Rather, it's a way of life that nurtures and respects children so that they become the people they are meant to be. We don't get to the end of unschooling and congratulate ourselves because it 'worked'. The fact is we don't get to the end of unschooling. It's a life process.

But back to being convinced. Perhaps we need to read a lot of books and blogs and forum posts. Immerse ourselves in unschooling. We can read other people's stories, see unschooling in action, find kindred spirits who will support and encourage us. Of course, there are some sites we should definitely avoid. There are lots of people who'll tell you unschooling is an irresponsible and lazy thing to do. Just google those words. Or perhaps not. They're wrong, but their words might creep into our heads and make us doubt.

How do I know these people are wrong? Usually, they haven't tried unschooling for themselves or given it a fair go. They don't really understand what it's all about. But they think they do. They have strong opinions which they can't back up with any practical experience. I always look at the language a writer uses. Is it factual or mere opinion, well-balanced or emotional? I try to find out a little about the author's background. Is there a particular reason they want to convince us unschooling isn't the way to go? (Of course, no one can sell curricula to unschoolers.) More often, I just click off a negative site and go somewhere else. Because there are plenty of good news stories elsewhere, written by people who do understand the principles of unschooling.

If we are convinced that children can be trusted, perhaps the next step is deciding whether we are being called to do it. For us, homeschooling wasn't working. We were not happy. My relationships with my children were suffering. When I look back, I am grateful we found our way to unschooling. I am guessing that most people who are transitioning to unschooling weren't happy with their previous situation. They are looking for something better. If everything was working, why change?

But still, it's a big step. We might feel it's better to stay with what we know, stick with the crowd, instead of setting off into the relatively unknown. When doubts arise, school or structured homeschooling can look like safer options. We try to convince ourselves that all the pain and sacrifice we were experiencing was just an inevitable part of a parent's duty. If something is worth doing, the pain is worth it, isn't it? Don't we have to endure the tough times as well as the good? Perhaps we bailed out too early. We just have to knuckle down and do what God expects of us, right? We have no choice.

But we do have a choice. I honestly don't think God intends for us to suffer while homeschooling. We will inevitably suffer in life, but we don't have to invite it in. We need strong, joyful, families in order to withstand the battles of life and remain faithful. If there is a better way for our family, maybe God wants us to choose it. Could He want us to trust?

Trust? Isn't this what God wants everyone to do every day? We have to live in the moment, take one day at a time, do our best but leave the future to God who will always look after us. He has a plan for each and every one of us, our children included. I think if we are doing what God wants us to do, He will ensure we are successful.

And I do believe that God wants me to unschool our children. It is such a loving, respectful and joyful way of life, in tune with every aspect of Christian life. I have learnt so much about love while we have been unschooling. And I'm still learning.

153

The treasures are continually being revealed. I only have to pull one of my girls onto my knee and hug her tight to know I am doing exactly what I'm meant to be doing. What is more important than love?

We believe in the principles of unschooling. We feel we are being called to do it. We have knowledge and friends to support us. But occasionally the thought goes through our heads: "Are they really learning anything?" The answer to this question will be obvious if we keep a homeschooling records book.

When I get out my records book and scroll through it, I can see without a doubt that my children are learning. So maybe keeping detailed records, which we can look back on whenever we are feeling insecure, will help us to trust. And these records don't necessarily need to contain evidence of projects and essays. We can observe so much just by looking, listening and talking to our children.

So do you think unschooling 'works'? Have you surrounded yourself with a support group? Are you noting down all the learning experiences your children are having? If you're doing all this, and you believe unschooling is what you're meant to do, then trust won't be a problem.

Give it time and trust will grow.

Acquiring Bucketfuls of Trust

Everyone knows we need loads of trust to unschool. But how do we get it? Where does it come from? Trust isn't something you can buy. It's not something you can apply your will to: *I want to trust; therefore, I trust.* It's something some people seem to have in abundance, and others have great difficulty acquiring.

So where does trust come from?

I could tell you that all we need to do is observe the fruits of trusting. But not everyone has grown up unschooled children. Not everyone can say, "I was right to trust. Look at my kids! They did okay."

I could tell you to look at other people's grown up unschooled children. But you might think, "But they're not my kids. All children are different. What if mine don't turn out so well?"

I could tell you to read as much as you can about unschooling, so you understand the principles. And this might be good except reading and real life could be two different things.

So what would I say? I'd say if you know, without a doubt, you are doing the right thing, then trust won't be an issue.

But how do we know what's the right thing to do? How do we know if unschooling is the right choice for us? Should we try it? Or maybe not?

I don't think we actually have to decide to unschool. We don't have to 'give unschooling a go' to see if it works for us. All we have to do is stop doing all the things that aren't working for our families.

It was easy for me to recognise the things that weren't working for my family. There were many times when I thought, "My kids won't do what I want if I don't yell or threaten or

155

punish." Life was stressful. I was often angry and upset. And unkind.

Yes, I was often unkind to my children, but I felt my unkindness was justified. It was my children's fault I acted without gentleness. If only they'd do what I told them. It was my duty as a mother to persist in pushing them, even when I didn't like what was happening to our relationships. I had to be tough and teach them what was right.

But then one day, I'd had enough. I decided that unkindness is never justified. But I also recognised that even if I acted with kindness by smiling gently and refusing to get upset when my kids protested, this wouldn't fix things. The problem was bigger than that. I realised that we just weren't living life the way it's meant to be lived. I should have been listening to my kids, and not to all those outside voices that bombarded me each and every day. So I changed things. I stopped making my kids do all those things other people told me were important. The conflict dissolved away. And without me realising, we became unschoolers.

Now some people might think I gave in. Maybe my kids rule the house? Perhaps they don't do anything now that I'm not pushing them. I might be a lazy mother who's avoiding the sometimes disagreeable job of disciplining her kids. But none of that's true. I could write a lot about how unschooled children work hard and are considerate and helpful. Those stories would back up my claim. But all I really have to say is this: if I were avoiding my duty and my kids were out of control, I would feel guilty. I wouldn't feel at peace. There would be no joy in our lives. And we have loads of love and peace and joy. Things feel right. I know this is the way we should be living.

So I trust because I'm not willing to *not* unschool. I am not willing to give up the joy, love and peace we have. I refuse to go back to a life where I often found myself being unkind because there was so much conflict within my family.

Where does trust come from? How do we get it? We consider the option of not trusting and choose to live the life that brings us peace.

So if someone said to me, "How will I ever trust enough?", this is what I'd suggest:

Throw out all the things that are coming between you and your children, one by one. And when you reach that peaceful state where joy and love reign, you'll never want to go back. You'll know what you're doing is right. And trust won't be an issue. You'll have it by the bucketful.

When I talk about peace, joy and love, I'm not implying an unschooling life is a perfectly happy life. Oh no! Sometimes life is tough and full of suffering. Unexpected things happen. But when relationships are strong, we can pull together, encouraging and supporting and loving each other through the difficult times.

How to Get Our Children to Trust Us

We know we need to trust our kids, but do they need to trust us? Are we trustworthy?

Gemma-Rose (9) shows one of her ballet paper dolls to Sophie (12), and says, "She's wearing a Firebird costume."

"I remember listening to that music!" says Sophie, with delight.

I remember too, so I say, "I could find that piece of music on YouTube if you like."

The girls nod and soon we are settled in front of my laptop watching a rather grandly dressed conductor directing the various instruments of the orchestra.

When the 10-minute clip comes to an end, I have another suggestion. "I wonder if there are any videos of the actual ballet." The girls sit impatiently while I search. There are lots of videos. We take our pick, and soon we are watching the firebird dance around the damsels in Kashchei's enchanted garden.

Sophie knows the story and asks if I can find the bit where the prince smashes the egg containing the evil ogre's soul. I can't find that small segment of the ballet, but I do discover a much longer 45-minute video of *The Firebird* ballet which looks very promising.

"Shall we watch that another day?" I ask. The girls nod.

And then someone remembers that the older kids drew pictures of the Firebird years ago. Sophie and Gemma-Rose gather pencils and paper, and soon they are busy drawing their own representations of this mythical creature.

I sit and think while they draw. This morning, we had no idea we were going to learn about Stravinsky and *The Firebird Suite* and the ballet. It just happened. I picked up on something

Gemma-Rose said and made a few suggestions which the girls were eager to follow.

I often say, "How about...?" or "Would you like...?" and "We could... " and my kids' eyes usually light up, and moments later, we find ourselves on a wonderful learning adventure together.

The other day, I even teased Gemma-Rose by saying, "We could do some maths," and she actually replied, "Okay." Yes, she was quite happy to listen to any suggestions I had.

I have been musing over the reason why my girls are so open to my suggestions. And this is what I've come up with:

My girls love learning. They know it's a natural part of life. Everyone does it, including adults. So when I make a suggestion, they know I am just sharing learning ideas that all of us might enjoy. Usually, we end up learning something new together.

And secondly, I think they trust me. Trust me? Isn't unschooling all about parents trusting their children, not the other way around? Here's what I am thinking:

We can say we trust our children and we are willing to let them direct their own learning, but sometimes we have a secret agenda. We try to sneak in certain learning experiences that we feel are essential, that we don't really trust our children to learn by themselves. We 'suggest' they might like to learn this maths concept or we might find a round-about way to test their spelling. Children are clever. They realise what we're doing. I guess they could become wary about our 'suggestions'. They no longer trust us.

When our suggestions become important to us, they end up not being suggestions at all. And children know they are not really free to pick and choose from the menu of experiences we are strewing their way. We all know mum is going to be disappointed if they turn around and say, "No, thanks! I prefer to do something different."

And maybe there's another way we can influence the effectiveness of our suggestions. It's all to do with control. Can you remember, as a child, asking a question and receiving a long lecture? Adults are good at seeing an opening and taking over. Children's eyes glaze over, and they lose interest. I try to gauge my children's level of interest and respond to their needs, not use the moment to swamp them in every piece of information that I think they need to know. If I didn't do this, I'm sure that if I suggested an activity they might think, "Oh no! We'd better not agree, or we'll be caught for hours!" Again, I would lose their trust.

On Monday, Sophie, Gemma-Rose and I are going to settle on the sofa and watch a longer version of the Firebird ballet together. I can't wait. I love learning new things. So do my daughters. I might point out a few things as we watch, but I certainly won't lecture. (They will probably point out a few things to me too.) Then afterwards, I won't test them by asking a hundred different questions. (I am sure they'll tell me all about the ballet without any prompting.) I will just let the girls enjoy.

Oh, yes, there's one other thing I will do. While we're watching, more suggestions for further adventures may occur to me. Learning happens that way all the time. I'll be sure to scribble any possible ideas down in my notebook. Then at an appropriate moment, I will be able to say, "How about we...?" And the girls might just say, "Wow! That sounds interesting. When can we do that?"

Or they might not. It really doesn't matter at all.

Part X: Freedom

Maybe many people don't trust kids because they think: "If kids can do whatever they like, they'll probably do nothing at all."

The next few stories are about how our kids are worthy of our trust, and why it's important that we give them the freedom to choose.

How Connection is Essential

Some ideas seem to make a lot of sense. For example, children have far less life experience than parents, so we are in a better position than them when it comes to decision making. If we give our kids too much freedom, they might make poor choices. Some mistakes might not be significant, but what about those that could affect their futures? Surely, a responsible parent will tell her kids what they should be doing? And many parents do exactly that because they love their kids, care about them, and want to do their best for them.

But, of course, if we are unschooling, we don't tell our kids what to do. Instead, we trust. We trust they will make the right choices. We trust they will learn what they need to know. We trust they will get where they want to go. Are we irresponsible? Perhaps we're side-stepping our parental duty?

We might be if we just step back and say, "Do what you like. I trust you will make the right choices." There is more to unschooling than that. We can't be uninvolved. Our kids need our guidance and help. But how can we guide our kids without telling them what to do? If we want to share our ideas, thoughts and experiences in order to help them, why should they listen to us?

We need to be connected with our kids if we want to pass on such things as our values, our sense of right and wrong, and any experiences we feel might be helpful. We also need to be in tune with our kids so that we know when is the right time to offer our help and how to do that in the best way. But how do we become connected? What do we need to do?

We need to respect our kids. Give them the same consideration that we'd give to an adult. We can't treat children as our property or mini-versions of ourselves. Children are not ours to do with as we like. We have to recognise that they are unique individuals with equal dignity to us. We need to speak to children with politeness and care. We can't order them around.

But respect isn't just about being polite. We also have to be sensitive to our kids' needs and moods. We have to imagine what it's like to be in their shoes instead of assuming we know how they're feeling. In other words, we have to show them empathy.

We should listen to children. Really listen with all our attention instead of giving them the impression that we have more important things to do.

We should take our children seriously. Their ideas, thoughts, needs, desires, ambitions, and dreams are important. They are part of who they are.

Of course, kids need guidance, especially when they are very young. We should consider it our privilege to help and support them, to give them what they need, to do what they might not be able to do for themselves. But as they grow, we need to be willing to step back more and more, respecting their choices, allowing them to do things for themselves.

Kids will make mistakes because of their inexperience or an inability to cope. And that's okay. We don't need to punish them. Instead, we must seek understanding.

We have to help our kids be aware of their needs and how they can best handle them. Eventually, they will know themselves better than we do. We can't get inside their heads. We don't know what it's like to live in their bodies or how they are feeling. We might not be aware of all the dreams that swirl inside them and how important they are. Of course, we'll get a fair idea by listening to our kids. They'll talk to us about the things that they value. If they trust us. If we are connected.

We have to accept our kids just as they are. Love them unconditionally. When we do that, they'll know they are important to us. And we'll be important to them. We'll be connected. And our kids will be willing to turn to us for guidance because why shouldn't children listen to the people who love and care about them the most?

Of course, even when kids are willing to listen, they still might choose to reject what we have to say. But this is okay. Kids have to be allowed to work things out for themselves.

And maybe what we say *should* be rejected. Parents aren't always right. That's something to consider. Kids have good ideas. They have a fresh outlook on life. They aren't held back by outdated, faulty ideas that have an inconvenient habit of echoing in our heads. If we let them, we can learn from our kids.

So we should give our kids the freedom they need and are entitled to. That's okay. It's the right thing to do. As long as we're connected.

Talking About Having the Freedom to Choose

"If parents give children the freedom to do whatever they want, will they choose to do nothing at all?" I ask my daughters.

Sophie smiles and says, "It's not possible to do nothing."

"But I've heard parents say to their kids, 'You've done nothing today!'" I insist.

Imogen joins the conversation: "Perhaps parents don't value whatever the child has been doing. To them, it's 'nothing'. It doesn't count."

I ask my girls what they choose to do with their time. And Sophie says, "Write, blog, redesign my blog, take photos and read." Imogen tells me that she likes to write, plan her writing, blog and read.

"You both do a lot of writing," I say. "You spend a lot of time on your computers. I could say, 'Stop writing! That's all you ever do.'"

My girls giggle. So do I. Stop writing? Isn't writing a valuable thing to do? We know lots of parents who worry because their kids don't like writing.

"What if you spent all day playing computer games?" I ask. My girls don't do this, but lots of unschooled kids do. "Do you think kids are learning while they're playing games? Are they doing something valuable?"

"Yes!"

"So a parent shouldn't judge what a child is doing? They shouldn't attach value only to certain things?"

"No."

"But surely a parent knows better than a child. They have more life experience. Shouldn't they have a better idea of what children should be doing?" I ask.

"In some ways, having experience is good," says Imogen. "Parents can use it to help a child, but they can't tell her what she should be interested in. Only a child knows what she values. Parents sometimes have definite ideas about who their children should be and what they should be doing. It's hard for them to accept their children the way they are."

"Maybe parents also worry about their kids," I say. "If they see them doing something like playing computer games, they might wonder if they'll be able to get jobs. They want their kids to spend their time doing something that will lead to a safe career. What their kids are interested in might not seem like a very secure option."

Sophie points out that everyone has unique talents which are developed through their interests. Kids should be allowed to follow their interests and see where they lead. It's irrelevant whether a child's choice is a safe option or not. Parents shouldn't tell kids they should be doing something else, something that isn't suitable for them.

"What a parent should be doing," says Imogen, "is encouraging and helping their kids with their interests so that if they want to turn them into a career further down the track, they've had the best possible start. This will help them to be successful, to do as well with their interests as they possibly can."

I have another question for my daughters: "A child might not seem to be doing anything valuable as far as a parent is concerned. But what if she doesn't seem to be doing anything at all. Sophie, you did say earlier that it's impossible to do nothing."

"A child could be thinking or resting or just stopping to appreciate life. Everyone needs quiet times when they're not doing anything visibly productive. Parents have quiet times. Why shouldn't kids have them too?"

"I think we're taught that we have to cram as much into our days as possible," I say. "And parents worry about how much their kids are doing. Are they doing enough? It makes them feel better if they can say at the end of each day, 'She's done this and this and this. What a productive day she's had!'"

And sometimes kids do look productive. But there are times when they don't seem to be interested in anything in particular. The girls and I chat about how these times are just a normal part of life. They're essential. None of us can work at full pace all the time. We all need quiet periods when on the surface, not much seems to be happening. But who knows what's going on subconsciously? Maybe quiet times are processing times. One day, the spark will reignite. And we're off digging deeper into our interests or chasing an entirely new one.

"Children should be made to do things they don't want to do so that they get used to it. Once they're adults, they're going to have to do a lot of things they don't want to do. Parents are only helping kids develop good habits." I wait to see how my girls will respond.

"Children don't need to be pushed to do such things," says Imogen. "They already do difficult and unpleasant things."

"Like?"

"Chores."

"I've heard of parents who would like to unschool," I say, "but they're worried that their kids will choose not to help with the chores if they have the choice. And they don't have the energy or inclination to do them all by themselves. What would you say to that?"

"Model what you'd like your child to do."

"We have to be prepared to do everything we want our kids to do?"

"Yes. And trust they will do it."

"When kids are trusted," says Sophie, "they want to live up to that trust."

We talk about a few more difficult things my kids do, such as practising the piano and reading dense books and getting up early each morning to run.

167

"Why would kids want to do difficult things?"

"Just because something is difficult doesn't mean it's not enjoyable. In fact, the more we have to work at something, the more satisfaction we get from it."

"Why do you run? Why do you roll out of bed even on cold days or when you're tired and run before breakfast?"

Imogen: "Running is a challenge. I enjoy pushing myself to run further and faster."

Sophie: "I can't stay home when everyone else goes running. I'll miss out. I want to be part of the team. It's good to celebrate the good runs and commiserate over the bad ones. It's a family thing."

"What if a parent does force a child to do things they don't want to do? Could this actually be bad for the child?"

"Yes," says Sophie. "When a parent makes a child do something, they're acting like an external motivator. They're not trusting that the child will make the right choices on her own."

"It's important that children are motivated to do what is right from within," says Imogen, "because when they grow up and leave home, when they're no longer living with their parents, and there's no one to make them do things, the difficult things won't get done. Instead of making their kids do hard things, parents should be giving them the opportunity to make their own choices. They should give them the encouragement and support they need to develop self-motivation."

"Will children follow the good example of a parent?"

"They'll pick up whatever they see around them. They'll learn what's important from the people they spend time with."

"So if a parent chooses to live a lazy way of life, and gives the children the freedom to do whatever they want, will they choose to live a lazy way of life too?

"If parents don't do much in a day, then children aren't going to see a reason to do anything much either."

"But we're talking about unschooling children. Do you think unschooling children are lazy?"

"Of course not!" My daughters are adamant.

I guess that means unschooling parents aren't lazy either. You might have been wondering about that. Years ago, I used to think, "Wouldn't it be good to unschool? I wouldn't have to do anything at all!" Oh my, I was so wrong.

It's funny how we can pick up the wrong ideas.

With So Much Freedom Will Children Choose to Be Lazy?

If a parent gives a child the freedom to choose what she wants to do every day, isn't there a risk she will choose to be lazy and not do anything at all? Or maybe she will decide to do what is easy, rather than what is challenging?

While we were driving to town this morning, I asked the girls if they'd brought along some books they could read, while waiting their turn to have their piano lessons.

"I've got *Les Miserables*," said fifteen-year-old Charlotte.

"Are you still reading that?" I asked.

"I know I'm going slowly, but I'm making progress. I'm definitely going to finish it." Then Charlotte added, "But I can't say it's one of my favourite books. The action keeps getting interrupted by long passages of history. I have read a lot about the French Revolution."

"It sounds like *Les Mis* is the ultimate info-dump novel," observed Imogen.

"Info-dump?" I asked.

"In novel writing, information can be given as part of the story, or it can be dumped in large chunks between passages of action."

"All that French Revolution stuff sure slows down the pace of the novel. I guess it's a good way to learn history, but I decided to read the book for the story," said Charlotte. "It really is hard work persisting sometimes."

"Are you tempted to give up?" I asked.

"No. I chose to read the book, and I'm going to finish what I started. I want to say, 'I read *Les Miserables*,'" said Charlotte. "I've also promised myself that when I get to the end of the novel, I will watch the film version. I'm looking forward to that."

"And the stage version," said Imogen. "That should be good as well."

I told the girls that Victor Hugo also wrote *The Hunchback of Notre Dame*, but I couldn't tempt Charlotte with this novel, at least not in the near future. "I think I will read something different next. How about reading another Charles Dickens, Imogen?"

"That sounds good. Which one? *Nicholas Nickleby*?"

The girls have set themselves the goal to read every single Charles Dickens novel. I guess they will.

I have never read any of Victor Hugo's novels. I did start *The Hunchback of Notre Dame*, but after a chapter or two, I lost interest. I have never even considered reading *Les Miserables*, unlike Charlotte. The girls are doing much better than me with Charles Dickens too. I've been reading *Bleak House* for what seems like years, (but I'm going to finish it!). Imogen and Charlotte finished that novel a long time ago. Just imagine if we adults had to do everything we'd like our children to do. Would I be able to keep up? I doubt it very much.

It seems to me that if unschoolers were lazy, they wouldn't voluntarily attempt to read such challenging literature as *Les Miserables*. And sometimes they even choose to persevere when the going gets tough.

Now I know not all unschoolers enjoy literature. This is only an example. Callum, a former unschooler, isn't doing any reading at the moment except car manuals. But you should see him under the bonnet of a car, working out how to fix various problems. In his spare time, he isn't sitting back doing nothing. He's busy learning new things. His energy and determination and ability to work things out impress me. He definitely enjoys a challenge, which is just as well because as he solves one problem, he discovers another and another.

Do unschoolers choose to be lazy? Are they inclined to take the easy option rather than the challenging? No, I don't think they do.

Do Unschoolers Choose to Do Difficult Things?

I often run down the main fire trail that winds its way through our local bush. The track descends gently at first but then drops away so steeply I have to take care not to lose my footing. After I have descended 57 metres from my starting elevation, I turn around, ready to make the return journey. It doesn't take long for the muscles in my legs to start burning as I climb back up the rock-strewn sandstone track. When I get to the midpoint of the ascent, I always have the same thought: *Why did I run down so far? This isn't fun at all. I'm never doing this again.* But, of course, I do.

I wonder why I put myself through such agony, time after time. It's not as if there's anyone watching me. No one would know if I cheated and didn't descend quite so far. I could stop running at any point, and it wouldn't matter at all. So why do I choose to do something so difficult?

My daughters Imogen, Charlotte, Sophie and Gemma-Rose also run down that steep hill. I don't make them. Like me, they just want to do it.

Hill running isn't the only hard thing my girls choose to do. Three times a year, they write novels during the various NaNoWriMo (National Novel Writing Month) months. They take up the challenge of writing 50,000 words in 30 days. At the beginning of the month, the words flow easily. It's fun. But as the days pass, writing becomes more and more difficult. There comes a time when they are tempted to give up.

"I can't wait to do something other than writing this novel," Sophie says. "I want to take more photos, write some blog posts, work on something different."

She could give up and fail the challenge. She could choose not to write another word. But she says, "I can't *not* finish." Something pushes her on.

Then there's music. I never have to push grumbling girls towards the piano to make them practise. Their fingers fly up and down the keyboard, playing scale after scale, over and over again. A certain section of music refuses to sound right, so it's played multiple times. It can be frustrating. But my girls choose to do it.

My daughters do a lot of things they don't have to do. They freely choose to do them. Why?

Are my children following my example? Is it all about wanting to be part of the Team? Or could it have something to do with personality? Perhaps Elvises are just stubborn and don't know how to give in. Or could there be something else influencing us?

Perhaps we all have an inbuilt need for a challenge. We need goals which will stretch us. We all want that wonderful, satisfying feeling which results from hard work.

I think back to our non-unschooling times. In those days, I set the goals for my children. They followed my expectations, which were often based on the expectations of others from outside our family. There was no need for my children to seek their own challenges. Maybe there wasn't time. Whatever the reason, they certainly didn't freely choose to do difficult things. They were more inclined to avoid work when the day's learning was over.

Of course, there are all kinds of difficult things. Parenting is one of them. What keeps us going when things get tough? It's love. And children also do things because of love. Maybe love is the greatest motivator of all.

So if no one pushes unschooling children, will they choose only to do what is easy? No. My unschooling children work hard without any pressure from me. I'm sure they're not unique. I think it's true to say: unschooling children choose to do difficult things.

Why We Don't Have to Push Kids to Work Hard

This morning, my husband Andy watched as our girls, and I got ready to go for a run. As we laced up our shoes, he grinned and said, "What a mean mother you are making everyone run before breakfast!"

Although Andy was joking, I'm sure many people might take his words seriously. Perhaps they would indeed think I am a mean mother because what other explanation is there? Surely four girls wouldn't choose to get up early, pull on their running gear and head out the door when they could stay in bed?

A few days ago, after I'd finished my morning run, I watched my daughters as they finished theirs. Despite having run about 6 km, they suddenly picked up speed. With determined looks on their faces, they sprinted towards me side by side.

A few moments later, as they eagerly upturned their bottles and gulped down water, I asked: "Why do you do it? Why do you always come running with me? You could choose to stay in bed."

"Well, I have to admit that sometimes the thought of running doesn't appeal. So I refuse to think. I just roll out of bed and get dressed. And then by the time I'm fully awake, I'm here. And that's good."

"Running is hard work. When I'm only halfway up a steep hill, and my legs are aching, I wonder why I do it. But the feeling afterwards? It's *so* good. It's worth all the effort."

"Running is a challenge. I get a huge sense of achievement from doing it."

"I like being part of the Team. If I stayed in bed and you all went without me, I'd be missing something. I'd be the only one who hadn't worked hard."

"I love being out here in the bush at this time of the morning when everyone else is still in bed. We're doing something no one else is doing!"

Once the girls' breathing had returned to normal, we gathered our hoodies and water bottles and plodded home. It was time to eat.

Listening to my girls, it seems to me that kids love challenges. They choose to work very hard without any prodding from us. Perhaps they even have an inner need to get their teeth (or feet!) into something difficult.

Unless, of course, we keep them busy doing things *we* think are important. Then there will be no reason for them to challenge themselves because we'll be doing it for them.

"So what are we having for breakfast?" Sophie asked as we approached our house.

"That reminds me," said Imogen. "Breakfast tastes so good after we've had a long run. I'd do it just for that!"

Of course, your kids might not run, but I bet they do like challenges. Perhaps we all have an inner need to do something that pushes us hard. What do you think?

Part XI: Screen Time and Technology

Watching TV, Playing Computer Games, Doing Nothing Much at All

We trust our kids and give them the freedom they need to explore their interests and become independent learners. We know they will challenge themselves, work hard, and do difficult things. But what if they choose to spend lots of time on their computers or watching TV? Is that really okay?

Perhaps you've started unschooling. All of a sudden, there are no plans to follow. You aren't saying, "This is what I want you to do today." You're hoping your children will be eager to follow their noses when it comes to learning. You've imagined them using their new freedom to pursue impressive projects. Other unschoolers are doing wonderful things. You're excited because soon your kids will be doing amazing things too.

But they don't. They're sitting on the sofa watching TV. When they're not doing that, they're playing computer games. Or they're lounging around, doing nothing much at all. And you're worried because this isn't what you had in mind when you said, "You're free to do what you want."

So what can you do?

Some people say kids need a deschooling period between schooling and homeschooling. Maybe they also need such a period when they are transitioning to unschooling from structured homeschooling. It takes time to get used to looking at learning in a completely different way.

Also, there are times in our lives when we all need a break, especially when we're experiencing a big life change. We need time to rest, think, and do nothing in particular. A time to adjust. A time when nothing much is expected of us. I have had difficult periods in my life. Getting through each day was enough for me without doing anything additional. Then one day, I woke up and felt ready to tackle new challenges, and I was off again, chasing new adventures. When we think about it, transitioning to unschooling isn't a small event, particularly if schooling or homeschooling was stressful, which it probably was, because if all had been going okay, why change?

But just say you've been patient and your kids still aren't showing any signs of making a move towards self-directed learning. Could it be they are already doing this? The problem may be their learning doesn't look anything like what you imagined.

The television and the computer are great learning tools. I can't see how our kids can fail to learn while using them. Both present information. The computer is also interactive. I am constantly amazed at what we can do with computers and the Internet. There are many wonderful opportunities to do many unbelievable things. These are some of the things my girls have been doing: animating, learning to code, editing videos, writing novels, designing blogs, blogging, watching videos, vlogging, designing games.

All this sounds good, but what if a child only wants to use the computer for games? Games are good too. I've tried playing some of the computer games my girls like, and I am hopeless. I can't think or react quickly enough. My brain doesn't make the right connections. I am absolutely sure that computer games are teaching my children to think creatively and to solve problems. We tend to dismiss things we have survived without or don't understand. Perhaps sitting next to children and asking them to explain a game will help us value what they are doing. I am always so delighted when someone wants to share my passions. It's very special when one of my kids takes an interest in what I'm doing. Why should it be any different for our children?

We might be able to accept that a computer is a valid tool for learning. We might even be happy to let our children play computer games. Perhaps the problem isn't actually the computer (or the TV). It could just be the amount of time a child spends using them. Maybe we worry when we see a child sitting in front of a screen hour after hour. We might feel like saying, "Go and do something else! Go outside and get some fresh air!" How do we get our kids to balance their screen time with other activities? Can we? And is it inevitable that every child will want to spend excessive time on their computers if we let them?

I can only tell you about my family. All my children have their own computers, and they use them whenever they like, for as long as they like, for whatever purpose they like. We have no computer (or any screen) rules. So do my girls spend all day on the computer? No. Not having rules doesn't necessarily mean no regulation. My children moderate their usage for themselves. They tell me they don't want to spend all their time in front of the computer because there are so many other interesting things they want to do: play the piano, sing, run, sew, draw, read, talk and other things as well.

Interesting things to do? Could we enrich our children's worlds, show them other possibilities, give them new ideas, expand their horizons by strewing? Could we invite them to share our own activities? If we are willing to share their computer worlds, they might be more inclined to share our interests too, or at least listen when we suggest alternate activities. Although my girls love using their computers, they also love spending time with me. If I say something like, "Let's walk to the village and buy ice cream" or "Shall we read together?" or "I could help you with that sewing", my girls will close their computers (unless they need time to return from their creative worlds). I wonder if all kids respond like this when we spend time nurturing our relationships. Or is it just a personality thing?

Could it be that some children might be overdosing on the computer because restrictions have suddenly been relaxed and they are hungrily catching up with what they feel they have missed out on? When they realise the computer won't suddenly disappear, they might pull back and start to moderate their usage naturally. I've heard this is some people's experience.

But I've also heard some parents say their children are addicted to the computer. Or they think addiction is a definite possibility and want to avoid it. I'm not saying parents shouldn't worry about such things. But maybe the problem isn't with the computer. Could a child who seems addicted have a need, such as loneliness, that the computer is fulfilling? All I am certain about is this: having no computer rules doesn't inevitably mean addiction because it hasn't happened to my children.

Then again, perhaps addictions do happen to everyone. It depends on how you look at it. We are all passionate about something. I love writing. You could say I'm addicted. Every opportunity I get, I open my computer and start composing. If my computer isn't handy, I scribble in a notebook. I have lots of notebooks. I grab whichever one I find first. I write when I'm supposed to be doing housework. I forget to eat. I write in my head while I'm lying in bed. I even dream about writing. It's most inconvenient when I'm in need of some good sleep. But most people would say writing is good. We all want our children to like writing. (Mine do.) So my addiction is probably acceptable. It is true that I do other things besides write. I run most mornings with my girls. I make sure I spend time with my children before I start writing. But once I have entered my creative world, I have effectively disappeared.

If I want my children to be willing to put aside their 'addictions', I must be willing to put aside mine. This means pulling myself out of my creative world whenever I am needed. This is hard. But because we are all writers in our family, we understand each other and make allowances for this. I don't often expect my children to interrupt their activities at a moment's notice. They are gentle with me too. This is why I think a time limit rule for computers is not appropriate.

So I spend a lot of time writing, and that might be acceptable. If I were practising the piano for hours or reading book after book that would be okay too. But what if I spent all that time playing on the computer instead? You'd probably tell me I have a problem. I suppose what we are talking about here is putting a value on different types of learning.

If we are unschoolers, we accept certain unschooling principles (or we are working towards accepting them). We trust a child will learn what he needs to know when he needs to know it. But do we always believe this? Or are we only at ease with unschooling when a child's choices match our own expectations?

Is it Really Okay to Give Kids Unlimited Access to Screens and the Internet?

I have shared how giving kids unlimited access to screens doesn't necessarily mean children will choose to spend all their time using them. All my kids have no trouble regulating their usage. So is that the end of the story? Is that all I've got to say about screens? Or should I recognise that some people might indeed have problems using screens and the Internet? Maybe I have a problem too.

Perhaps you've been reading about unschooling, and you like the idea, but there's one thing that makes you feel uneasy: unlimited screen time. What if your child spends an excessive amount of time on their computers or phones? Perhaps you feel they're wasting their time? What if their screens seem to be causing them to behave in a way you don't feel is healthy?

There are lots of unschooling articles that will reassure you about screens. Their message: if we allow our kids to have as much screen access as they like, they will learn to self-regulate their usage. We just need to let go of control and trust our children. They'll work it out for themselves. And I have found this to be true. My children have always had free access to screens. I have never made any rules. And they all use their screens in productive and balanced ways.

But are my children representative of all kids? Is it okay for me to say, "Look at my family? Follow our example. Your fears are groundless." Or are you right to worry about the effect of such things as screens, the Internet, social media and computer games on your children?

Even though my kids handle these things well, I don't. I have got very entangled with the Internet, and it's affecting my life. Not so long ago, I faced up to the fact that I need to make some changes. I want to regain my peace and my concentration, which affects my ability to do worthwhile work. I also want to strengthen my face-to-face relationships. These have been suffering because my attention has been online rather than offline.

Screen time. How do we feel about this word? Does it make a difference what type of screen our kids are using? And are we more comfortable letting them have access to a screen if we feel they are doing something worthwhile with it? For example, we might be happy for our children to do research using the Internet or complete an online course or belong to an online book study group. We might be willing for them to spend a lot of time on their computers if they are writing.

But what if our kids are on social media or playing computer games or watching YouTube videos? Perhaps we label these activities as time-wasters because we don't see the value in them. However, we learn from everything in life, and we all have different interests, so maybe our kids should be allowed to spend time doing the things that are important to them, regardless of our feelings. If we accept this idea, we should let our kids have free access to screens. It's the right and respectful thing to do.

But what if we let go of control and our kids go wild (in our opinion) and don't want to do anything except sit in front of a screen? We might reassure ourselves that once they realise we're not going to take away the screens, they'll relax and slow down. It's all a novelty at first, but after a while, they'll want to do other things as well. They're not always going to want to spend every available hour on their computers or tablets or in front of the TV.

However, despite what other people tell us, we might not really be convinced this will happen. Deep down, we don't trust our kids will be able to self-regulate. Do children pick up on these feelings of doubt? When we say, "You can spend as much time on your computer as you want," we could also pass on the message, "I'm not sure I'm happy about this situation." Are we waiting for the first opportunity to grab back control? Kids know when we don't feel comfortable. They don't trust us just like we don't trust them. So maybe if we aren't 100% committed to an idea, it won't work. We'll end up changing our minds about unschooling.

Why do we fear letting go of control? Why do we feel very uncomfortable when we are asked to trust our kids? Do our own experiences affect how we feel? Are we untrustworthy? If we don't trust ourselves to behave sensibly when we're using our computers, how can we ever trust our kids?

What is sensible screen behaviour? We might all have different ideas about this. Do we think it's okay for everyone to live life with one eye always on a screen? Are we happy living in a society where most people communicate via their screens instead of having face-to-face relationships? Do screens and the Internet bring great value to our lives? They allow us to be constantly connected with information and each other regardless of where we are in the world. Is society evolving in a positive way because of technology?

Or do we yearn for more face-to-face conversations? Do we need to do things with our bodies? Do we need to connect physically with other people? Perhaps we feel technology such as the Internet is distracting us from living real life and doing deep work.

There is no doubt that technology has enhanced our lives in many ways. And we can't go backwards. This is the world we live in, the world where our kids will one day get jobs. We can't close our eyes to technology even if we, at times, don't like it. But do we need to be careful when using it? Do we need to guide our kids when they want to use such things as the Internet?

I guess a lot depends on whether we think the Internet holds any dangers for our children. Are we happy exposing them to it? Or do we worry they will become addicted to it and therefore become unhappy?

Is there really such a thing as Internet addiction? I don't think it's inevitable that our kids or we will become addicted to the Internet (or even computer games). But maybe some of us will have more problems with it than others. Could the Internet fulfil certain needs within us? For example, maybe we overuse social media because we're lonely. Perhaps it's easier to browse the Internet and play games online instead of getting down to serious work. Is it worth pondering why we feel pulled towards the Internet when there isn't a good reason to use it?

A while ago, I decided to reduce my online time. I deleted my Facebook account. I'm making an effort not to hop aimlessly around the Internet. I've deleted some phone apps. I'm no longer constantly checking my emails and other notifications. I want to regain control of my online life so that I have a better offline one.

The Internet hasn't always dictated my behaviour. Not so long ago, I used to be like my children. I'd purposefully use the Internet. I had good concentration skills. I did valuable and deep work. I spent far more time offline than online. So what went wrong?

"Why can't I handle the Internet and you can?" I ask my daughter Imogen.

"Your work is online, Mum. You're expected to use the Internet. That's where you meet people and do things. It's easier for us because we don't have to be online as much as you."

Yes, once we get involved with the Internet, its hold of us can get tighter and tighter. There's always one more email to answer, one more article to read, one more comment to write, one more photo to post, one more story to share, one more problem to ponder, one more person to help, one more... It's never-ending. I justify the time I spend online: I'm doing worthwhile work. But sometimes we have to step back and reclaim our lives. We can't do good work when we feel overwhelmed and unhappy.

So if adults can have screen regulation problems, is it reasonable to think that some children might have them too? And if they do, how can we help them? Should we limit their screen time? Should we let them use their screens only for certain purposes? Perhaps we need to exert our parental control? This might be the responsible thing to do.

Or do rules about such things not work? Do they result in battles? Will kids look for ways to break the rules? Will they try to use screens without our knowledge?

I'd rather my kids were free to do things in front of me rather than in secret. I want us all to be honest with each other. So I don't make any screen rules and limits. But if we don't make rules, how do we ensure kids don't get themselves into situations where they become unhappy because they are unable to deal with their screens? Maybe connection is the answer.

We can't say to our kids, "Go and do what you like," and then step back and let them get on with it. Unless, of course, we have strong connections with them. Maybe we need to build up the bonds between us so that our kids value our opinions and look to us for guidance. We can then talk about our own experiences, our struggles, the dangers that we face, and how we're dealing with them. Of course, we should also listen to our kids as they share their opinions, thoughts, ideas, and what's important to them. Parents also have to be good examples. We might have to make changes in our behaviour if necessary. And maybe we have to help some of our kids determine what their needs are and how they can fulfil them in ways other than by spending excessive time online.

Perhaps we have to guide and support our kids towards self-regulation in a respectful way. Doing this gives them the opportunity to learn about themselves and their needs and work out their own ways of dealing with screens, ways that allow them to do what is important to them without compromising their happiness and health. And isn't that better than just making a lot of rules?

So is it really okay to give unschooling kids unlimited access to screens and the Internet?

I say to Imogen, "Most unschoolers state that if we trust our kids and let them have free access to such things as the computer and the Internet, they will learn to self-regulate their usage. Do you agree?"

"Yes."

"And if kids seem to be overdosing on their computers when the restrictions are lifted, this will pass once the novelty wears off."

"Yes, that makes sense."

I then say, "I've never made any screen rules, and none of you has a problem. It's all very simple, isn't it? Or maybe it's not. I've been thinking about how I have free access to the computer, and I'm having trouble controlling my behaviour. I waste time online. I get distracted. I feel unhappy with how I keep checking my phone. So if adults like me can show addictive behaviour online, perhaps kids can as well. Maybe it's not enough to reassure other parents that if they let go of control, everything will be okay."

After listening to me, Imogen has something of her own to add: "If parents are worried that their kids are using their screens in a way detrimental to their health and happiness, they can't just say, 'Turn off the computer and go do something else.' It's not that easy. What will kids do? It's important parents build up an offline life full of rich experiences that a child will want to be part of. A parent has to do something. They can't just stand back and make rules.

"And what if parents have been using technology as a babysitter? They might be happy for their kids to use it when it suits them. But then they complain when kids want to use it at other times. Is that fair?"

"Perhaps parents have to work on their connections so that their kids trust them and value their opinions. This will also ensure parents know their kids very well. If we all have strong bonds of connection, maybe we can allow our kids free access to their screens, and there won't be any problems."

Our conversation continues. There's a lot to say. It's a complicated issue.

Why I Don't Restrict My Children's Time on the Computer

Parents might limit screen time thinking they are doing the right thing for their kids. However, kids need time to do the work that's important to them. Being told they have to get off the computer can be very frustrating.

"How long have you been on your computer, Mum?" asks my daughter Imogen. "You'll be getting rectangular eyes if you're not careful."

"Not long," I say hurriedly. "Oh, all right, I admit it. I've been on here quite a while, but you should see what I've been doing."

The girls gather around, and I proudly show them an animation I'm working on.

"Look! My sprite is moving across the screen, and then it turns around and comes back," I say with a big grin on my face.

Yesterday, the girls and I discovered a new programming website. All evening, Sophie, Gemma-Rose and I sat side by side trying to work out the basics of using code to make an animation. It wasn't long before we had sprites moving across the screen, but they were gliding rather than walking. We just couldn't work out how to move their legs.

The girls went off to bed, but I continued experimenting. Suddenly I knew what to do. I got very excited. There was no way I was going to be able to wait until the morning to share my cleverness with the girls. I ran to their room: "Are you still awake? I've worked it out. I know how to make a sprite walk!"

This morning, I shared my new animating knowledge with my daughters. Soon fish and aliens and people were all swimming and marching and strolling back and forth across the screen. Then we moved onto new problems. Sophie wanted to add conversation to her animation, and I experimented with music. Gemma-Rose has been modifying sprites, customising them to her taste. I predict we will be spending lots of hours on the computer as we try to conquer the skill of coding.

Lots of hours on the computer? That sounds rather frightening, doesn't it? Do we want our children spending so much time in front of the screen? Perhaps we should limit them to half an hour or an hour of computer time a day?

"Mum, your hour is up. I'm sorry, but you've got to go and do something else now," orders Imogen.

"But... but... I've almost solved this problem. I can't leave my code right now."

"No buts, Mum! I want to see you outside, getting some fresh air."

I huff, and I puff, and I glare at the girls.

Imogen bursts into giggles. "Oh, okay! Just joking, Mum. If you want to keep working, you can."

I giggle too. But I also think about how frustrating it would have been to interrupt my thought processes and stop work when I was right in the middle of a challenge.

I spend a lot of time on the computer, usually not making animations but writing. I enter my creative world as I write, and it is often difficult to return to the real world at a moment's notice. I understand when my girls are also absorbed in their writing. Now I'm wondering if the same thing happens when kids get involved with computer games and animations and other activities.

But do we consider animating and game playing and game design as worthwhile activities for children to be involved with? Are we willing to let them work for as long as they want?

Work? Or a waste of time? I guess that's the big question. Kids would certainly say they're doing worthwhile work. I think I would too. It's problem-solving. It involves creative thinking skills. And like it or not, computer technology is part of our world, something our children need to know about. It also happens to be very enjoyable.

Perhaps you're not sure about all this, and you're worried about how much time your kids are spending on the computer. If so, get on there with them. Ask them to share their passion. See what's absorbing their interest. Join in and have some fun.

If we share our children's interests, perhaps they'll share ours. Well, that's how it seems to happen in our family. We're always sharing each other's passions and learning from each other. We have loads of things we like to do. And right at the moment, we are enjoying animation. But not exclusively.

"I'm off to have a run," I say, as I close my computer. "I'll finish that animation later." I have decided, without any prompting from my bossy children, that it's time to do something else.

"While you're running, I'll practise the piano," says Sophie.

Gemma-Rose continues fiddling about with her sprite. That's okay. I understand: Animation is absorbing. A time will come when she feels satisfied. And then she'll move on.

Are Computer Games a Waste of Time?

Does your child like to play computer games? Maybe you wish he'd do something else because you think he's wasting his time doing nothing much at all.

The other day, my girls were playing a computer game.

"What game are you playing?" I asked.

"*Run*," said Gemma-Rose. "It's great. *Run 2* is even better."

"Can I have a go?" I asked.

"Oh, yes!"

A moment later, I had the computer on my knee and my fingers on the keyboard. Sophie and Gemma-Rose explained exactly what I needed to do.

"Ready, Mum?"

I nodded. This was going to be easy. All I had to do was direct the little alien down a tunnel, avoiding all the rectangular shaped pits along the way. I only had three controls to worry about: the left and right keys and the space bar, which was for jumping.

The game began. My little creature approached a pit. I pressed the space bar. He flew through the air. He landed safely on the other side. He ran around the next hole and over another. Soon he was at the end of the tunnel. I'd completed level 1. I grinned. I was still grinning a few levels later.

"You're doing very well, Mum!" congratulated Sophie.

Those words were scarcely out of her mouth before things fell apart. I pressed the space bar. My alien shot up into the air and then disappeared down the very first hole. Game over. Back to the start. My alien set off again. I pressed the space bar. He shot up into the air and disappeared down the very first hole. Game over. Back to the start.

"Jump at the corner, Mum, and rotate the wall with your left key."

"Keep your touch on the keys light."

My daughters' suggestions didn't seem to make any difference. I couldn't move my little alien safely all the way through the tunnel.

Gemma-Rose sensed I was getting frustrated, so she said, "Would you like me to do this level for you?"

"No," I said firmly. "I'm going to do this myself." And a long time later, I did.

On to the next level. And the next. I wiped my brow. I breathed deeply. I stretched my aching fingers. I was working hard.

"I thought this would be easy," I confessed between levels. "I just don't have the right skills."

"You need good concentration and memory," said Sophie.

"I think my biggest problem is I lack the necessary connections in my brain. I just can't think quickly enough. I can't do everything I need to do all at the same time."

After a while, my head started hurting from all the effort. "I think I've had enough for one day," I said at last.

"You did very well, Mum!" Both my daughters were grinning at me with delight. "And you'll get better with practice."

I learnt a lot from this experience. Children certainly aren't doing nothing when they're playing computer games. They're concentrating hard. They're building connections in their brains. They're learning how to think and act quickly. Depending on the game, they might be doing a whole lot of other things too.

And there's something else I found out: children love sharing their computer games.

One more thing: until we share our children's experiences, how can we really know what they're doing?

So if you're worried your child isn't doing much at all while he's playing a computer game, then how about asking if you can have a go? Sit side by side. Enter your child's world. See what it's all about. You could end up having a lot of fun. (I suppose you might also get a sore head!)

"What's *Run 2* like?" I ask my daughters.

"*Run 2* is like the original game except you can skate as well as run."

I'm looking at the game description:

This game requires enormous concentration and memorisation!

I don't think I'm going to conquer this game any time soon. But what if I worked at it? I might gain 'enormous concentration and memorisation.' Now wouldn't those skills be worth having?

Should Unschooling Kids Live Balanced Lives?

You might agree that our kids are doing worthwhile work when they're using their screens and the Internet. But you could still be worried. If kids are glued to their screens all day, will they miss out on other things? Shouldn't kids live balanced lives?

I often hear stories about parents who are concerned because their kids don't seem to be living balanced lives. "My child wants to play on the computer all day. She spends hours doing only one thing. I'd like her life to be more balanced."

Usually, unschoolers are reassuring: Balance is a parent idea, maybe even a school one. Slicing our days up into sections so we can fit in a bit of this and a bit of that is artificial. That's not how life is. Kids know what they need and want to do. They know how much time they need to do it all. They should be allowed to immerse themselves in their interests and passions without being interrupted.

And I agree. It can be frustrating having to leave an activity just because someone decides you need to do something else. We shouldn't make kids swap activities when they're working deeply on something. It breaks their concentration. Kids don't need to do a variety of things each day. They can stick with one thing all day if they like. All week, or even all month if that's what they want to do. I have found that over time, my kids learn about an enormous amount of things. It just doesn't happen evenly. Interests come and go and return and then disappear again. Kids learn the skills they need. They just do it in their way and in their time. They don't need their learning to be timetabled. Yes, we don't need to worry about balance.

However, perhaps we can think about balance in a different kind of way. To be healthy and productive, I know I need balance in all areas of my life: family, work, health, recreation, and spiritual. When one of these is out of balance, I get into a mess. I end up doing nothing properly, and I don't feel very peaceful either. And maybe it's the same for our kids.

So how do I encourage my children to live balanced lives?

I can't say, "Go outside and exercise!" I've tried that. It results in a sullen child who digs in her heels and thinks it's no business of mine whether she exercises or not.

I can't insist my kids pray with me.

I can't make them relax and have quiet times and maybe go to bed early if they need to catch up with their sleep.

I can't make them swap the digital noise of the Internet for the beauty and quiet of nature.

But I do want my kids to be healthy, physically and mentally. I don't want them to feel stressed and overwhelmed. I'd like all parts of their lives to work together so that they are happy and productive people

So what can I do? I can live a balanced life myself. Be a good example. Exercise. Delight in nature. Have quiet times. Go early to bed when I need to. Turn off my computer. Let my actions reflect what I think is important and hope what's important to me will become important to my children. This might happen if we remain connected.

Perhaps I can also talk about these things, sharing what I discover. I might invite my kids to join me when I'm doing such things as exercising and praying. I could create a general atmosphere of balance in our home.

And if I'm concerned that one of my kids is living an unbalanced life, if I can see that her actions are leading to problems with such things as her health, I can talk to her. By talking, I don't mean I should jump in and tell her what I think she should do. Instead, I can find out how she's feeling. Is she fitting in all she'd like to do? How are things going? Listen and then reflect back. Help her decide what's important and how to achieve what she wants to do.

Because it's all about our child, not us. Unless, of course, we're talking about our own lives. Yes, perhaps we need to be prepared to make some changes in our lives too. How many times do we get concerned about our kids without first looking at ourselves?

Is living a balanced life important? I think it is. If it's the right kind of balance.

An Unschooling Day at Home

The phone alarm beeps at 6.10 am. A few minutes later, I swing my legs over the side of the bed and pad down the hall to the girls' bedrooms. I open their doors and say, "Anyone want to come running with me?" I can see vague shapes stirring in the semi-darkness.

Soon after 6.30 am, Charlotte (16), Sophie (13), Gemma-Rose (10) and I are walking down the road to the park. It's quiet and cool, the best time of the day. We run 5 or 6 kilometres of our bush track circuit, up and down the hills, in and out of the trees. Finally, I say, "Good work, Team! Let's go home for breakfast."

As soon as we arrive home, Charlotte grabs a large pan and begins making porridge. I disappear into the shower. Showers, breakfast, and morning chores. We wash dishes, clean bathrooms, make beds, sweep floors and fill the washing machine before we say morning prayers together.

We gather in the living room. My eldest son Duncan joins us. He's still on his university break. Andy and Callum are at work. Imogen (19) is away from home, visiting a friend for three days. Prayers, Bible reading and a meditation. We chat about the day ahead of us. "What shall we have for dinner? Do we need to get some meat out of the freezer? Does anyone have any plans for the day? Does anyone need me to do anything special for them?"

The washing machine has come to the end of its cycle. The girls follow me into the garden, and we hang out the clothes. It's pleasant in the sun, but it looks like it's going to be a hot day.

The postman arrives with two books that I ordered online a couple of weeks ago. One of them is called *Secret Garden*. It's a sophisticated colouring-in book containing page after page of intricate drawings of flowers and leaves and birds. I show the book to the girls and tell them that I'm going to use some of the pictures as embroidery designs. "I saw this idea on someone's blog," I say as I open my computer to show them.

Charlotte disappears into her bedroom. She has things she wants to do. She has a pile of books to read, an online art class to work on, and a science video she is going to watch. Sophie and Gemma-Rose and I settle ourselves on the sofas in the family room.

"What do you want to do?" I ask my younger girls.

"Will you read to us, please?" asks Sophie. I nod and reach for our current book, Jackie French's *The Road to Gundagai*. Sophie takes up her sewing, and Gemma-Rose grabs her sketchbook. They like to keep their fingers busy while listening.

I come to the end of a chapter, and I look up. I know Sophie is going to plead with me to keep reading. I decide to read until it's time for morning tea. 10 o'clock arrives. I fill the kettle and make coffee and pour glasses of milk. Gemma-Rose opens a container sitting on the kitchen bench. It's full of scones that she baked yesterday.

While we munch and sip, I check my emails. I visit Facebook for a few minutes and 'like' a few posts. The girls open a book or have a look at their blogs. Charlotte appears. I close my computer and invite her to sit down and tell me about what she's been doing. She shows me some cereal box paper dolls she's working on. She tells me how much she enjoyed reading *The Drovers Road Collection*. We all discuss the book, remembering how much it made us laugh when I read it to the younger girls a while ago. We compare what we know about New Zealand (the book's setting) to our own country, Australia. "I'm going to write a blog post about the book," says Charlotte.

Gemma-Rose already has a blog post ready to publish. She wrote it yesterday. It's about a doll she made. She hits 'publish' and then I visit Facebook briefly to post a link to it on my page.

"Mum, did you read my chapter of our novel?" Sophie asks. I did. Now it's my turn to write the next part of the story we're writing together. We discuss the plot, so I know what I'm doing.

I have another book I'm reading aloud to the younger girls: *Refuge*. This is also by Australian author Jackie French but completely different from the one we were reading earlier. There are only a couple of chapters left, so I read them both. I also read the author's notes at the back of the book. The themes of the book are immigration and asylum seekers. We find ourselves discussing these issues. We talk about why not everyone coming to Australia is allowed to stay, and who can stay and why. And aren't we fortunate living in a free and peaceful country?

We wonder: what is Australia's population density compared to other countries? We look up the population for Australia, Japan and the UK, and then the areas of each of these countries. Sophie takes a piece of paper and a calculator, and soon she's worked out the population densities.

"Wow! We have far fewer people per square kilometre than those other countries. Only about three people per square kilometre (using data from 2013). There's plenty of room for more immigrants!"

Yes, we are a sparsely populated nation even though a large part of our country is desert. The girls can see that when we look at a map.

While the map is out, the girls find Christmas Island where there is an asylum seekers' detention centre. Both girls use the grid coordinates to pinpoint the island. We notice a key to one side of the atlas page, and soon we are locating capital cities, major towns, airports, agriculture and industries.

Sophie is thinking about the *Secret Garden* book that arrived in the mail this morning. "Do you think I could embroider a design from the book too?" She decides to write a blog post about her plan.

I hop over to Facebook quickly and post a link to the book while I remember. I want to thank Kelly for recommending *Secret Garden* on her blog.

"Can I read to you, Mum?" asks Gemma-Rose. She already has her book on her lap: *A Little House of Their Own*. It's the last book in the Caroline Years, one of the Little House book series. We sit side by side on the sofa and enjoy a chapter together.

Just before lunch, someone asks the question, "Where did the metre come from? How do we know all metres are the same?" I do some research while the girls make lunch, and then while we sit around the table eating, we have a great discussion about the imperial, the metric and the US systems of measurement. We laugh over the mental image of King Henry I extending his arm out to the side and saying, "The distance from my nose to my thumb is exactly one yard."

After we've washed the dishes, Sophie practices the piano. I find Charlotte sitting on the sofa rereading *The Road to Gundagai*. "Which bit are you up to?" she asks. She stole away our book a few days ago and read it to herself quickly. But the book must have been good because she is back for a second look.

I take some time to answer a few blog comments and emails. Before I finish, Sophie appears and says, "If I had some chocolate, I could make some chocolate oaties."

"Put on some sunscreen, and when I've finished replying to these comments, we can walk to the village and buy some." Ten minutes later, Sophie, Gemma-Rose and I are enjoying a stroll to the village store. Charlotte chooses to stay at home. She is practising her singing.

Sophie begins cooking as soon as we return. I'm not sure what Gemma-Rose is doing. She could be writing or reading or drawing. I know what Charlotte is doing. I can hear her. It's her turn to use the piano.

I decide to edit another of my children's stories. It's been a long time since I last looked at the manuscript for my book *The Angels of Gum Tree Road*.

Charlotte interrupts me at my computer. "I'm about to start dinner. What shall we have with our burgers?"

"Do we have any salad?" We don't. "Do we have any potatoes?" We do. I volunteer to chop some potato wedges. Gemma-Rose decides to help me. Sophie has finished baking the oaties. We each sample one. Then Sophie makes some yoghurt. We wash a few dishes. It's almost time for dinner. There's just time to bring in the washing, tidy up a little, and set the table.

My husband Andy goes to the gym on his way home from work. Callum is at TAFE (Technical and Further Education) doing his welding course. Imogen isn't due home until Friday. So only the three younger girls, Duncan and I sit down to eat.

More dishes to wash and then Charlotte decides to watch a movie. The other girls ask if they can borrow my tablet so they can play a game together. I return to my computer and my editing.

Then Andy arrives home. While he eats dinner, he tells us about his day. Then he wants to know everything we've done. After relaxing for a while, Andy prepares his lessons. The younger girls announce they're off to bed. I ask, "Do you want me to wake you for a run in the morning?" They nod. I have my diary to write. Charlotte comes to say good night. We spend some time chatting about her day and what she has achieved.

It's the end of another unschooling day.

But before I climb into bed, I grab my homeschool records book. I want to make sure I record all the day's learning experiences. I translate everything into schoolish language under such headings as English, Maths, Creative Arts, and Science.

I think about what we did today:

We ran and walked. We prayed and read the Bible. We cleaned and washed and tidied the house. We baked and cooked dinner together. We did lots of writing and editing, reading and listening. We discussed and researched. We looked at maps and manipulated real life numbers. We explored the world and its issues. We drew and sewed, practised the piano and sang. We imagined and dreamed and hoped.

Today we spent lots of time together. We learnt a lot. We laughed and enjoyed. I guess that makes today a typical unschooling day at home.

Part XII: Maths

Maths can be a stumbling block for potential unschoolers. Can kids really learn the maths they need without formal instruction? What if we feel unable to let go of maths? Can we still call ourselves unschoolers? And what about higher maths? Even if kids aren't interested, shouldn't they learn it just in case? What if they want to go to university some day and need more maths?

Being Honest About Unschool Maths

Unschooling except for maths? Is that really unschooling?

I want to discuss that question, but first: why is it so hard to let go of maths? I've never heard anyone say, "We unschool except for history or creative arts or science. Why do many of us cling to old and false ideas about learning when it comes to maths? Do we not believe our kids will pick up all the maths they need by living life?

Or maybe we don't think that's enough maths. Although we may never have used it, perhaps we think our kids should learn higher maths just in case. Just in case of what? If our kids ever need more maths than they know, they can always learn it. It's never too late.

We might tell ourselves that even if our kids never use all this maths, it's a good mental exercise. They might not retain everything, but it won't be a waste of time and effort because their brains will have got a workout.

And maybe we think that because we survived higher maths, it won't hurt our kids to do it too.

I've also been pondering another idea: perhaps some of us don't want to let go of maths, both primary and high school, because it would make our homeschool record-keeping more difficult.

My daughter Charlotte completed part of a higher maths course. Her story illustrates how we can fool ourselves. I won't say we are dishonest, but we know that if we look too closely at a situation, we may discover something we don't want to deal with. So we don't look.

I told everyone Charlotte loves maths. "I love maths. My kids love it too. We're a maths family. We like playing around with numbers." This explained (I hoped) why my kids did structured maths courses even though we called ourselves unschoolers. I told everyone that my children enjoyed these courses. But did Charlotte really like working her way through the many levels of higher maths? For a long time, I didn't know because I didn't ask her. She never complained about doing maths. Therefore I assumed that she enjoyed this subject because it was convenient for me to believe this.

Yes, sometimes we can look at things with half-closed eyes because it's convenient. Charlotte's online maths course records provided an easy way for me to prove she was doing the required maths for homeschool registration purposes. If she gave up her course, what was I going to do? I'd have to find other evidence that she was learning maths. Could I do that? Maybe but it would certainly be much more difficult than running some maths worksheets and progress reports under the homeschool registration visitor's eyes. So I continued not to examine the situation too closely. And my kids continued learning maths in a formal way. We weren't 'unschooling, but I require my kids to do maths'. I didn't require maths. Oh no, my kids wanted to do it. They loved this subject.

Except they didn't. One day, my daughter Sophie said, "I hate maths." And eventually, I got brave and asked Charlotte how she felt, and she confessed she wasn't enjoying her course as I had hoped. I knew I had to do something: I let go of maths.

I want to go back to that question: Can we call ourselves unschoolers if we require our kids to do maths?

If we think of unschooling as a pathway that we progress along as we learn more about this philosophy, I think it's quite okay for us to require maths and still call ourselves unschoolers. The particular point where we are standing at the moment is the one just right for our family. And maybe we'll stay there. Or perhaps we won't.

But we all have to keep our minds open. Keep thinking. Keep learning. And be honest. Ask the question: are we really at the correct point for our family? Do we need to be brave and examine what's really going on rather than what we hope is happening? Perhaps we're doing something a certain way because it's convenient and not because it's right. If we find out that our kids' learning is being negatively affected, we have to face the something about it. We can't stand still and say, "This is what suits our family," when really it might only suit us, the parents, and not our children at all.

So I decided to be honest about maths. I listened to my kids, and then we let go of it. I lost the convenience of having lots of formal maths records. But that was okay. We still manage to get through our homeschool registration visits. I've discovered something: if we think about things long enough, there's usually another way.

My Older Children's Maths Story

I'm going to share my family's maths story. It will show you how I changed my thinking about maths. It took me a long time but eventually, I stopped making my kids 'do maths'. Why? Because I had to.

Many years ago, my kids used workbooks or textbooks to learn maths. When they were small, they didn't complain. Filling in a few pages of maths was just part of their day. They knew that once this subject was out of the way, they could move onto something more interesting.

On the surface, I was happy with this situation. I thought that it was good for my children to practice maths for a short time each day. But there was a problem that I didn't really want to face: my children were filling in a lot of worksheet pages in an impressive manner, but were they remembering much? I suspected they weren't. However, I turned a blind eye. The filled-in pages showed that my kids had done their maths. I was able to tick off maths in the homeschool records book.

As my kids got older, things became more complicated. They were no longer content to do maths because it was expected. They didn't think that was a good enough reason. It didn't make sense to them. They started saying, "Why do I have to do this? When will I need all this maths?" And my answer was always the same: "All this maths might come in handy one day. You just never know." What I really meant was, "I don't know when you're going to use it, but I had to learn it. Everybody does. It's just the way things are. So you're going to learn it too. Just in case because we don't know what's ahead of us." And I thought that was a pretty good reason. Yes, just in case.

I had a lot of battles with my three eldest children. They protested that *just in case* wasn't a good enough reason. I knew deep down they were right. Eventually, my teenagers wore me down. I was tired of fighting with them. I knew we had to make a change. As a compromise, I suggested my children swap their advanced maths courses for a general maths course that included such topics as banking and taxes. They couldn't protest that this kind of maths wasn't relevant to their lives. One day they'd have to use these skills. So my teenagers soldiered on for a little longer, but none of them finished their courses.

I expected my daughter, Imogen, to follow in her older siblings' footsteps. I thought she'd also say, "Why do I need to learn all this maths? I'll never need it." But she didn't. Imogen was different. She decided for herself that she wanted to do an advanced maths course. "I want to go to university, Mum. Maybe I'll apply to do a medical degree. I think I'll need maths for this course." There was also another big incentive: "I'm going to be the first Elvis child to complete this course!" When you are fourth in line, there are not many things left that haven't already been achieved by an older sibling.

So how did Imogen learn advanced maths? She started with a textbook and then we discovered an online course. Imogen liked the video lessons, the summaries of essential skills, the concise worksheets, and the records that showed her at a glance how far she'd progressed through the course and what grades she was achieving. All went well for a time, and then Imogen came to a section that we felt wasn't adequately explained by the video lessons. I could see Imogen's confidence falling. I thought soon she's going to say, "I don't want to do this anymore. When am I ever going to need all this maths?"

So for a few weeks, I spent extra time searching the Internet for more information and trying to work through the maths examples with Imogen. Doing this meant that I was spending less time with the other girls. I decided that there had to be a better way.

One day, I discovered that a friend in our parish is a high school maths tutor. Instantly, I could see the maths problem disappearing. Would John tutor Imogen? Yes. He was more than happy to give her a weekly 2-hour lesson for free.

John set the tone from day one. Imogen appeared after the first class with a broad smile on her face. "John said that if I were in school, I'd be in the top few percent of my class. He thinks I'm very capable." Full of confidence, she tackled the course her siblings had hated and failed to complete. John's lessons ended up being one of the highlights of her week. After three terms with John, Imogen completed the advanced maths course at the age of 16.

This sounds like a very successful maths story, doesn't it? Yes, Imogen completed the maths course with an excellent grade at a young age. But did she retain all the knowledge that John had helped her to learn?

A couple of years after finishing the course, I asked Imogen how much of it she remembered, and she said she'd forgotten most of what she'd learnt. She remembers the feeling of satisfaction that came from completing the course, but she's forgotten the actual content. That's because she changed her mind about doing a medical degree. She didn't use the knowledge she'd gained because she ended up studying an arts degree. The maths wasn't needed.

I've also forgotten a lot of the higher maths I learnt as a child, but I can remember how satisfied I used to feel when I worked through a problem and got the right answer. It didn't matter to me whether the maths I was learning was useful or not. I just liked the black and white nature of formal school maths. I either got the right answer, or I didn't.

I was very disappointed when all of my older children failed to like maths as much as I do. I couldn't understand why they weren't excited about this subject. Did they just have different interests to me? Different interests for different people? Or was there more to it than that? I wondered whether the way my children learnt maths had put them off it. But then again, my fifth child Charlotte seemed to enjoy maths.

I once wrote: "Charlotte, like Imogen, has decided for herself that she wants to complete the advanced maths course..." But Charlotte never did finish that course. One day, I had to face the fact that, although she was enthusiastic at the beginning, she, like my older children, began to wonder, "When will I use all this maths?" But unlike her older siblings, Charlotte didn't complain. And I didn't ask even though I suspected all was not well. You see, I rather liked Charlotte doing a formal maths course. Her worksheets provided me with easy evidence that she was learning this required subject. Yes, I had lots of maths records to present at homeschool registration time.

But eventually, I faced facts. I asked Charlotte how she was getting on. She screwed up her face and said, "When am I ever going to need to know such things as trigonometry?"

And that was the end of her formal high school maths studies.

Were my children who never finished a high school maths course disadvantaged? No. All of them have studied at university level. One son even completed a Master's of Teaching (primary) degree. They all have the mathematical skills that they need.

It's funny how we worry about such things as maths, isn't it? Why is maths such a big deal?

Why My High School Unschooler Isn't Going to Learn Any More Maths

I didn't use trigonometry today. I didn't use it yesterday. I don't suppose I'll get an opportunity to use it tomorrow. Sometimes I wonder why I ever sweated over it, memorising all those cosine, sine and tangent facts. What a waste of time that was! Or was it? You never know: a trigonometry opportunity may be just around the corner. I might get up next week, and it will be the perfect trigonometry day. I'll say, "Hey! It's just as well I learnt trigonometry. I'd be stuck if I hadn't. I'm so glad I spent all that time learning the facts all those years ago!"

All those years ago? It's been rather a long time since I last sat down and worked out a maths problem using trigonometry. I don't actually remember much about it. I spent a long time learning it, and I have forgotten everything I ever knew. What am I to do?

I guess if that trigonometry situation does arise, I could always google 'trigonometry'. How long do you think it would take me to learn what I need to know? If I really need to know it, I'm thinking not long at all.

So why did I waste all that time at school learning trigonometry? Well, I didn't have much choice. I was made to 'learn' it. Except I didn't really learn it at all. I memorised enough to get me through the maths exam and then promptly forgot it. You see, I had no use for it. It didn't seem worth retaining all those facts.

But I got a good grade in maths. Surely that was an achievement? Yes, I can say, "I did advanced maths, and I got into the top percentile when comparing my results with all the other students in my year." That sounds impressive, doesn't it? Not everyone can say that. I can still boast about it, even today. But it's an empty boast. "Let's sit down and do some trigonometry," someone might say. "I'm much too busy to do that," I protest. I wouldn't like him to find out that I know nothing about the subject. All that's left of my knowledge is a vague memory of angles and calculators.

If one day, when we're sitting in our aeroplane seats flying over Australia, one of my daughters turns to me and says, "Mum, what distance did our plane travel before taking off?" I could always google the formula I need to work it out, assuming I have Internet access from my seat. If I am unable to google straight-away, I might wish I'd memorised the facts. But it wouldn't make much difference if I did have an intimate knowledge of trigonometry because I'd have to wait for another piece of important information. I would need to ask the pilot what angle his plane took off at, relative to the ground, wouldn't I? I can hardly do that when the plane is in mid-air.

And if a neighbour leaves a ladder leaning against his house with its top rung level with the intersection of the wall and roof, and one of my girls notices as we stroll by on our way to the village store, and asks, "How long do you think that ladder is, Mum?" I might be able to tell her if I again know the right formula. Of course, I'd need to know the height of the house and the angle the ladder makes with the wall. Wait a minute! Wouldn't it be easier to lay the ladder down on the ground and measure it with a tape measure?

I discovered these two examples of trigonometry by googling 'everyday use of trigonometry'. Everyday use? I don't think I have ever come across problems such as these in my everyday life.

But what about my career life? There was no need for me to know trigonometry when I worked in a research lab in a veterinary physiology department of a university. But what if I'd had a different job? What if I'd needed that information? Wouldn't I have been grateful that I'd learnt all those formulae? For, of course, school was my one and only opportunity to learn such things. Or was it? If I had suddenly decided to enter a field where advanced maths skills were needed, I could have done a course there and then, couldn't I?

Charlotte (16) and I are talking about what she wants to learn about this year. "How about maths? Do you want to do the higher maths course?"

Charlotte screws up her face. "When am I ever going to need to know such things as trigonometry?"

"Well, you never know," I reply. "You could learn it just in case."

What am I saying?

"What if you need it in the future?"

"Then I'll learn it then. It's never too late."

"So you feel you know enough maths for now?"

Charlotte nods her head.

You don't want to learn more just for the fun of it?"

"No."

Sophie might choose to explore maths simply because she enjoys it but not Charlotte.

What will everyone say when they find out my 16-year-old daughter is not going to finish the Higher School Certificate maths course?

"She might need maths."

"It's a good mental exercise."

"Isn't she clever enough to do it?"

Oh, Charlotte is clever all right. She's cleverer than most people. She's not going to waste her time on something that might never be needed when there are so many other things she wants to do. And if she ever does need higher maths, she's clever enough to learn it quickly without all those years of repetitive examples.

And I think I'm quite happy about that. I'm letting go of old ideas and other people's expectations.

Giving Up and Letting My Kids Unschool Maths

One day, when my daughter Sophie was about nine or ten, she told me she hated maths. She also told me she wasn't very good at it. I immediately said, "Of course you're good at maths!" I hoped these words would solve the problem. Just be positive and offer lots of encouragement and everything would be okay. But it wasn't. My heart sank. I could see Sophie following in the footsteps of her older siblings. I could see years and years of battles ahead of us. Sophie would go through the motions of learning maths, not enjoying it but doing it because it was required. I didn't want to go down that road again. Surely there was a better way?

Again, I wondered if the problem was more to do with the method of learning maths rather than the subject itself. I decided we'd have to change our approach to maths. Was there a more interesting way of exposing my girls to this subject? I wanted to find out. Perhaps I could try a few different things to see if I could interest Sophie in the topic.

So I went looking for something better than workbooks, and I discovered online maths courses. I thought this was the answer to our problem. These courses looked very attractive. Maths concepts were taught using games and other interactive activities, which were colourful and fast moving. They looked like a lot of fun. I hoped my girls would look at the course and think, "Wow! I'll enjoy doing this!" Maybe they would like having an avatar. They could change their hair colour and style, and dress them in different clothes. Also, there were virtual worlds that they could build: zoos, bedrooms, gardens and other places. The girls could earn points by working through the maths activities, and they could spend them on furniture, animals, toys, and other things to add to their virtual worlds. There was another aspect of the online courses that appealed to me: the girls could earn certificates as their point scores grew. I could print them off. I knew they'd look good in a folder and we could use them for homeschool registration purposes.

So I signed my daughters up for the online maths course. And for a while, Sophie was happy to sign into her account, do the activities, and earn the reward points and also some certificates that I could put into her homeschool record portfolio. With her reward points, she built up her virtual worlds. Every day she changed her avatar. She actually raced through the activities gathering points. At first, I had a huge smile on my face. I thought, "This is working very well. Sophie is learning so much!"

Then one day, Sophie started saying once again, "I hate maths. I'm no good at it." My heart sank again. I realised that swapping a workbook approach for an online maths course wasn't the answer. However attractive these courses were, they weren't convincing Sophie that maths is an interesting subject. They weren't giving her confidence in her ability to learn and use maths skills.

So what was the problem? The online maths courses were just dressed up versions of the workbooks Sophie had previously been using. Both approaches relied on a reward system to motivate kids to learn. With workbooks, the rewards were ticks and gold stars and the satisfaction that came from filling in the answers and then turning the page knowing the task had been completed. The rewards offered by the online course looked more attractive. For a time, they did motivate Sophie to learn. But eventually, they also lost their attraction. She no longer wanted to change her avatar. She didn't want to buy something new for her virtual worlds. She'd been there and done that and was no longer interested in collecting points. Learning once again came to a halt.

There was another problem: Sophie had raced so fast through the activities, collecting points along the way, that she hadn't absorbed the concepts properly. That was why she was saying, "I'm not very good at maths."

So we were back to square one. Sophie was once again telling me she hated maths. I could have just told her to get on with it: "I don't care how you feel. Maths needs to be done. Look how lucky you are. I found you an online course. I paid for it. It's much better than workbooks. Maths is the only thing I require you to do." But I didn't actually say any of these things. What I wanted to do was give Sophie another opportunity to discover whether she could enjoy maths. I know that not everyone does enjoy maths, but I wanted to find out whether she truly didn't like it or whether it was just the way I was presenting it to her. Perhaps I still hadn't found the right approach.

So the next step was unschool maths. I had to be brave and let Sophie experience maths in an unschool way.

Now, this might seem like a big step to many people. A bit risky, maybe. How will kids learn all they need to know about maths unless the concepts are presented to them in a logical and formal way? Risky or not, I knew I had no choice. If I didn't let go of maths, I'd have to face more years of another child telling me she hated maths. Sophie and I would battle every day. And what would be the result at the end? We would have loads of maths notes in my homeschool records book, and it would look like she'd done a lot of maths and we'd fulfil the homeschool registration requirements. But it would all be a waste of time because Sophie wouldn't get much out of her learning. Yes, she might pick up the basic maths concepts, but she wouldn't remember much else.

And so I decided to let my youngest children, Sophie and Gemma-Rose, learn maths in a real way as part of life rather than force them to do a formal maths course.

How do unschooled children learn maths as part of life? Some parents step back and let their kids work out the mathematical concepts by themselves confident they will do this. And this approach is successful. Kids do have the ability to learn all they need to know. However, I haven't done this. I want to do more. I know my girls will learn all the maths skills they need just from living life, but if I expose them to other mathematical experiences, perhaps they will want to learn more. They could become fascinated with this subject and want to learn about it just because they're interested.

So I strew maths in front of my children just like I strew everything else. I find maths-related books, videos, podcasts and documentaries. I show them real-life maths they may not have noticed. I share the maths that's part of my life. There's no shortage of things to strew because the world is full of maths. We just need to start looking with the right eyes. When I find

216

something interesting, I strew it. Sometimes my girls want to look. Sometimes they don't. Whatever they decide is quite okay with me.

Some people might say that maths is different from other subjects. We have to learn it systematically. It's not something that can be picked up piece by piece in a seemingly random way. But that's how I'm presenting maths to my children. We're approaching it from many different angles using a variety of resources, and we haven't been anywhere near a textbook for a long time. Even though we're not starting at the beginning and working our way through the concepts in order, my children are learning a lot of maths. And they're enjoying it too.

I once said to Sophie: "I'm thinking about making a podcast about unschool maths. Do you have anything to say about this topic?"

"Oh, yes!" she replied. "You're talking to the girl who hated maths and then turned around and now absolutely loves it. I have LOTS to say about unschool maths!"

Those words made me smile. I guess Sophie no longer hates maths. She no longer thinks she can't do it.

Thinking About Maths Creatively

It seems to me that there are three main ways of learning maths: the workbook way, the real-life maths way, and the messing-about-with-numbers way.

Sophie once learnt maths the workbook way. She started with paper books. Then she moved on to an online structured maths course. The course looked attractive, even exciting. There were flashing and colourful interactive activities, cute avatars to change each day, and virtual rewards and points to collect. But really, online maths courses are just dressed up versions of workbooks. A child works through them in an orderly fashion, working out endless problems in the hope that the concepts will seep into their memories never to be forgotten.

Sophie enjoyed her online course for a short while, and then the avatars and clever interactive activities lost their appeal. They were novelties hiding rote learning. Sophie reluctantly signed into her account each day, until one day she announced, "I hate maths. I'm no good at it."

It was time to rethink maths, and this is when we tried the second method of learning maths: real-life maths. I realised that children need to see a use for all the maths they learn. So I went searching for real-life maths experiences. Sophie baked and counted her money. She drew geometric patterns for fun. She calculated the distance she ran each day. From time to time, I strewed interesting maths resources and books under her nose. I tempted her with computer games and other activities which at first glance didn't look like maths. I found maths in the most unexpected places like computer science courses. We viewed videos and tried out maths gizmos. And all this worked very well. Sophie started to say, "I like maths!" She began to take an interest in anything mathematical.

Sophie (11) is still very interested in real life maths, but just recently, I have realised she is also learning maths in a third way.

It all started when I bought Sophie Bill Handley's book, *Teach Your Children Tables*. Sophie learnt to do such things as work out her times tables without memorising them and to multiply big numbers in her head. It was all very impressive. It gave her confidence. She was having fun. One day she said, "I think I'm turning into Skye Penderwick!" and she grinned, liking this idea very much.

Bill Handley approaches maths in a totally different way to traditional maths learning. Using his methods, a child can solve a problem quickly, and accurately, with better understanding, and at the same time, have fun. I must admit I thought, "Why learn a new way of doing things when the old way works too?" But I am getting older, and new thinking isn't as easy for me as it is for Sophie. Even if these new ways of solving problems are never adopted, there is real value in trying them out because they encourage thinking skills and creativity. Not everything has to be done the same way automatically.

A couple of days ago, I noticed an old Mega Math workbook sitting in the dust on the top of one of our bookshelves. I bought it years ago at a secondhand store, and no one has ever used it. I showed the book to Sophie, and her eyes lit up. It was written by Scott Flansburg, who is known as the Human Calculator. We found a YouTube video of Scott showing off his mental maths skills, and Sophie was impressed.

"Would you like to be a human calculator?" I asked. Sophie nodded her head, emphatically.

Is there really any call for superfast mental skills? Does it matter if a child can manipulate numbers quickly or not? Is it just a gimmick?

I have been thinking about this, and conclude the value is not so much in impressing others with superior maths handling skills. The real value is loving numbers so much that you just can't help thinking about them, and experimenting with them, seeing what you can do with them. It's possible to be as creative with numbers as some people are with words or a basket full of fabric or a piano full of keys.

Imagine adding up the cost of all the food items a them in a shopping basket. Or seeing a random street ı telephone number and working out all its factors. Or counting the number of waves breaking on the shore in 10 minutes and calculating the number that will wash up on the shore in 24 hours. Or trying to beat a record of adding as many numbers as possible in 60 seconds. Imagine doing such calculations purely out of enjoyment, doing them instinctively because you are curious and love manipulating numbers. When she reaches this stage, a child is learning maths not because it's expected, and not because he can see a need for it. He is being creative with numbers for their own sake. He just loves messing about with them.

Maybe it's like English. You can learn the rules from a book or learn how English works by using the language in real life situations. Or you can love manipulating and experimenting with words so much, you will write just for pure love. You will enter that delightful creative world as often as possible and not really want to return when other things beckon. As a writer, I can relate to all of this. I just never imagined such creativity could be applied to maths. I always assumed maths was very black and white. And now I am beginning to see that it is very colourful indeed.

So Sophie is learning maths the real-life way. (She has at times seen the value of a bit of old fashioned memory work too.) But her real love is playing with numbers. She likes working out puzzles, attempting to add up long lists of numbers without resorting to paper, and thinking about numbers at odd moments for no reason other than enjoyment. Yes, I think she is turning into Skye Penderwick.

Yesterday Sophie said to me, "I don't suppose there are many jobs in the world for mathematicians."

"Oh yes, there are," I replied. "A lot of people haven't discovered how interesting maths is. A lot of people are looking for other people to do their maths and their thinking for them."

"Do you think I could be a mathematician?"

"Of course!"

A short while ago, I would never have imagined Sophie wanting to become a mathematician. Now it is a real possibility. It all came about because she spent time, not with workbooks or even real life problems, but because she started messing about with numbers.

These days Sophie no longer says, "I hate maths!" She is enjoying it. She is confident. And she is good at it too.

Disguising Maths Practice as Fun

I once bought a book containing loads of ideas for making maths games. I was very excited at the thought of printing off some paper game boards, finding a pack of cards, and then saying to my children, "Hey, would you like to play a game with me?" I imagined them learning their times tables or common number additions while they were enjoying themselves. They wouldn't even know they were 'doing maths'.

They wouldn't even know they were 'doing maths'? To me, that sounds a bit deceitful. Would I be tricking my kids into learning maths? This makes me feel uneasy. Maybe that's why I never actually used the book. It sat on our bookshelf until Andy discovered it. "I can use this at school!" my teacher husband said with enthusiasm. Yes, it's the perfect book for schooling. But maybe not unschooling where I want our children to pursue knowledge either out of love or need or both. I don't want to sneak it into them.

The other day, my girls went catalogue shopping. I gave them some catalogues that I'd found in our mailbox and some virtual money and suggested they buy a virtual gift for each member of the family. Yes, this activity was a suggestion. My girls voluntarily decided to go ahead and do it. But part of me disapproves of my idea, despite Sophie (13) and Gemma-Rose (10) saying they enjoyed themselves.

Catalogue shopping is real. Many of us love browsing through the bright glossy pages dreaming about what we'd like to buy. We might even circle a few things we're going to get next time we go into town. We probably add up the cost of what we're going to purchase to make sure we can afford it.

But my girls weren't really shopping. They were doing a maths exercise that I'd disguised as fun. Gemma-Rose enjoyed choosing gifts for the family using the junk mail catalogues. But I don't think she cared how much her purchases cost, even though she didn't complain about having to add them up. Actually, she was very clever. She left most of the addition to Sophie, who likes doing such things.

The junk mail catalogue shopping idea was a success. I'm not sorry I suggested it. So what's the problem? The problem is that I know I could easily get carried away with similar ideas. Like this one that I tried yesterday...

"How about you both choose a new recipe from the Aldi cookbook," I said to Sophie and Gemma-Rose. "You could make a list of ingredients and then go to the Aldi website and work out the cost of everything. You can tell me how much money you'll need to make your dinners. Then we can go shopping, buy the ingredients, and you can cook the meals."

Well, the girls liked the idea of choosing a new recipe. Their eyes lit up at the thought of shopping and preparing a meal of their own. But did they like the idea of pricing the ingredients and working out the cost of each meal? They didn't protest at first. Maybe they thought, "If I want to cook, I'm going to have to do the maths first." They had to fulfil a condition before getting to the part they were actually interested in. But after a while, I could see Gemma-Rose was getting frustrated by what was really a boring exercise. She knows I never work out the cost of all the ingredients in a recipe before I go shopping, so why should she? I concluded that giving her such exercises to do will eventually put her off maths. Maybe she will even come to hate it.

I remember trying to teach Gemma-Rose how to tell the time. That was a bit frustrating. I looked for fun activities to help her understand what time is all about. I thought she'd enjoy all the games that taught this skill. But she didn't. She ended up doing a lot of groaning and complaining. In the end, I bought her a clock and fixed it to her bedroom wall. I then stepped back and forgot all about time. That was a year and a half or so ago. The other day I said, "Gemma-Rose, can you tell the time?" She rolled her eyes and said, "Of course I can!" I didn't need to find a fun way of teaching her about time. She learnt about it herself when she realised she wanted to use her clock.

I think back to those time learning games. Games aren't the same as adding up columns of numbers. They should be a lot more fun. So why didn't Gemma-Rose enjoy them? Maybe it was all to do with the type of game I presented her with. We can use maths to play a game, or we can play a game to learn maths. There's a subtle difference. Both might improve our maths skills, but the second kind of game is really a maths exercise in disguise. And kids are very clever. It doesn't take them long to discover our trickery. They know we don't trust them to learn what they need to know when they need it. We want them to learn NOW. The sooner they have those maths facts memorised, the better. Our child might start to feel pressured.

Now, I don't think we should stand back, afraid to tempt our kids with some maths experiences. There are many wonderful ways of strewing maths. Maths is interesting. It can be fun purely for its own sake.

"Would you like to watch this video? I'm not sure exactly what it's about, but I found it on the Numberphile website, and it could be interesting."

"I discovered a new way to add a long list of numbers without getting into a muddle. Do you want to see?'

"I found another video of *The Human Calculator*!"

"Do you want to play Sudoku? I found an online generator."

"This book looks good. How about we have a look at it together?"

We can include our children in all our own real-life maths experiences:

"Do you want to help me sort out these bills?"

And our children will come across maths experiences all by themselves:

"I just did the 'measure ingredients for baking' challenge for the baker's badge on the DIY website."

Children will ponder and ask questions. Sophie might even have wondered, without any prompting from me, how much money she'd need to buy her junk mail catalogue gifts.

Yes, there are so many wonderful ways to enrich our children's world with maths. And they will be fascinated by maths, or they will see a need for it, or perhaps both. We don't need to trick them into learning it.

So how are my children going to learn the maths skills they will need? If I observe and listen to my children, I should be able to find out.

"The best way to learn maths is to use it with your interests," says Sophie. "But I don't mind adding up numbers for no particular reason because I find numbers interesting."

"I don't," says Gemma-Rose. "Adding up lots of numbers is boring. You write it all on a piece of paper which is filed away and never seen again. What's the point?"

"It helps you to learn maths. What if you need to add up something?" I ask.

Gemma-Rose grins. "I'll get someone else to do it for me!"

"She can add up really," says Sophie. "I've seen her do it. She adds up her money all the time. She just doesn't want to do it for no reason."

"But some activities are useful. They help you learn maths. You practise what you need to know," I say.

But Gemma-Rose is not convinced. "I'll just pick maths up as I go along," she says.

You know, if I resist the temptation to pressure her, I believe she will.

The Problem with Real Life Maths Resources

I often go looking for real life maths resources to strew under the noses of my girls. Yes, I like to tempt them with different maths experiences, hoping they'll think, "Wow, maths is so interesting and useful as well!"

So when I have a few free minutes, I can often be found at my computer, googling the words 'real life maths' or even 'real world maths'. And as soon as I hit 'search', pages of resources appear on my screen. This might sound absolutely wonderful to anyone interested in unschool maths. But could there be a problem with real life maths resources?

Real life maths resources. I have nothing against the 'real life' bit. No, I'm sure children learn maths from their own real-life experiences all the time. If they need maths, they will soon learn how to manipulate those numbers and come up with the necessary answer. The maths is relevant. It has a use. There's a reason for working out what maths is all about.

It's the 'resources' bit that I have trouble with. Real life resources are different from personal real-life experiences.

Some time ago, after googling 'real life maths', I ended up on a real-life maths website that promises to provide teachers and students with maths that's relevant to the world.

Doesn't that sound good? If the maths is relevant to the world, it's useful, and therefore it's worth learning. I got excited: *This is the perfect way for my children to learn maths.* At least that's what I thought at first. It wasn't long before I began to wonder whose world the maths is relevant to. And the answer came back: not my child's. It's relevant to someone else's.

This doesn't mean I don't like this website and other similar resources. I do think they are interesting, and so do my girls. We've enjoyed discovering how other people use maths in the world.

Someone has to calculate how much waste is produced by a cruise ship of tourists.

Someone else has to keep an eye on the profits produced by the various movies. Which studio is more successful, and why?

Then there are the people who are tracking the Ebola virus. They need to look at the mathematical figures to become informed about the risks, the likely causes, and the possible solutions to this medical emergency.

And what about Mardi Gras beads? How many beads are distributed each year? How many are recycled? Someone works out these problems.

Yes, real-life maths is fascinating. We've really enjoyed discovering what other people are using maths for. We've even watched associated videos and followed links to find out more about the various real-life situations. Maths can lead us on other adventures.

We found out that the environment might or might not be at risk from cruise ship waste, depending on whether you consult an environmentalist or a cruise ship owner.

We looked at the Rotten Tomato ratings and discovered a few movies which might be worth watching and lots that are probably not worth bothering with.

We decided we are safe from the Ebola virus but learnt a lot about how it's transmitted.

And we agreed we'd like to see a Mardi Gras parade one day and wear strings of beads.

The bit I don't like about this real-life maths website is the worksheets, the mathematical exercises which accompany the interesting stuff. They are no different from traditional worksheets. They are just based on real-life situations.

Now it might be interesting working out how someone determined the volume of waste on a cruise ship. But when I see a whole page of similar problems, my heart sinks. This isn't real work. We're just working out something that someone else has already done, to see if we can get the same answers. I'm guessing if my heart sinks at the thought of doing this so will my child's.

So do I think real life maths resources aren't useful? Not at all. We dip into them all the time. We use what we like and ignore what we don't.

Of course, if your children are learning maths in a more structured way, you might find real-life maths websites a wonderful alternative to traditional textbooks and workbooks. Relevant real-life problems are always more interesting than made up ones.

And there is no doubt some children enjoy the challenge of working out maths problems. Even Sophie sometimes feels like doing this. But not all the time. And certainly not if it is 'required'.

Approaching Maths Backwards

The other day, I made a big mistake. I uttered the word 'maths' in Gemma-Rose's presence. Oh my! She instantly became stiff and prickly. "What's wrong with maths?" I asked.

"It's boring. It's just a lot of numbers."

"You don't like numbers?"

"No."

I attempted a little nudge: "Numbers can be fun. We could play a game together. Maybe a computer game."

Gemma-Rose (10) flung herself down on the sofa next to me with a huge sigh. I opened my computer, and soon we were on the games page of a maths website. "What would you like to play?" Gemma-Rose told me I could choose. I clicked on the first game on the page and waited while three other 'players' joined us. Then Gemma-Rose began dutifully working out problems, while a character in a hot air balloon floated across the screen. Many problems later, the game finally ended, and these words flashed up on the screen: "You finished third."

Third? Every problem was solved correctly, and Gemma-Rose finished *third*? What a stupid game.

"You have to get the answers faster," I said. Then I added, "Do you think being timed helps children learn maths?"

"No! Being timed just makes me feel like panicking."

"Let me have a go," I said, as I chose a different game to play. Soon I was clicking and calculating and clicking. It wasn't long before I was sighing and saying, "This is so boring! Do people think kids are stupid or something? This isn't a game. This is just a maths exercise in disguise. It's trickery."

Gemma-Rose grinned. "I told you maths is boring!"

But it's not. And I know Gemma-Rose isn't really bored by the subject. I've seen her interested in such things as the Fibonacci sequence and Pi.

I wonder if we can approach maths backwards? Could we offer the big picture, show children how fascinating and interesting maths is, and then wait for a child to wonder about the details? Maybe it's a bit like writing. We expose a child to the big picture by introducing them to great writing when we read to them. A lot of children are then inspired to compose their own stories. But if we spend a lot of time making a child work on her spelling and grammar, she might lose interest. She can learn the details as she writes.

I've been pondering something else: can maths concepts be approached from many different directions? For example, we could tell our children what Pi is and how to use it to calculate the area of a circle (which I am sure they've been impatiently waiting to do!) and then set them some problems. Or we could treat Pi as something very interesting in its own right, and return to it again and again, just a little at a time, from different directions: a video, a book, a mention in a conversation, a pie! Each time a child comes into contact with Pi, they learn more about it.

So I have a daughter who can tell you about Pi and Fibonacci and even Pythagoras, but she's still not 100% accurate when it comes to times tables (though she knows how to work them out given enough time). And you'd better not ask her to do long division.

Some people might say, "Just make her sit down and get those maths facts learnt, once and for all!" I am tempted to agree. That would make life a lot easier. But I can't do that. Why not? Because that would threaten our relationship. I'd lose Gemma-Rose's trust, a barrier would go up, and she would stop listening to me.

"Who's in charge here?" someone else might add. Gemma-Rose is. She knows what she needs to know right at this moment. I've discovered it's impossible to force kids to learn anything they don't want to know about. That doesn't stop parents trying though. Or teachers.

I know if I am heavy-handed, my daughter will probably run a mile from maths. But letting her learn maths in her own way, in her own time, may very well lead to something very exciting.

Of course, real life is already teaching Gemma-Rose a lot of the details of maths. I've been thinking about this too.

"You use maths all the time," I said to Gemma-Rose. "It's all around us."

"It is?" She seemed surprised.

Maybe many of us are like Gemma-Rose: We just don't notice the maths that surrounds us. We don't realise we're using maths skills all the time.

"Why don't we watch out for maths experiences?" I said. "We can wear our maths detective eyes."

So that's what we did. Did we find many experiences? Oh yes!

Becoming Real Life Maths Detectives

"We use maths all the time," I say to my daughter Gemma-Rose (10). "Maths is everywhere."

Everywhere? She doesn't look convinced.

"You use maths to count your money," says Sophie, "and when you're cooking."

Cooking? How many times have you heard this example when real life maths is mentioned? "Real life maths? You know, cooking."

My girls cook all the time. I have lots and lots of cooking entries in my homeschool records book. They all say similar things: my girls measured the mass and volume of solid and liquid ingredients. They used grams and maybe kilograms, metric cups, millilitres and litres. They multiplied and divided. They recognised fractions. They used the oven and noted the temperature in degrees Celsius. Yes, there's a lot of maths there. But real life maths isn't only about cooking.

"Let's be maths detectives," I suggest. "Let's watch out for someone using maths."

It isn't long before we notice Imogen measuring out our puppy's food. She uses a metric measuring cup. Imogen tells us how much food the puppy eats for each of her three meals. We quickly work out how much food she eats in a day.

Then Gemma-Rose spots Callum's retractable tape measure which he tossed on the table and forgot about. She pulls out the end of the metal tape to measure the table in centimetres, noting she could have used inches instead.

It's my turn. Can I spot some maths? Charlotte is making coffee. She splashes some milk into each mug, and I say, "I wonder how much milk Charlotte used." I'm too lazy to get up to perform an experiment to find out. Anyway, it's not an appropriate time: I have a cup of coffee to drink before it gets cold.

Instead, I say, "I wonder how much milk is in each of those individual UHT milk portions, the ones you get in motels." I do some googling and discover that each milk portion contains 15 ml. We decide Charlotte would have used more than 15 ml because she is more generous than a packaged portion. It doesn't take me very long to work out how many 15 ml portions there are in a 2 L bottle of milk (133). I google the price of bottled milk, and I already have the price of a 240 pack of individual portions. I do a price comparison. Of course, bottled milk is the better buy. We wonder why anyone would buy the more expensive individual portions and come up with some answers. Of course, we note that hardly anyone would use only 15ml of milk in their coffee if given a choice. If everyone did, 133 people would be able to use one bottle of milk, and I have never known that happen. We've all witnessed lots of people putting milk into their coffee at homeschool camps.

Sophie, Gemma-Rose and I sip our coffee or milk while we chat about these things. We're not having a maths lesson. We're wondering and pondering.

I tell the girls about a time when I used to buy sugar in individual portions. They don't remember because they were very young when I did this. They want to hear all about my attempt to slow down our family's intake of sugar. "Even though the sugar cost more per kilo by buying it in individual sachets, we ate less of it, so it ended up cheaper in the long run."

We finish our coffee and swallow the last crumbs of our homemade biscuits. While the girls return the cups to the kitchen, I open my homeschool records notebook and quickly type in all the real-life maths we have discussed.

"I wonder what other real-life maths we can spot," I say. "Shall we keep our eyes open?" The girls are agreeable. They are going to use their maths eyes. "If you want to, you can use my phone to take photos of any maths you find." This is just a suggestion.

I'm looking around. Do you know what I'm seeing? Lots and lots of maths I never usually notice, maths we use without even thinking about it. I can see maths I can share with my daughters. Maybe we can have more maths conversations. (Aren't conversations a great way to learn? They're enjoyable too.) We could wonder and ponder. We could take some photos. Perhaps we could do a little research if we feel the need. It might be interesting as long as it doesn't turn into a maths lesson.

It could be a big temptation to turn every interesting conversation into a maths exercise. I know maths problems will appear while we're chatting. (They did while we were chatting about portions of UHT milk.) I also know if I insist my girls work them all out on their own, it will take lots of time. They will soon lose interest. They won't want to talk maths with me. I wonder if I could do any workings out aloud, allowing my girls to see what I'm doing. Of course, I wouldn't stop them helping if they feel so inclined. Do you think that will work?

Yes, maths exercises are not what this is all about. This is about looking at the world together, with wondering eyes. It's about showing my girls maths can be a very interesting and relevant subject.

Perhaps you're not convinced maths is everywhere. Could you be passing over lots of everyday experiences without seeing them? How about putting on your maths detective eyes? Look around. Notice. Ponder. Wonder. And enjoy!

Giving My Unschoolers a Maths Test

I had a brilliant idea. Well, I thought it was a pretty good idea until this morning. It was all to do with maths. How do we prove our children are covering the required maths syllabus, and achieving the necessary outcomes, when they don't use a formal maths program? I've been thinking about this for a while.

My husband Andy is a school teacher. Every year his year 3 and year 5 students have to sit the dreaded NAPLAN test (National Assessment Program – Literacy and Numeracy).

NAPLAN tests the sorts of skills that are essential for every child to progress through school and life, such as reading, writing, spelling and numeracy.

So I had this idea: If my girls do the maths part of the NAPLAN test and pass, then I can say they have age appropriate maths skills. (They would be in years 3 and 5 if they attended school.) I could file the results in my records book as proof they are learning maths despite the lack of a formal program. I could continue tempting them with real books about real maths, finding maths games for them to play, and looking for every opportunity to expose them to real maths in our everyday life.

I asked Andy to bring home some NAPLAN papers, and this morning I asked the girls if they'd like to do the test. I can't say Sophie (11), and Gemma-Rose (8) jumped up and down with excitement when I explained what they had to do. But they were agreeable. They'd never done a test before. This was a new experience.

Ten minutes into the new experience, Gemma-Rose had had enough. She was making a lot of unhappy noises. She did lots of huffing and puffing. She was clearly unimpressed. I don't think she saw the point to all the questions. Sophie just got down to work.

A while later, they'd both finished. I marked Sophie's paper first. She smiled as I gave a tick to one question after another. Then she got a few wrong, and by the time I got to the last page, she was crying.

"But you did okay," I assured Sophie. "You got 85% right. That's good."

But Sophie wasn't convinced. She usually works at a problem until she has the right answer. Today her time was over. She couldn't go back and try again. Her final score is unchangeable. No one cares if she puts in further work and perfects her score and learns from her mistakes. That's the way of tests.

By this time, my enthusiasm for the test had waned considerably. I had two unhappy girls, and I hadn't even marked Gemma-Rose's paper.

"Let's forget the test," I told Gemma-Rose. "We don't need to mark it."

But Gemma-Rose surprised me by saying, "You might as well mark it and see what I got."

So I marked the paper, and she got 77%, which didn't please or displease her. Marks don't mean much to her.

What do I do next? Am I tempted to pull out the maths textbooks so the girls can fill in the gaps in their maths education? Or am I satisfied with the results? Will I be giving them further tests at regular intervals to prove they have age-appropriate maths skills?

As I mull these questions over, I wonder about the value of testing. I am sure that the ability to take a test is a skill of its own. Working out problems in real life has nothing to do with how you fill in a paper under a time constraint. I've also just remembered that students usually revise before a test. They do it while the material is fresh in their minds. My girls only got a few seconds' warning. So was the test fair?

"Shall we start studying for the next test?" I ask Sophie and Gemma-Rose. "We could grab those textbooks off the shelf and start work." They look at me. Am I serious? No, I'm smiling. The girls look relieved.

It would be so easy to take those textbooks and insist the girls use them. Maybe everyone wonders why I don't do this. I could satisfy the educational authorities. My girls would learn maths, and I wouldn't have to worry about proving it. Easy.

But I know I would be saying, "I don't trust you to learn what you need to know. I need to intervene just in case. I am more concerned about outside expectations than I am about you. I don't really believe in the principles of unschooling."

Will I be giving the girls any more tests? I spent years trying to remember things just to pass tests. And then forgetting everything as soon as the test was over. I want something better for my children. I want their learning to be real. So I won't be giving them any more tests.

I will continue strewing maths in front of the girls, and I will take delight in their delight as they learn.

And I will look for another way to satisfy the educational authorities.

Making Kids Learn Maths Just in Case

Should we make our unschooled kids learn maths in a formal way just in case? Is this sensible? We never know when they might need to prove they have covered all the skills presented in maths courses. What if they want to apply for a university degree course that has a maths prerequisite? What if our kids decide they'd like to go to school and so have to slot back into the system with their age peers?

These are situations some unschoolers have told me they've had to deal with. They've let go of maths and then later, they've regretted their decision because their kids have been behind in maths.

When responding to concerns about maths, I always say that maths can be learnt whenever a child needs it. It's never too late for kids to acquire any necessary skill and catch up to where they need to be. Of course, catching up takes time. A child can't learn everything overnight. But usually, when we have a need for knowledge, we learn at a fast rate. If there's a particular reason for learning something, we're prepared to put in a lot of effort.

But even knowing that it's possible for kids to catch up, some parents are still anxious. Maybe they're worried about time. Could there be a reason why their kids don't want to spend extra time learning the required maths skills? Are they working to a rigid timetable?

For most kids, time shouldn't matter. The window of opportunity to get into university (at least in Australia) isn't small. Anybody of any age can apply to do a degree course. No one misses out because they are too old. However, maybe we've got into the habit of thinking that kids must apply to university as soon as they finish school which is usually when they are 18. They work hard and complete their courses, and then they get jobs. It's the way things are usually done. But kids don't have to work to this timetable. They could continue studying for the skills they need after they have reached the official school-leaving age. If for some reason, continuing to study full time isn't an option, could a child work and study part-time? There's more than one way of doing things. There really isn't any need to panic because time is running out.

But time might matter when we're talking about school. If kids enter the school system, they're expected to be at the same level as their age peers. And unschooled kids might indeed be behind when it comes to maths. Catching up might not only be hard work, but it could also be discouraging as well. Wouldn't it be better if all unschooled kids formally learnt maths just in case they want to go to school?

I wonder if having one eye on school compromises our unschooling lives. Does it lessen our commitment? Does it prevent us from immersing ourselves fully in this way of life? Our family never talks about school. For us, it's not an option.

However, even if parents are fully committed to unschooling, shouldn't kids be free to choose? What if one of my kids wants to go to school? I don't think this is likely to happen because our life is too good to give up for the experience of school. But yes, my children are free to choose, and anything is possible. If one of them wanted to go to school and they were behind with maths, we'd probably talk about what they would have to achieve to fit in with their age grade. Are they willing to work hard to catch up? Should they do this before entering school? If school is important enough, kids will find a way of getting there. This applies to university as well.

Of course, there are times when our unschooled kids learn maths in a traditional way just in case, and it has nothing to do with us. Parents don't have to force them to do it. There are no battles: *Why do I have to learn maths? I'll never need it.* We don't have to point out that, despite appearances, the maths may be useful. No, sometimes our children freely choose to do a maths course.

When my daughter Imogen was about 15, she did an advanced maths course. At the time, she was interested in many things, including medicine. She knew the medical degree course had a maths prerequisite so she asked me to find her a suitable course to complete just in case she decided that she'd follow this passion. By the time she finished the maths course, Imogen was no longer thinking about a career in medicine. Instead, she wanted to study writing.

Imogen didn't need maths to apply for her Bachelor of Arts degree in Professional Writing and Publishing. So was completing the higher maths course a waste of time? Does Imogen regret doing it? It depends on how you look at it. Imogen is rather pleased that she is the only Elvis child who has ever completed an advanced maths course. But, a few years down the track, does she remember much of what she learnt? No.

"I never used the maths," says Imogen, "so now I've forgotten most of what I learnt."

Imogen's maths result is a bit like my science degree. We both ended up with meaningless bits of paper. We did our courses but remember little of what we learnt.

Sometimes I wonder what interesting things kids could be doing instead of spending time learning stuff just in case.

When an Unschooler Isn't Interested in Maths

What if our children moan and groan every time we mention the word 'maths'? What if they say they hate it and can't do it? What if they're just not interested?

We could insist our children do some maths whether they like it or not. Basic maths skills are essential. What if someone finds out that our children don't know such things as the times tables? Will they criticise us and our decision to unschool? Perhaps we feel we have to keep pushing our children even if we end up battling with them. And what about homeschool registration? We might need to prove our children are learning maths. If a child doesn't do any, what are we going to write in the homeschool records book?

Or we could ignore these outside expectations, and maybe our own worries, and resist taking control of the situation. We could remind ourselves that our kids will learn all they need to know in their own time. All we have to do is surround them with a rich and interesting environment, and trust. They will get there when they're ready.

I've been taking the latter approach with my youngest daughter, Gemma-Rose (14). For some reason, she has always had a great aversion to the word 'maths'. Just mention it, and she closes up. I'm not sure how her dislike of maths came about. I did insist Gemma-Rose do some formal maths for a year or so when she was about six or seven. She hated the worksheets. She hated the 'fun' interactive activities. Most of all, she hated the timed exercises. Could this have affected her so deeply? It probably did.

Whatever the reason, Gemma-Rose has always had a problem with maths. Some people tell me that I should just sit her down and make her get on with it: everyone has to do things that they don't want to do. She needs to realise this. Maths is essential. She'll be at a disadvantage if I don't insist she learns it. But it's

241

impossible to force kids to learn without their cooperation. Of course, I could have given her some incentive to learn by using rewards or punishments or shame. But I didn't want to use these. That's not the way to encourage real learning. I was also worried that the more I pushed, the stronger Gemma-Rose's dislike for maths would become. I was hoping I could give her a new perspective on this subject.

I wondered if Gemma-Rose disliked maths because she had a false idea of what it is. Maths isn't worksheets. It's not having to remember the right answers in a certain amount of time. It's not having a *You Failed* message flash on the screen when you don't manage to do the required tasks. Instead, maths is a fascinating language that infiltrates every part of our world. For the past few years, my mission has been to strew maths, a bit here and there, to give Gemma-Rose a proper taste for it. Give her a different view of this subject. Most times, she has soaked it up without realising she is actually experiencing maths.

I've also been observing Gemma-Rose using maths in her everyday life. This has meant looking carefully because I think most of us pass over many maths moments. We just don't notice them. And I've been offering maths information in a light-handed way whenever an appropriate moment has arisen, and Gemma-Rose has seemed in a receptive mood. I've discovered that sometimes it's okay to give her a little nudge. At other times, it's far better to back off.

There's been a side benefit from strewing maths and observing Gemma-Rose using it: I have been able to add lots of maths notes to our homeschool records book.

Sometimes when I've been explaining my approach to maths, I've said such things as, "Gemma-Rose doesn't like maths. She's not very good at it. She's just not a maths person." Then one day, I stopped and examined those words. Were they really true? And I decided they weren't. Gemma-Rose is very proficient at maths. She uses it all the time. She has no trouble working out all the mathematical problems that arise in her life.

Here's an example:

One day, I saw an opportunity to introduce decimals to Gemma-Rose. I was hoping she was ready to learn about them. So for a few minutes, I explained all about the decimal point and place values and how to add and subtract. Then I looked at my daughter. She was squirming, and she had a familiar closed off look on her face. "Just relax," I told her. "It's not that hard to understand." But it seems it was. I gave up. I wondered if Gemma-Rose would ever want to learn about such things.

Later on, I realised I'd been blind. I hadn't seen something very obvious. Gemma-Rose uses decimals all the time when she's running. She has no trouble working out her distances and speed and all the other interesting data she wants to know about. How does she do the maths involved? I don't know. What goes on inside her head is a mystery to me. All I know is that she's got her own way of doing things. She doesn't use the conventional methods and language that most of us associate with maths.

It seems to me that children are quite capable of finding their own ways to work out mathematical problems without first having to learn all the rules of multiplication and addition and fractions and everything else we try and drum into them.

Recently, there's been a new development in my daughter's maths story. A couple of months or so ago, Gemma-Rose said, "Mum, can you find me a maths course to work through?"

My jaw dropped. Gemma-Rose wanted to do a maths course?

"I think it's time I learnt maths properly."

"Are you sure you want to do a course? I could find a more interesting way for you to do maths."

"I just want to learn maths. I don't need it to be turned into a game or something fun."

Gemma-Rose had decided for herself that she was ready to learn maths in a conventional way. She thinks it's time she learnt the language everyone else is using.

So I searched for an appropriate online maths course and then presented Gemma-Rose with a few options. She looked at them all and then chose one.

"Would you like me to watch the videos with you and help you with the quizzes?" I asked.

"No, thank you, Mum. I can do this by myself."

Can a child who has had hardly any formal maths experience do a maths course by herself? Yes, she can. I've been very surprised. There have been a couple of occasions when Gemma-Rose has asked for my help, but basically, she is working through the program on her own.

Where did Gemma-Rose start with the course? At the beginning? No, we looked at the questions together, and then Gemma-Rose decided to start with a year 7 unit. That's high school maths (in Australia). And that seems to be the right place for her. Gemma-Rose is less than one year behind her school-age peers. That's not bad, is it? It just goes to show that she picked up all the primary school maths skills on her own just by living life with a bit of maths strewing thrown in for interest and information.

What's ahead? I don't know. Gemma-Rose will decide. I trust she knows what she's doing.

So what do we do when our unschoolers aren't interested in maths? We could push them to do it anyway. But if I had done this, would Gemma-Rose's aversion to maths have increased? Would she never have come to the point where she is willing to know more? I think it's very likely that the trust between us would have been destroyed. And I'm sure this would have flowed over into other aspects of our lives.

Instead, I think it's far better to listen to our kids, support them, and trust they will learn what they need to know in their own time.

Part XIII: Reading

Learning to Read

Can children learn to read without being taught formally? Yes, I'm sure they can. Have I got some stories that will reassure parents that this will happen? Well, I can share the mistakes I made and what I learnt while my kids were learning to read. Sometimes we can look back and wish we'd done things a bit differently.

How did I encourage my kids to learn to read in a natural way? I'm often asked this question, and I'd like to say that I just relaxed and didn't worry about reading. My kids taught themselves to read when they were ready. It was no big deal. But that's not true.

Like most parents, I couldn't wait for the time when my children could read. Reading is magical. Books allow us to experience the world. Yes, being able to read is a wonderful thing. Reading was something I wanted to share with my kids. And so I was anxious that they learn this skill quickly.

I think most parents want their kids to learn to read as soon as possible. And that's not just because they're impatient for their children to experience the delights of reading. No, many of us feel pressured to impart this skill to them. We might have to prove to an educational authority that we are competent to teach our kids at home. Perhaps we have family and friends watching over our shoulders, poised to criticise us at the first opportunity. Could our children's ability to read be seen as a reflection of our ability to be a homeschooling parent?

And then there's the pressure that results from comparing children. We might get anxious if someone else's child who is younger than ours is reading and ours isn't.

So reading can feel like a big deal.

When our first child, Felicity, was about five years old, I decided it was time for her to learn to read. Things went very smoothly. We sat side by side for a few weeks. I gave Felicity some pointers on reading. We read a lot together. Before I knew it, she was a fluent reader. It was a painless process.

I thought, "Wow! I'm such a good teacher. Look, I've taught my very first child to read in a matter of weeks." (What was everyone else doing wrong?)

Felicity read the whole of the *Anne of Green Gables* series by herself at the age of six. And, of course, I wasn't reluctant to share this with my homeschooling friends. "My daughter is only six years old, and already she has read all these books!"

I came down to earth with our second child Duncan. Things didn't fall into place so easily for him. Soon I realised that I hadn't taught my first child to read at all. Felicity had learnt to read despite me. It was all her own doing. She was ready to read. She wanted to read. She asked the appropriate questions. I gave her the information. And yes, soon she was reading.

When Duncan was about five, I decided it was time for him to learn to read. Looking back, I can see that he wasn't ready. I had to register him as a homeschooler, and I thought it would be expected that he should be reading by a certain age. I got anxious and decided I couldn't wait until Duncan showed an interest in reading. I had to push him to acquire this skill.

So Duncan and I spent some very frustrating times together as I tried to teach him to read. He just wasn't picking it up at all. It got to the point where I got very angry with him. I would say things like, "What's wrong with you? Why can't you remember what that word says?" When he couldn't read a word, I refused to tell him what it was. I wanted him to sound everything out. I would jump up and down and make a big fuss about the whole thing. I couldn't understand why he was so slow. Of course, he must remember what that word says. I only gave it to him a few minutes ago. I was sure he was just being a trouble to me.

I didn't feel good about the way I was treating Duncan. I knew that learning shouldn't be like this. But I found it very hard to relax and let Duncan learn in his own time and way. I felt I had to push him on. So I didn't give up trying to teach him, but I did wonder if I should change my approach. If what we were doing together wasn't working, was there another way to help him learn to read?

I searched the library for books about teaching children to read and found one about shared reading. I decided to give this method a go.

I put aside the uninteresting graded readers I'd been using with Duncan. Instead, I asked him to choose a real book, one that he wanted to read. Then we sat side by side with the chosen book. I volunteered to read it to him. Duncan didn't have to read it to me, but if he did want to have a go, all he had to do was tap on the page or my knee to indicate he'd like a turn in the driving seat. With the pressure taken off, Duncan did decide he'd like to try and read.

Whenever Duncan came to a word he didn't know, I didn't make him sound it out. No longer did we sit for long, excruciating moments while I'd try and force him to remember what the word was. Instead, I'd instantly give him the word. And then I would return to the reader's driving seat and naturally continue the story. The story was the main focus. We wanted to enjoy reading it. When he felt ready, Duncan could tap my knee again and then take over the reading. We continued doing this, going back and forth, taking turns. As his confidence grew, Duncan would tap my knee almost instantly after I'd said any words he didn't know and then start reading. We read like this for quite a few months. And although he wasn't a fluent reader on his own, we did enjoy a lot of books together. The bad feelings associated with reading disappeared.

When Duncan was almost eight, we had a homeschool registration visit scheduled. Our AP (Authorised Person) from the education department was coming to see us. It had been two years since her last visit. I knew she would want to see our records and progress reports for all areas, including reading.

I wondered how I would explain to the AP that Duncan wasn't yet a fluent reader even though he was eight years old. Would she think this was a problem? I decided to be confident and bluff my way through it. I planned to say, "He's well on his way to learning to read. He enjoys reading. I'm sure it will happen any day now." I thought that was all I could do.

248

But something unexpected happened. Three or four days before the AP came to see us, Duncan brought me a book and said, "Mum, can I read to you?" He sat down, and he started to read. And he didn't stop. He read page after page after page. His reading skills had all fallen into place. He was a fluent reader.

So it does happen. A child just needs time. Children will learn to read when they're ready.

As you can see, I did a lot wrong while trying to help my children learn to read. But we learn from our mistakes.

Here's what I learnt:

- A child needs to be ready and willing to learn; otherwise, it's frustrating for everyone and a waste of time.
- The 'right' age to read is different for different children. A child's readiness to read must be respected.
- It's okay to offer help to a child who wants to learn to read. We can find some appropriate resources and give some pointers, but we have to do this on our child's terms and back off if he's not interested.
- The way we help, the resources we might use, has to take into account the needs of our child. There are lots of different options and some suit some children more than others.
- A structured course isn't essential.
- Learning to read by reading real books is better than using readers.
- Maybe some children find reading more difficult than others, and extra help might be needed. We should work with our child instead of forcing our help upon her.
- But then again, some children might just need more time. Sometimes lots of time is needed (or what feels like lots of time).
- If our child wants our help, we should give it to him when he needs it. We should tell a child what a word says instead of making him sound it out.
- It doesn't help when we become frustrated and angry and impatient. If we find ourselves tempted to say such things as, "What's wrong with you? When will you ever learn?" it's time to back off and leave reading for a later date. Perhaps our child isn't ready to learn. Unkind words that

result from frustration can hurt children and can damage their confidence. They can also damage the parent-child relationship.

- Children who learn to read at a later-than-average age catch up quickly.
- It's impossible to tell which of my children were early readers and which weren't.
- Even if a child isn't reading, this doesn't mean she's not learning other things. Focus on what she knows rather than what she still has to learn. Relax and enjoy doing things other than reading.
- We should ignore the opinions of people around us. Don't listen to them but instead listen to our child. Nobody is more important than him. He will get there in the end.

Can a child learn to read entirely on her own? I am sure the answer is yes.

A Slow Learner

It doesn't seem that long ago that I was helping my daughter Gemma-Rose learn to read. She'd choose a book, and we'd sit side by side on the sofa, and we'd enjoy the story together.

To be honest, I don't know if 'enjoy' is the right word. Reading was a very slow process. We hardly ever got to the end of a book. I'd think, "Will Gemma-Rose ever read fluently?" which was a very silly question because I'd already experienced six other learner readers. Of course, she'd learn to read. In her time. Not mine.

For some reason, our shared reading sessions came to an end. Perhaps we just got busy with other things. Maybe I subconsciously decided I couldn't stand any more slow, painful reading sessions. Or did I suddenly become a very patient mother, willing to allow her child to learn at her own pace?

For a long time, I read to Gemma-Rose, but she didn't read much to me. Then one day, she said, "Mum, can I read you a story?"

I looked at the book in her hand. It was a short chapter book, not a picture book. "That might be a little difficult," I replied. (I know: I wasn't exactly encouraging, was I?)

"I can read it," insisted Gemma-Rose as she snuggled up next to me on the sofa and opened the book at the beginning of the first chapter. "'Isn't it a lovely day, Mum?' Kirsty Tate said happily, as she gazed out of the car window at the blue sky and sunshine...'" Gemma-Rose was off, and she didn't stop. I sat delighted and surprised as she read chapter after chapter to me.

"When did you learn to read?" I asked her, and she just grinned and shrugged her shoulders as if reading is the most natural thing in the world to do.

On Friday, Gemma-Rose (7) appeared with a huge stack of picture books. "I've chosen some books, and I'm going to read all

251

these to you." Obviously, she'd planned a special event for me. So she settled herself on the sofa, and I climbed onto her lap (only joking) and my youngest daughter treated me to all those old favourites I hadn't heard for some time. She read each one clearly and accurately, with lots of expression, in between plenty of giggles. She was enjoying the tales too.

"Last time I heard these stories, I was reading them to you," I pointed out. Yes, it wasn't that long ago that I was in the reader's chair. It wasn't that long ago that I'd had to remind myself that Gemma-Rose would read when she was ready. Now she is in the reader's chair, and she took no longer to get to the fluent reading stage than any of my other learner readers.

So I have come to this conclusion: it was just as well I was too busy to worry about Gemma-Rose's reading. I might have intervened and messed things up. Or was I not too busy? Could I be learning? Perhaps I trusted Gemma-Rose to go at her own pace. Could I have finally got it right with my very last child?

Sometimes it is me who is the slow learner.

The Reading Out Loud Experiment

I have to admit that listening to stories being read out loud isn't my favourite activity. My mind tends to wander, and I miss half the words. But my kids are different from me. They love reading aloud time. Even though most of my children are grown up, they still like to gather whenever anyone opens a book and says, "Do you want to listen?"

I wonder why my kids love listening, and I don't. Perhaps it's got something to do with the fact that they associate reading books together as a happy family time experience. There's no pressure to listen. It's not a formal learning experience. It's just something pleasurable that draws us all together.

When I was a child, I was read to by teachers who always wanted to check whether I was listening properly. They'd ask questions after they'd read out loud. They sometimes asked me to write something about the book. I'd have to be ready with the right answers. I couldn't just relax and enjoy the story.

But even though I don't particularly like listening, I do like reading aloud times. Usually, I'm in the reader's chair. I have the book and can see the words, so my mind has less chance of slipping away to other things. And I just love seeing my kids' faces light up as they hear the words of a wonderful story. And then afterwards, even though I don't ask any questions, my kids will still want to share their thoughts. There is always something they want to discuss.

A day arrived for each of my kids when they wanted to occupy the reader's chair. And even though I prefer reading to listening, I had to be willing to vacate my seat. Yes, it was my child's turn to read.

Some time ago, Gemma-Rose asked, "Can I read to you, Mum?" She settled herself next to me on the sofa, excited because she was in the reader's chair. She smiled at me and then started the first chapter of the book she'd chosen.

"Hey! Slow down," I said, almost immediately. "I can't hear all the words. When you're reading out loud, you have an audience. They need to be able to understand every single word."

Gemma-Rose stiffened. She flashed her eyes at me and then read the next sentence in a gruff voice very, very slowly.

"Well, if you're going to read like that, perhaps we should leave it for another day."

I received another scowl before Gemma-Rose picked up the pace and began reading in a more normal voice.

Then she mispronounced a word, and I corrected her. My youngest daughter grunted the word back at me.

"Don't you want to know the right way to say the words?" I asked.

"I guess so," she muttered.

Gemma-Rose continued reading, and anticipating she might not know a word in the next sentence, I jumped in and said it for her.

"I knew how to say that word!"

"Sorry!"

Reading went smoothly for a time and then as Gemma-Rose became engrossed in the story, she forgot to say all the words. Maybe she read them in her head, but I couldn't hear them.

"You missed out some words!"

Gemma-Rose huffed and puffed before continuing.

And then she ended a sentence with a wrong word. She did it more than once. "That's not what the author wrote. You have to read the words as they are written."

Occasionally she left out a whole line by mistake.

Oh my, things were not going well! Gemma-Rose was no longer bouncing about with excitement. She was stiff and very, very grumpy. And I wasn't very happy either. I wondered if perhaps we should just forget reading out loud together. Then I had another idea. I decided to do a reading aloud experiment.

What would happen if I didn't correct Gemma-Rose anymore, just let her enjoy the reading experience? Would her reading aloud skills improve without any interference from me? Would she gradually come to moderate her pace and say the correct words on her own? I thought it was worthwhile trying this experiment. What was the alternative? Gemma-Rose would start to hate her reading out loud times with me and not want to do it. No, we didn't have much to lose.

So for 18 months Gemma-Rose and I settled ourselves on the sofa together each morning with a book. And as she was reading, I tried to ignore all the mistakes she was making. Instead, I just observed. I thought about the mechanics of reading. One day I began to wonder if her 'mistakes' were all that significant after all.

Gemma-Rose read too fast and sometimes left out words. Was this because she was engrossed in the story? Her mind was probably racing along at a furious pace. Sometimes she left out a whole line of words and didn't even realise. Was she scanning a few lines at a time? Probably, she'd read the missing words in her head, so she didn't even notice she hadn't said them out loud.

Gemma-Rose ended a sentence with a wrong word. Could her mind have been jumping ahead, trying to make sense of the sentence? I think she was anticipating a likely word. Maybe she was right most of the time. But those times she was wrong, her sentences still made sense. The author could have chosen the word she supplied.

And when Gemma-Rose did make a mistake which didn't make sense at all, she always backtracked without any prompting from me. "That's better! It makes sense now," she'd smile, pleased she'd corrected her error.

I could have placed my finger under every single word, and then Gemma-Rose would have read them all perfectly, I'm sure. I could have smiled and felt proud of her reading ability. But I don't think perfect word-for-word reading actually says much about a child's reading skills.

My husband Andy is a primary school teacher. Every now and then, he has to give his students a standardised reading test. The student reads, and Andy notes all the words that she mispronounces or leaves out or is unable to read or substitutes with different words. He notes the rate of reading. To get a perfect score, the student has to read the story as the author wrote it, word-for-word in a certain amount of time.

I don't think this kind of reading test tells us if a child is reading for meaning. A good reader will be scanning ahead quickly, making guesses as to what word is going to come up next, thinking about the words as belonging to sentences. I think this standardised test might as well be given as a list of individual words. It says nothing about the real ability of a child to read for comprehension and enjoyment.

Yesterday morning...

"Shall we find out what happens in the next chapter of your book?" I ask Gemma-Rose.

"Oh, yes!"

Soon we are settled side by side with the book between us.

Half an hour later, I say, "Wow! You're a good reader! Do you remember when you used to leave out words?"

Gemma-Rose grins. "Well, it didn't matter. You could read them for yourself. You could see the page too."

"But now I can listen with my eyes shut."

Yes, Gemma-Rose, who was always a good reader, can now read out loud very capably. And all I did to help her was to sit back and not interfere.

"Is it your turn to read to me now?" asks Gemma-Rose.

Oh yes, I did do one other thing. I kept reading to her.

Listening

When I was an eleven-year-old student, our teacher got out her tape recorder and played us a current affairs radio program. It was a hot summer's afternoon, late in the day, and I felt sleepy. I didn't even try to concentrate on the program. I spent the 30 minutes that I should have been listening, daydreaming instead. Apparently, almost all of my fellow students did the same thing. And the teacher must have suspected that our minds were not on the world news. Once she'd turned off the recording, she looked sternly at us and then gave us an impromptu quiz. I had absolutely no idea about the answers. It was a horrifying moment. I'd been caught out completely.

I think about listening skills. I don't ever remember, as a child, listening with enjoyment while someone read out loud to me. Oh, I certainly liked to read to myself, but I don't think I had many opportunities to concentrate my full attention, in a non-threatening way, on the skill of listening. By contrast, my girls look forward to listening to me reading out loud every day. We have at least four books 'on the go' at once. That's a lot of reading-out-loud time. Our reading times are certainly the highlight of our day.

I have been musing over a few questions:

Should we read out loud to our children? How can we encourage them to listen? What are the good things about listening to a story together? And is anyone ever too old to listen?

As I am reading to my children, I glance up now and then and watch them. I can see they are completely absorbed in the story. Gemma-Rose sits on the edge of her seat during the exciting parts. She smiles with delight at a funny remark. She draws back and looks frightened when danger approaches. She even begs me not to read any more when the climax is near, but I reassure her everything will turn out well in the end and soon she is once again smiling. It doesn't seem like my children's minds wander at all. I don't have to quiz them like my old teacher did to know they hear every word. Is this because I read stories that are exciting and that capture their imagination? Perhaps. But maybe there is more to it than that. Could the fact that I don't quiz my kids encourage them to listen carefully? My kids aren't under any pressure to learn and remember. They are free to enjoy. And so they have discovered the pleasures of listening.

I love sharing books with the girls. Because we are all listening to the same story, we can discuss it as we go along. I also think that a pleasure shared is definitely a pleasure multiplied. Someone only has to quote a line or two, and we are all transported back into a scene from the book.

Regularly Sophie brings me a book and asks, "Can I read something to you, Mum?" She likes climbing into the reader's chair and having an audience. She tries hard to change the pace of her sentences; she emphasises certain words; she uses different character voices. Sophie is, in fact, following Andy's and my example and becoming a good reader in her own right. Listening is teaching her how to read out loud skilfully. And if she mispronounces a word, I have the opportunity to (gently) share the correct way of saying it. (It's amazing the number of words I had to learn how to pronounce as an adult. I read them in books as a child, but never actually heard them said out loud!)

I have strewed a number of books under Sophie's and Gemma-Rose's noses, and they have shown no interest in them at all. One example is *Anne of Green Gables.* Perhaps they opened the book and looked at all the long sentences and paragraphs and were put off. So I suggested I read the Anne series out loud and now the girls are enjoying these books. We have almost finished *Anne of Windy Willows,* and their interest shows no sign of letting up. I guess reading out loud introduces our children to stories that might be just a little too difficult for them to read on their own.

I do not doubt that when we finally make it to the end of the Anne series, the girls will whisk the books away to some private corner and read them all over again. They will no longer seem a too formidable challenge for individual reading. I have seen them do this time and again with other read-aloud books.

Do children get too old for listening? The other day Sophie asked Andy, "Dad, will you please read *The Lord of the Rings* to us? We were too young to listen last time you read it out loud." Andy has agreed, and the girls are getting excited. They are anticipating some cosy evenings sitting together in the family room, while Andy brings Tolkien's books alive for them in his own special way. I bet the older children join the younger ones, even though they are already very familiar with the stories. Too old for listening? Never!

Although I see lots of benefits to reading books out loud, maybe there are some children who just don't like sitting still and listening. This is okay. We don't all have to be the same, do we?

Part XIV: Writing

My Writing Unrules

Will my child write? This seems to be a fairly common worry for parents. Some children want to write, and some are more reluctant.

All my children are writers and always have been. Is this because I am a writer and they are following my example which they have grown up with? Or do they have writing genes? I often muse this over, trying to work it out. Despite my ponderings, I haven't come to any firm conclusions. Maybe a bit of both?

We aren't all alike. Each of us has different strengths and talents, so I think it is safe to assume that some children won't have the same interest in writing as others. Their talents will lie in other directions. And this is okay. The ability to write creatively isn't a superior talent.

But there is no doubt we can't get through life without writing, so children need some level of writing skills. So should we push them along and insist they write? Or will they eventually learn when they realise they need these skills?

I wonder if we can actively encourage our children to take an interest in writing, creating an atmosphere where they might feel excited by the possibility of writing? Could the following points encourage a child to give writing a go?

- Be a writer ourselves. Model the skill. Share our writings. Talk about the process.
- Read a lot to children so they can hear good examples of writing. Read picture books, novels, poetry, non-fiction, magazines, comics, billboards, junk mail, anything. Our kids may be inspired to copy their favourite authors or want to write stories like those they love. Gemma-Rose went through a phase where she only wanted to write about princesses and mermaids. At her age, I did the same. After imitating other authors and learning from them, children may go on to develop their own writing styles.

- Have lively discussions, encouraging children to join in and share their ideas and interests. Talking may turn into writing. We all need something to write about. Quite often, I come away from the dinner table, where we've been chatting together, and head straight to my computer with an idea for a story. The same thing happens with my children.
- Don't pressure children to write. This leads to frustration on both sides. It's quite okay for children to have times when they aren't interested in writing. The desire to write will probably return. In the meantime, read or do something else.
- Don't worry about spelling. Having to spell all words correctly turns writing into a chore. It slows down writing and dampens the creative urge. I have found that spelling improves the more a child writes, without any intervention from me. If it doesn't, it's no big deal. Good spelling isn't an indicator of intelligence. There's always spell-check!
- Don't worry about backward letters or poor handwriting. These also improve with time. Don't worry if a child doesn't want to learn how to write cursively. This skill can be learnt at any age if a child is interested.
- Let children use a computer if they don't want to write by hand. Duncan used to use an old typewriter when he was about six.
- Let them dictate if they can't write well enough. It's more important to nurture creativity than worry about the mechanics.
- Children's writings can take many forms: letters, stories, emails, poems, comic strips, magazines, shopping lists, journal entries. All forms of writing are valuable.
- Look out for real writing opportunities such as letters, blog posts, shopping lists. These are better than set writing exercises as long as we're not making a child write them.
- Writing is a serious business. It should be valued. It's real work. Children are writers, even if they are still learning. We're all still learning!
- Take the time to read children's writings if they are offered for sharing, or get children to read them out loud. (This helps when the spelling is a bit mysterious!) Take the writings seriously. Comment positively and don't criticise.

262

I'd hate my writings to be pulled apart and criticised. Why should children feel any different?

- Save a child's writings. Place them in a folder and treat them as special. They are! I have a few folders of Felicity's and Duncan's earliest stories and poems. They are real treasures.

- If a child doesn't want to share her writings, that's quite okay. We don't have an automatic right to read our children's words. Writing can be a very personal thing. Sometimes we just don't want anyone to read our words. If we insist on reading our children's work, they may stop writing.

I have written this as a list of Dos and Don'ts, but of course, these are only points for consideration, not Sue Elvis' Writing Rules!

Wanting to Learn How to Spell

Gemma-Rose (8) isn't a defiant child, so when she said to me, "You can't make me learn anything I don't want to learn," I stopped and listened.

We were talking about spelling. Did Gemma-Rose want me to enrol her in an online spelling program?

"No, thank you, Mum."

"Well, how will you learn how to spell?"

"I'll pick it up as I go along," she answered confidently.

"But wouldn't it be easier to do a proper program. Don't you think it's a fun way to learn to spell?"

"Not really. And if I don't want to do it, I won't learn, so it's a waste of time."

I didn't enrol Gemma-Rose in a spelling program. She is going to pick it up as she goes along.

Actually, all my other children have also picked up spelling as they've gone along: I answered their spelling questions and pointed out a few patterns here and there, and they learnt some words on their own because they liked them. And they're all good spellers. I don't know why I was distracted by the idea of an online website for my youngest child. New things come along, and sometimes they are worthy of consideration. We try them out and then return to what we know works for us.

We are reading *Anne of Green Gables*. Gemma-Rose is sitting on the edge of her seat, her whole body quivering with enjoyment. As I read Anne's long speeches, Gemma-Rose's face lights up, and she can't resist interrupting: "Anne is such a chatterbox!" Now and then she asks me a question: "What's an alabaster brow, Mum?... alabaster... alabaster..." Gemma-Rose rolls the word off her tongue, delighting in the sound. When we come to the word 'excruciatingly' she is absolutely delighted. She repeats this word a few times too, asks me its meaning and wonders when she can use the word herself.

A few days pass, and Gemma-Rose appears and announces: "When I fell over when we went running this morning, it was excruciatingly painful!" A huge grin spreads across her face and then she adds, "It didn't hurt that much really, but I wanted to use 'excruciatingly'. Isn't it a wonderful word?"

A few more days pass, and Gemma-Rose asks me: "Do you think you could write me a list of spelling words? I want some nice long, interesting ones like 'excruciatingly' and 'Australia'. If I could spell them, I could use them in my stories." I write her a list of interesting words.

For the last couple of weeks, Gemma-Rose has been writing a stage play for an online challenge. Every day she has been working by herself, writing page after page of script.

"Do you want to read what I've written so far, Mum?"

I glance over Gemma-Rose's shoulder, and I'm surprised. I can read everything she's written, and most of it is spelt correctly. And it hasn't even been through the spellchecker.

I conclude that there's more than one way to learn how to spell. The picking-it-up-as you-go-along method is working for Gemma-Rose. She wants to learn the spelling of the words she wants to use.

Now I have to admit that one of my children was not a good speller. I tried organised spelling lists and phonics-based spelling and still, he spelt things his own way. I talked this 'problem' over with an educational representative who reassured me that many very intelligent people can't spell. Many are so successful in their fields, they can employ someone to spell for them. Or they use a spellchecker. So I stopped worrying. I did, however, notice something very interesting. When that child started participating in online university discussion boards, his spelling miraculously underwent a transformation. Almost overnight he could spell. I guess it comes back to need.

The other day my husband Andy texted me while we were driving. Imogen read out the message: "Tonight's parish council meeting has been cancelled."

"Excellent," I said. "Now we don't have to hurry home from our day out."

Imogen texted Andy: "Mum says exellent."

The reply came instantly back: "You missed out the 'c' in excellent."

"Dad! You can tell he's a school teacher," groaned Imogen. "It was only a text message. I do really know how to spell."

And Gemma-Rose will know how to spell soon too, not because she's using a fabulous spelling program, but because she wants to learn.

Why Do Some Children Love Writing?

The other day, Sophie appeared with a huge smile on her face. "I've written a blog post," she announced, and then added, "I wrote it your way. It's like one of your stories."

"Tell me about it," I encouraged.

"Well, I mentioned my feelings as well as the action... and I used the present tense like you sometimes do. I like the present tense. It puts the reader right in the middle of what's going on." Sophie is right. I use this tense a lot. I love it too.

Sophie handed me her computer so I could read what she'd written. Here's her post:

I am excited. Mum has arranged for me to have piano lessons. For the past few years, Imogen has been teaching me. She is a good teacher, but being taught by your sister is not the same as having a professional teacher.

Imogen, Charlotte and I troop up to the front door. I am ready to impress my new teacher. Our teacher opens the door smiling. She is a kind woman, and she says that I can have the first lesson.

I am a bit nervous. Will I be good enough? Have I practised enough? All these thoughts run through my head as I enter the music room.

I have only ever played on an upright piano, but my teacher has a grand one. I wonder what it will be like to play on it.

The teacher asks me what scales I can play, and soon I am enjoying myself, showing my teacher what I have learnt and what I am learning.

She patiently listens to what I play and fixes up the mistakes. She starts to make things more fun and exciting than I ever thought possible and I listen, all ears, and try to do as she says.

All too soon, my lesson is over. It is Charlotte's turn to be taught. I start picking up my books and folder. My teacher picks up a chocolate and hands it to me. I cannot believe it. Nor can Imogen and Charlotte. In all the years that they had been having piano lessons, they have never got chocolates. I feel very happy and special.

Piano is more fun than work now. I can't wait for my next lesson.

What do you think? That's not bad for an 11-year-old girl who's never been taught to write, is it?

Sophie hasn't done any punctuation or grammar or comprehension exercises. She has never written a set composition. I haven't even taught her all the different uses for writing. She just listened and read and observed other family members writing and discussing writing. Then she went away, eager to follow our example, and write herself.

I think about all the complicated learn-to-write methods my husband uses with his primary school class: all those worksheets and activities that concentrate on one skill at a time. Are they really necessary for homeschoolers? Or is it enough to provide an environment where there is enthusiasm, good example, and reasons to write?

All my children write. They write for pleasure as well as need. Is that because they are following my example? Do they get caught up in my excitement? Maybe they assume writing is something everyone does because those around them do it. Or could it be the literature we read or the discussions we enjoy? Maybe we just have lots of thoughts we want to put into words. Do we all have lots of real reasons for writing, and so it seems a valuable skill to have? Or is the desire to write purely hereditary? Were my children and I meant to be writers? Perhaps I am just one of the lucky mothers who doesn't have to worry her children won't write, because we all have the right genes. What do you think?

I sometimes wonder what would happen if a non-writing parent suddenly became an enthusiastic writer. Would her children follow suit? That would be a very interesting experiment. Or are there enthusiastic child writers whose parents hate writing? They could have other mentors, I suppose.

And I also wonder what skills my children don't have just because I've never been interested enough to try and gain them, and model them myself.

"Would you like to listen to a chapter of my novel, Mum?" asks Sophie. Soon I am enjoying the latest tale of the Bean family.

"So who is your favourite character?" Sophie asks as she closes her computer. She is eager to hear my reply.

"Mr Cracker! Yes, I really love Mr Cracker," I answer.

Sophie smiles widely. "Do you know the best thing about writing?"

I think I do. It's having someone to share it with. I guess we all enjoy sharing things we love, don't we?

A Passion for Writing

I love writing. It's one of my passions. And all of my children love writing too. They observe me sitting at the computer with my head down, in a world of my own, tapping away. Then:

"Hey! I've finished. Read this and let me know what you think." I step back, and the girls crowd in, eager to share what I have created. I watch their faces.

"What do you think? Is it okay?" I ask anxiously.

"I like how you..."

"Yeah, that's good!"

"I love it!"

I can always rely on my family!

My children have noticed how much I enjoy playing around with words. They have seen me jumping up and down with excitement when I have been successful in finding the right words to express my thoughts. And they have wanted to try too. They have wanted to write.

All my girls have their own blogs. I created mine, and then they decided they'd like to have blogs of their own as well. It's great. We share so much.

"I can't think what to write a blog post about, Mum. Any ideas?"

"What do you think, Mum? Do you think it makes sense? Does it have a central idea?"

"Oh! When did you write that? I've just discovered your new post. I love it!"

We are all very critical of our own work, and very encouraging about each others'.

We all want to improve our writing skills. I have borrowed most of the how-to-write books in our library. My girls have borrowed a few too.

Last term Imogen said, "Mum, do you remember those writing exercises you did with the older kids some years ago? Could you do something like that with Charlotte and me, please?"

I remembered. I borrowed a library book. It had lots of information about bringing writing alive by creating images in the minds of readers.

So the other week, I went away to search for a suitable book to use with Imogen and Charlotte. I happened to find the same book I used years ago. (It wouldn't have mattered if that book hadn't been available. I think most how-to-write books contain something worth sharing.) And this is what we did:

I skimmed the book looking for sections the girls would find interesting and useful. I don't believe in wading through everything in a book, working through it in order.

I read an interesting section out loud. I stopped every now and then, and we discussed the ideas and tried out some examples. Then I looked at the end-of-chapter exercises and asked, "Which one sounds appealing?"

After choosing an exercise and discussing it, the girls went to their computers deep in thought. Soon they were tapping on the keys. Sometimes it was difficult to begin writing and a couple of times, Charlotte and I had to do some brainstorming. But her imagination soon moved into gear. Intense looks of concentration appeared on the girls' faces as the words started to spill onto their computer screens. I could see they'd entered that other magical creative world.

A few days passed: "Are your stories finished? Do you want to share them?" And the girls hurried to find the right files on their computers. I read their pieces out loud, and we discussed them as we went. We pointed out the bits that worked and tactfully made suggestions for improvements. The girls didn't mind these suggestions. That is the whole point. We're all working to improve our skills. Imogen and Charlotte made alterations until they were satisfied with their work.

So far, we have discussed such topics as active and passive verbs. We've described smells, (have you ever tried to describe a smell?) and sounds and tastes, and abstract things like feelings and emotions. We've used specific nouns, added action to all our imagined scenes, and reduced our surplus words. We've 'shown' not 'told'.

When the girls have finished their stories, they post them on their blogs.

I've noticed a few unschooling principles in action here:

Children learn a lot by sharing family passions. They are eager to try out things that they can see adults doing.

It is quite okay to use books and do a 'course' of learning if that is what children want to do. My writing course was very amateurish, but it fulfilled their needs, and they had a lot of fun.

And my girls' writing turned into real work because they published their stories on their blogs. There is so much satisfaction gained from working on something that will ultimately be shared.

I have been working with Imogen and Charlotte, who are 16 and 13, but I have written with the younger girls too. Years ago, Felicity wanted to write poetry, and we spent a long time playing around with words together. She even entered a poetry competition and won a prize. But that is another story!

All my kids have had a lot of fun writing. And that I think is the secret. Everyone has to want to get involved. They have to want to write.

So if you're wondering how you can encourage your kids to write, perhaps you can show them how much you enjoy writing. Offer to share what you're doing. Invite them to join you. Who knows? If you're having fun, the chances are your kids will want to write too. And if not, that's okay. Not everyone has a passion for writing.

An Unschooler Learns How to Write

My daughter Imogen loves writing. It's part of who she is.

"When did you start writing?" I ask.

"I can't remember a time when I wasn't writing."

My fourth child was writing stories long before she knew how to form letters into words.

"Do you remember how Charlotte and I would sit side by side at the kitchen table and draw our stories?" says Imogen. "We'd chat about what was happening and then draw it. Then we'd chat again. And then we'd draw some more. When the page was full, we'd turn it over. Sometimes we'd end up with a stack of more than fifty pages."

"Do you think drawing is a good introduction to writing?" I ask.

"Oh, yes!" Imogen's eyes are aglow as she remembers those wonderful story drawing days. "When kids are drawing, they are exercising their imaginations. They're discovering what storytelling is all about. If a child is used to telling stories, later on, she will find it easier to write. She'll want to write."

Imogen tells me that a day arrived when she wanted to use words to write her stories down on paper. "It seemed like the next logical step." But did she have the necessary skills? Perhaps she first had to learn all the basics such as grammar, punctuation and spelling by doing a course with lots of exercises? No, she learnt all these skills while she was actually writing.

"It's much better to learn about such things as spelling while you're writing," says Imogen. "When you want to write, you want to know more to improve your writing. You have something to say, and you want to say it the best way you can.

Writing courses, workbooks and websites that try and teach spelling, punctuation and grammar aren't the way to encourage a child's love of writing. Kids can't see why these skills are important if they're not using them. If they're made to learn them, without needing them, they won't remember them very well."

Imogen has something else to add, "Anyway, there's something far more important than writing skills. Kids need something to write about."

Yes, we can have the best writing skills in the world, but if we have nothing to write about, those skills aren't going to be much use.

Something to write about? We are back to Imogen's childhood drawing stories. They were the start of her writing passion.

So Imogen taught herself to write. She read widely and experimented with different techniques. She wrote and wrote and wrote. And her skills improved enormously. But that wasn't enough for her. She completed a Bachelor of Arts degree in Professional Writing and Publishing because she wanted to learn even more. This course involved writing a number of essays.

"How many essays did you write before you started your university course?" I ask.

"Two and they were terrible!" says Imogen with a grin.

Was my daughter at a disadvantage because she didn't have any essay writing skills? Was she ill-prepared for university learning?

I shall answer those questions in the next story!

What if Unschoolers Don't Know How to Write Essays?

My daughter Imogen taught herself to write. After learning the basics, she read widely, observing the example of good authors. She experimented with different styles and techniques. She wrote and wrote and wrote. I wasn't surprised when Imogen announced she wanted to study writing at a tertiary level. She decided to complete a Bachelor of Arts degree in Professional Writing and Publishing.

Imogen's degree course involved writing lots of essays.

"How many essays did you write before you started your university course?" I ask.

"Two and they were terrible!" says Imogen with a grin.

"I can't even remember those essays," I say.

"You had a weak moment. You said, 'You're going to need to know how to write essays when you go to university so you'd better write some as practice.'"

Do you ever have weak moments when your confidence is in danger of seeping away? I've had a few. I used to look around at what other people were doing or listen to their ideas, which were different from mine. What if they were right? Perhaps I should make my unschoolers write a few essays. It wouldn't hurt, would it?

"So I wrote a couple of essays," says Imogen, "but they didn't turn out very well. I didn't enjoy writing them, so we gave up on essay writing."

We gave up? Or did I just come to my senses?

Imogen continues, "You said, 'You're a good writer. You'll pick up essay writing when you need it.'"

So Imogen started her university education with two bad essays under her belt. "Did you feel ill-prepared as you began your degree course?"

"No. One of the first things I learnt at uni was that the high school essay and the university essay are two completely different things. Even if I'd been able to write a perfect high school essay, that's not what they wanted. Not knowing what I was doing was actually good. I learnt to write an essay the way the university wanted it. Unlike the other students, I didn't have to relearn this skill."

Imogen wasn't expected to know how to write an essay before she started university. She was taught this skill in her very first unit, *Tertiary Learning Strategies*. But what if this unit hadn't been available? Imogen could have done a similar preparation module online.

"The best time to learn about essay writing," says Imogen, "is just before or as you start a university degree."

"We shouldn't make kids write an essay every week or so during the high school years to prepare them for uni?"

"No. Let kids write what they want. They'll soon pick up essay writing when they need it. An essay is just a different framework for your words. The most important thing is knowing what you want to say."

I have a final question for my daughter. It's a big one. "Are you passing your university essays?"

Imogen grins and says, "Yes, I can write a good essay. I'm having no problems at all!"

I had this conversation with Imogen several years ago. She has now finished her degree course with excellent results. Isn't that good to know?

If unschoolers don't know how to write essays, will they be ill-prepared for university? No, they'll be fine!

Part XV: University

Can unschoolers get into university? Yes, if that's what they want to do. Five of my children have studied at university level. Duncan has a Bachelor of Arts degree and a Master's of Teaching. Imogen also has a Bachelor of Arts degree, and Charlotte almost has one. Soon she will finish her course. Felicity completed several university units without any problems, but she didn't want to go on and do a whole degree. Callum enrolled in a Bachelor of Nursing degree, and studied successfully for a year or two before deciding that nursing wasn't for him after all.

Imogen's Unschool Plan to Get into University

At the beginning of her final official year of registered homeschooling, Imogen thought carefully about what she wanted to do in the future. Having so many passions, it was a tough decision choosing one area she wanted to focus on. But eventually, Imogen said, "I think I'd like to write," and I replied, "Words can change the world." She agreed. "I'd like to go to university and complete a writing degree."

But how was Imogen going to get onto the course of her choice? Together we formulated a plan, the first plan of Imogen's unschooling career. The plan, not only had to result in a place at university, but it also had to take into account her desire to continue indulging her other passions.

So what exactly did Imogen do?

Imogen was certainly not doing the same things as most students of her age. School students were busy learning and memorising all the information they were likely to be tested on in the final exam of their schooling career: the HSC (Higher School Certificate).

Even if Imogen had wanted to do what the school kids were doing, it wasn't possible. Homeschooled students are not eligible to sit for all the subjects that make up the HSC, the qualification most commonly used to compete for university places.

As Imogen wanted to go onto tertiary studies, she had to achieve an equivalent qualification, an HSC alternative. So she decided to complete three (online) Open University units, the results of which would give her a 'score' that could be used to compete for a university place. And while she did this formal external study, she also hoped she'd have plenty of free time to do such things as continue to learn and play music, write novels, run kilometres, and watch Shakespeare.

So this is what Imogen did last year, her equivalent year 12:

She...

- Completed three Open University units, one unit per semester: *Tertiary Learning Strategies, Critical Thinking* and *Introduction to Writing.*
- Continued singing and piano lessons and prepared for a piano exam.
- Sang with the church choir as soloist and choir member, and practised and performed with a second choir.
- Increased her musicianship knowledge.
- Listened to music.
- Taught piano to her siblings.
- Taught singing to her siblings.
- Wrote three draft novels during three separate NaNoWriMo (National Novel Writing Month) months.
- Edited her writings.
- Wrote posts for her writing blog.
- Participated in online writing forums.
- Read numerous writing books to learn more about planning a novel and editing.
- Read, watched and discussed all the Shakespeare plays the rest of the family were passionate about.
- Watched and discussed all the Gilbert and Sullivan operettas the rest of the family were enjoying. Sang songs from the operettas.
- Enjoyed other musical DVDs.
- Joined in with family prayers and other devotions, Bible readings and meditations, spiritual readings and talks.
- Enjoyed her drawing and doodling, improving her skills and filling numerous journals.
- Sewed her own clothes.
- Cooked the majority of the family meals.
- Became a 5 km runner and ran with the family a few times a week.
- Participated in indoor soccer competitions.
- Watched many documentaries with the rest of the family.
- Watched lots of movies worthy of discussion.

- Participated in all the outings and excursions the rest of us went on, including museums and galleries, the beach and the bush.
- Read classics such as Dickens, Austen, Bronte, Gaskell and watched mini-series and movie versions.
- Read many books. I could never list them all.
- Took an interest in everything that her siblings were learning.
- Discussed anything and everything.

Imogen might have done maths and Latin, but she finished the courses earlier than expected.

I have just listed these achievements off the top of my head to give an idea of what Imogen did the year before she applied to go to university.

So Imogen had a great year. Her 'plan' allowed her to continue following her passions, in an unschooling way, while at the same time, she was able to work towards an HSC alternative qualification.

So how did she go? Was Imogen able to do the degree course of her choice? Yes! Imogen completed three Open University units with excellent results. She then looked around at the various writing courses offered by both on-campus and online universities to see which one best suited her needs. She decided that she wanted to continue with the Open University option and complete a Bachelor of Arts degree in Professional Writing and Publishing.

Studying online was a great fit for Imogen. And it was good for the rest of the family too. Because she was still at home with us, Imogen didn't have to give up her unschooling life. She continued sharing and chatting and playing and watching and reading and discussing with us as she'd always done. Life didn't change much. That was good for all of us!

Supporting Our Kids' Decisions

I found the following words on my daughter Imogen's old blog. She wrote them a few years ago.

At the beginning of this year, I started my dream university course. I'd love to be able to say that it was what I had always wanted to study for, but sadly, no. You see, I used to have this mistaken idea that I wanted to be a doctor.

For years and years, I kept up the idea that I was going to be a doctor. Okay, so I couldn't name you a single thing about being a doctor that really drew me in, and I couldn't think of a single area that I would work in, but that was a small matter really. Obviously, I was meant to be a doctor.

Until I got to thinking, did I really want to be a doctor? I spent my last school years studying chemistry (which I was very bad at), biology (that was okay), and advanced maths. And I was pretty sure that I was ready to jump into this doctor's degree.

Only, I suddenly realised that that wasn't the right thing to do. Did I really want to be a doctor? I couldn't be a surgeon. Even thinking about cutting people up made me feel sick. And looking after a person for more than a day was never my thing either. No, I was pretty sure that I didn't want to be a doctor after all.

And that's when I realised that if I didn't have to be a doctor, I could be something else. Something exciting. Like a writer, or an editor. Yes, for someone like me, who's always working on some piece of writing that sounded just perfect. Imogen Elvis, author and editor. That sounded pretty good to me.

So now I'm studying writing and publishing. I might not enjoy the sociology side of things, but I know that somewhere in the future, the writing lurks. And I'm working towards the degree that I want. And what could be better than working toward the right dream?

After reading this post, I wondered why Imogen thought she should be a doctor. I felt rather confused because haven't we always given our kids plenty of space to explore possible interests? They've always had the freedom to do what they want. We've always supported their decisions.

"Imogen, why did you think you had to be a doctor?" I ask. "Did I push you in that direction?"

"No, you never did that. It was other people."

For many years, Imogen was a St John Ambulance cadet. She was a good one. She had the necessary knowledge and could treat wounds and injuries. She had compassion and confidence. She was a leader, teaching and inspiring the younger cadets. She was hardworking and reliable and supported the older St John Ambulance officers. Yes, Imogen knew what she was doing, and she enjoyed being a cadet.

"Everyone at St John's said I should study medicine," says Imogen. "I was good at first-aid, and I could do even more if I became a doctor. They said, 'We need more doctors.' They thought it would be a good thing to do. And at first, I thought they were right. Get a good job that pays well. Do something that everyone would approve of."

And then one day, Imogen realised she didn't really want to be a doctor. Although she enjoyed working with St John Ambulance, she didn't want to go further and have full responsibility for any patients. She couldn't see herself doing that. What she really wanted to do was write.

"When I told people I was interested in medicine, they were all very enthusiastic. But when I told them I'd changed my mind and was going to study writing instead, they tried to discourage me. 'There's no money in writing. You can't make a living out of it. Not many people get their books published.' Doing medicine is a safer option."

I'm sure for many people, Imogen's decision made no sense. But when they realised she was serious about writing, they had their own ideas about how she could go about it: "You should be a journalist. I know someone who did that, and she's doing very well." I guess it was kind of people to offer their thoughts and suggestions. They were only trying to help. But Imogen's dreams didn't lie in the direction of journalism.

Imogen studied for a Bachelor of Arts in Professional Writing and Publishing. She enjoyed her course immensely. And when she was finished, people wanted to know what her next step was going to be.

"What are you going to do next? Get a job with a publishing company?"

"No, I'm going to write novels." Imogen explained how she was going to edit the novels she'd been writing and how she was going to publish them herself.

"How are you going to support yourself while you do that?"

"By living frugally." And giving piano lessons and helping our family in return for our help.

People stopped commenting. But Imogen didn't stop writing, and recently, she published her very first novel.

It can be hard to ignore all the advice caring family and friends are eager to share. But that was the right thing to do. Although many people are passionate about medicine and therefore should follow this pathway, it wasn't for Imogen. She's a writer.

Sometimes it's hard to go our own way and do what we feel is right for us. As parents, we know this. But what about our children? Perhaps we need to be aware that they have to deal with this as well. They need us to stand up for them. We have to speak out. We must surround our children with the love and support that they need to go out there into the world and do what they should.

Use their talents. Follow their dreams. Make a difference.

We have to be willing to put up with possible criticism. Put our kids first. Because wouldn't it be sad if our kids felt like they had little support and so ended up doing something that pleased other people but was entirely wrong for them?

"What's Imogen doing?" a friend asks.

"She's published her first novel. Now she's writing the sequel," I reply. "She's also working in a cafe part-time so that she can support herself."

What is my friend thinking? It doesn't really matter. Imogen is doing okay.

An Unschooler Talks About Passions, University and Work

I'm talking to my son Callum about his experience of university and work.

"Why did you decide to study nursing?" I ask.

"I thought about a career in the health care industry because of my involvement with St John Ambulance. I thought nursing would be a good way to continue my interest in first-aid."

Callum joined St John Ambulance as a cadet. He spent many years with the organisation, increasing his skills and taking on new roles. He loved going out on duty, setting up first-aid stations, and then dealing with injuries. Callum also enjoyed training the younger cadets.

"Did you have any trouble getting into university?" I ask.

"Not really." And then Callum grins and says, "Actually, I had no trouble at all!"

Callum completed several Open University units online. He chose a basic introduction to tertiary learning unit, a critical thinking one, and one about human biology. The results of these units were combined to give Callum a 'score' which he used when he applied to do a Bachelor of Nursing at an on-campus university.

"Do you remember how we also got together a few documents, such as your St John cadet of the year certificates, and some references from other St John Ambulance officers, to put with your application? Your practical experience and your passion might have helped you."

"Oh yes, definitely. I had some good references. I was very fortunate."

So Callum got onto the degree course of his choice without a problem. And then he began a new phase of his life.

"Going to uni is totally different from homeschooling," I say. "Tell me about your experience."

"I think my university experience was very different from the other students. The very first lecture we went to, the tutors told us that university would be much less structured than we were used to. That might have been true for the students who'd just left school. But for me, it was almost like taking a step backwards. University learning was more structured than what I'd been doing. And then there were the essays and other work I was expected to do."

I don't remember Callum writing many essays while he was homeschooling. So did he cope when it came time to write his university essays?

"Oh yes," he says. "I could write because I did a lot of creative writing at home. Writing an essay is just another form of writing. It's very formulaic and logical. It was very easy to adjust."

Many years ago, I went to university because this was the expected thing to do. I didn't have any better plan, so I found myself studying something I wasn't very passionate about. I wonder if many of the students on Callum's course did this as well. Perhaps most of them weren't gripped by a passion, unlike Callum.

"Do you remember how being passionate about your subject got you in trouble?" I ask.

Callum laughs. "Yes, sometimes, I went beyond the expectations of the teachers. I wanted to know more than the information they were giving me. I wanted to know all the ins and outs of how everything worked. Maybe I was supposed to learn it at a later point, but I couldn't wait."

Callum was curious, and so he asked too many questions. He held up the class and got quite a name for himself.

"Do you remember the day the tutor asked a question, and she said anyone could answer it but not that homeschooled student?"

There was one tutor in particular who had very negative views about homeschooling. When she found out, at the first tutorial, that Callum hadn't gone to school like all the other students, she instantly said, "You obviously have no social skills and no knowledge." But by the end of the semester, she had changed her mind. She and Callum actually became friends.

"Were you a very social person?" I ask.

"Yes, I had no trouble talking to anyone of any age. I enjoyed talking to both the students and the lecturers at the university."

Even though Callum had never been to a learning institution before, he found it quite easy to be part of the class, and he coped with the lectures.

"I found a group of like-minded students who were really driven to do their work," says Callum. "We got on together and worked well. And I was also able to go and talk to the tutors and lecturers."

While Callum was studying for a Bachelor of Nursing, he was also working part-time as a store assistant at a supermarket.

Then one day, Callum stopped studying. After about a year and a half, he dropped out of the Bachelor of Nursing degree. He changed his mind about what he wanted to do. He decided that nursing wasn't really for him after all.

"Some people might say that you should have persevered until the end," I say. "It's not good to throw in the towel. We have to finish what we start. What do you think about that?"

"I disagree. It would have been a waste of time because I wouldn't have been happy working in the healthcare industry. It wasn't the practical side. I still do enjoy helping people. I like administering first-aid. It was the politics, the way the healthcare system works. I don't think I'd have been happy working within that system. You need to enjoy your work."

"So it's okay to change your mind? When we realise we've made a mistake, the sensible thing to do is to acknowledge that and to pursue a different pathway?"

Callum nods. "It's never too late to start again especially..."

"...especially when you're only 20?" I finish Callum's sentence for him, and then we both laugh.

Callum and I talk about how everything we do is valuable. Nothing is ever wasted. What we learn from one experience we take with us when we move forward to the next.

So what did Callum do once he'd left university? He went to his boss at the supermarket and asked if there was any chance he could get some full-time work.

"She offered me a position as a trainee store manager."

So my son started a new career. But I wonder: is a supermarket store manager a very challenging job? Is it interesting enough for Callum?

"Certainly for the three or four years that I've been working there, it's been challenging and enjoyable. Of course, it's not a job that I'm passionate about. I think I could continue working there for a while longer, but eventually, I want to move on to something else."

"What sort of things have you learnt while working in the supermarket?"

"A lot of social skills, working with the customers and the employees. Time management. Working to standards. High standards are demanded from the staff. Also, I've been driving myself to achieve and perform. I'm pushing myself to work better within the company and have seen good results, I believe."

A lot of people say that unschoolers are undisciplined. For example, they can't get up on time in the morning. They don't know how to work hard. I mention this to Callum, and he smiles. "When I was working as a trainee manager, I'd get up at 4:30, work through the day until the store closed at 7:30 and I'd get home at about 8 pm. I worked all day with only a half hour break in the middle."

"That's a long day," I say. "So you don't think unschoolers are lazy. They're very hardworking. And when you have to be up early to do something, you can do it, is that right?"

288

My son agrees.

Working at the supermarket, not only gave Callum the opportunity to learn a few new skills, but it also gave him an income that allowed him to pursue another passion. Callum invested the money from all those extra hours of work in his interest in cars: repairs and modifications.

"Tell me about the time when someone came up to you and said, 'How does someone learn how to fix a car without doing a recognised course?'"

"One of the guys I work with, he knows that I have a couple of cars that I'm working on. He asked me if I'd had any training in car mechanics. I told him I hadn't. I'd just picked it all up along the way. He couldn't understand how I could do that. That seemed rather remarkable to him."

Callum's interest in fixing cars started with an old Commodore station wagon. He used to take this car to the repair shop every time something needed fixing. And that was expensive. When Callum bought his next car, he decided he'd learn how to repair it himself. At that time, fortunately for Callum, a car mechanic was living next door to us. He was very friendly and didn't mind helping Callum diagnose his car problems. Callum then went away and did the repairs himself.

"1970's Holden Kingswoods are my particular interest," says Callum. "Their engines are beautiful and simple, very easy to work on. They were a great way to learn how an engine goes together. A more modern engine works using the same principles. They are just slightly more complicated."

"So you taught yourself car mechanics by finding out the right information by reading books, searching the Internet, and joining in with forums?"

"Yes, that's right."

"So really you were unschooling?"

Callum agrees, and we talk about how he's continuing to learn even though he's no longer a school-aged child. He's continuing to follow his passions. I want to know if one of his interests will eventually turn into a career.

"Hopefully. That's what I'm working towards at the minute. Yes, I never stop looking for info. I keep reading and trying to find out more about the things I'm interested in. I've started looking at ways I could turn my hobby into a job. I investigated being a mechanic, but my greatest interest is not actually repairing cars. It's the modification and the performance and the restoration of older cars in particular. So I've enrolled in a fabrication course at TAFE." (Technical and Further Education)

"Do you think people should follow their interests and see if they lead to a career?" I ask.

"I think so. Working with an interest is enjoyable regardless of what happens as far as a career goes. But I know you can make anything work so long as it's truly what you want to do and what you're interested in."

"A lot of people play safe and choose a secure career. They'd tell you that only a few people succeed in the industry you're interested in. Only a few people have the job you want. Is that a good reason for not pursuing your dream?"

"If you don't take risks, you don't get the rewards." There are some jobs that only a few people have. But why shouldn't we be one of those people? If we're passionate, if we are prepared to work hard and keep learning, who knows what will happen? We can at least, give it our best effort. Because we'll never know unless we try.

What About My Perfect Homeschooling Success Story?

"Did you get a place?" I asked eagerly. Had my son been accepted on the university course of his choice?

"I haven't yet worked up the courage to log into my account and have a look," Callum admitted. But a few minutes later, he emerged from his room, a huge smile on his face, "I did it! I'm on the course!"

I remember how elated we felt that night. I walked around feeling like the best homeschooling mother ever. My job was over. I'd guided Callum perfectly, and now he was on the pathway to his dream career. He was going to be a nurse. One day he would be working in the casualty department of a hospital, calmly dealing with any emergency the ambulance delivered. I could imagine it all.

Callum grinned, and I smiled, and we couldn't wait to share the news.

Callum accepted the place, and he decided to study part-time and continue working as well. The first year went exceedingly well. Callum stood out from the crowd. He was the only student with practical experience due to his excellent St John Ambulance record. He was also the only homeschooled student, and he impressed and annoyed the tutors with his persistent questions and knowledge.

"Callum, draw the patient in the correct position." Soon a perfectly proportioned, realistic looking man was lying in the required position on the whiteboard.

"I suppose you learnt art while you were homeschooling," sighed the tutor. He'd been expecting a stick figure.

"Does anyone know what this Latin word means? No? You tell us, Callum. I assume you learnt Latin while homeschooling."

"Not another question, Callum! Homeschooled students want to know too much. You're not supposed to think. You're supposed to sit quietly and listen!"

Yes, Callum was proving to be a headache for his tutors, but they couldn't deny he was set for a brilliant nursing career. Or was that only his proud mother's opinion?

Then things changed. One day, during the long summer break, I realised that Callum didn't look happy. He was rather grumpy and hard to live with. I wondered if he was just fed up with the holidays. Maybe he'd feel better once the university semester began and he could get back to work. But that wasn't the problem.

"I don't think I want to be a nurse, after all, Mum," Callum confessed one day.

"But Callum, you are so good with people. And you loved your work with St John Ambulance. You said you wanted to do something worthwhile to help others."

"I don't know, Mum."

"Perhaps you should have studied full-time. This would have been your final year. Have you just had enough of studying?"

"It's not that, Mum. I just don't know if I want to do nursing anymore."

My vision of my son with a stethoscope around his neck, working in the casualty unit, dealing with all the emergencies in his calm and confident and compassionate way, was fast disappearing. And I didn't want it to.

"If you persevere, you could have such a wonderful career. There are so many options within the nursing profession." I knew from Callum's face I couldn't convince him.

I could have argued and debated with Callum:

"You need to learn to stick with things."

"You'll regret giving up your course in the future. You should take advantage of your chance to get a university education."

"You've come so far; you ought to finish."

"Don't give up your dream because it's got hard."

"Every course has its boring basic units. Just wait till you get to the practical units. That's where you'll excel."

Don't take away my dream.

What about my homeschooling success story?

I remember chatting to Callum a few years ago. "I'm sorry, Callum, I'm not praying for a perfect life for you. Life's not like that. There will be struggles. Difficulties are the only way you will grow. They'll help you develop into the person you are meant to be."

Callum just grinned and said, "Why didn't I get a regular mother who just wants her children to be happy?" I could see he understood.

Yes, life isn't perfect. Sons change their minds. Mothers' dreams evaporate. But that's okay.

A few days ago, Callum arrived home, bursting with something he wanted to share.

"Okay. Tell me," I said, seeing Callum couldn't wait a moment longer to share his news.

"When my boss heard I'm no longer studying, she wanted to know if I would be interested in a store manager apprenticeship."

"Is that what you want to do?"

"It sounds good at the moment."

"Then it's fine with me."

Then today...

Callum again arrives home bursting with something he wants to share. "Okay. Tell me," I say.

"Hey, Mum! I had my employee review today. I got full marks for customer service. Apparently, all the customers like chatting to me."

"You're supposed to be an unsocialised homeschooling graduate, Callum! You shouldn't know how to talk to people of all ages and situations."

We both smile.

So my son is going to lavish his charming smiles and caring bedside manner on all the customers who come into the supermarket looking for a bit of human contact in their day. And I can accept that. It's Callum's life, not mine. This isn't about perfect homeschooling success stories, or perfect mothers, or what other people think. No. My job is over, and I'm letting Callum go.

The future? That is in God's hands, not mine, just the way it should be.

Choosing Not to Go to University

I ask Sophie if she is planning to go to university and she tells me she doesn't want to go just because it's the next expected stage of her life.

"If a university course would further one of my passions and help me get where I want to go, I'd do one," she says. "But at the moment, going to university isn't the right thing for me. And then there's the matter of money. I don't want to get into debt without a good reason." Yes, a university education isn't cheap.

So Sophie is not following in the footsteps of her older siblings who have completed their degrees. She doesn't even want to do a couple of Open University units so that she has a Higher School Certificate alternative. She's going to do without the piece of paper that tells everyone she has attained a certain level of education. But that doesn't mean that Sophie doesn't want to do some further study. She does. She knows what she wants to do, and she thinks she has found a way to get there, one that won't land her in debt.

For the last couple of years, Sophie has been working in the hospitality industry. She waits tables, makes excellent coffee and helps in the kitchen.

"What do people think when they hear you're working full-time in a cafe?" I ask.

"They think I've dropped out of school. That I have no ambitions. They ask, 'Is working in a cafe all you want to do with your life?' Of course, I don't want to make coffee forever. My cafe job is a means to an end. It's giving me the money I need to do what I really want to do."

Sophie has been saving her wages. She has saved enough to pay for a course of her choice upfront. So she'll have no debt at the end of her study.

So what is she studying? Sophie has enrolled in a certificate course. Not a degree course. Not a diploma course. A certificate course. Maybe we pass over this kind of course thinking that our kids should aim higher.

"When I finished school," I say, "I was expected to go to university. Anyone who got high enough marks in their final exams was expected to go on and do some further study. We had to complete our education. Only the kids who weren't so clever did a non-university course. And if you didn't do very well at school, you didn't even think about further study. You went out and looked for a job instead."

Does Sophie not want to go to university because she's afraid she won't be able to keep up with all the other students? "Do you think you could successfully do a university course?" I ask.

"Oh yes, I think I could write essays and do assignments," says Sophie. "I'm not bypassing university because I'm less clever than my siblings." Then she grins and says, "Actually, I think I'm very clever. I've found an alternate way to do what I want, and I'm not going to get into debt getting there."

There is no doubt that a university degree course is necessary for some careers. No one is going to find employment as a teacher or a doctor or someone similar if they don't have the right official qualifications. But sometimes there are other pathways for other careers.

Sophie is passionate about health and fitness. So she has enrolled in a certificate course in fitness.

"If you were interested in fitness research, a degree course might be appropriate," I say.

"But I'm more interested in the practical side of fitness. So a certificate course is a better way to go. And then after I have completed this course, I could do another one, such as a nutrition certificate."

"And if you suddenly decide you would like to do something like fitness research, you can always use the certificate course as a stepping stone to a degree course," I say. Yes, many certificate courses are accepted in place of a school leaver's certificate when applying to a university. Credit is even given for any studies already completed. Just because a child doesn't choose to do a degree course straightaway doesn't mean they're closing the door on this type of formal education forever.

But at the moment, Sophie can't see a reason for going to university. She's not interested in a career that needs that particular qualification.

"When I went to university," I say, "I didn't really know what I wanted to do with my life. I chose to do a science degree majoring in botany, but I wasn't passionate about that subject. I got accepted on the course, so I did it. Studying at university put off the moment when I had to decide on a career and then go out there into the world and earn some money. I guess I was just filling in time."

I think a lot of kids go to university with this mindset. Yes, they use university as a delaying tactic. But Sophie doesn't need a three-year gap that will allow her to think and consider her options. She's already done a lot of thinking. And experimenting. She's been exploring her passions and trying out her ideas for years. And now Sophie knows what she wants to do. (For now, because passions and careers can change over a lifetime. And that's quite okay.)

"I want to be a personal trainer," says Sophie.

Now some people might think that this doesn't sound like a very lofty ambition. It might not be their idea of a good career. And I admit it does seem a bit unconventional. Not your usual choice of work, especially if you are clever enough to study at university level. However, I'm fully supportive of Sophie's plan. I know her. I am familiar with her passions. I realise that she has a dream.

Being fit and healthy is important. It's not something that's popular one day and out of fashion the next. Everyone needs to maintain a reasonable level of fitness regardless of their age for the rest of their lives. Of course, the way we get fit, the programs we use, the fitness gurus we follow, the clothes that we wear, and the equipment we buy does change. But people with good knowledge who want to help will always be needed. And so I think Sophie will have no shortage of clients. She could be a very successive personal trainer. But that's not all she wants to do.

Sophie would like to write her own fitness programs, put together healthy food recipe books, maybe run a few classes as well as have some personal clients. She wants to use her skills as a vlogger, videographer and photographer to promote her own fitness business and become a fitness influencer.

"It sounds like you'll be using all your big passions," I say.

Sophie grins. "Oh, yes! Won't that be amazing?"

"What do the girls you work with think of your plan?" I ask.

"I haven't shared all my plans, but they certainly don't envy me working full-time at the cafe. They're still at school. They work to earn pocket money. They're not ready to support themselves. They're in a different stage of life to me. They go to school during the week. They work for a few hours at the weekend. They spend their free time going out with their friends. They expect to go to university but haven't really got any idea what they want to do with their lives. They're going to do things the conventional way."

"You're the same age as the other girls (17), but you're not in school. You have the freedom to do whatever you like. They don't envy that?"

"No, they don't understand what I'm doing."

"Do you envy them? Would you like someone else to be totally responsible for you? Do you wish the money you earn was your pocket money? Perhaps you'd just like to spend your time with friends. Travel the expected pathway. "

"Oh no, I don't envy those girls at all. I'm on my way to doing something amazing. And if I'm going to be completely honest, I feel like I'm a couple of steps ahead of them. I'm not missing out. I've moved on. I'm onto the next stage of my life." And that feels good.

So my daughter Sophie isn't going to university. She's not following the same pathway as her fellow workers who are still at school. She's not even choosing to do what her older siblings have done. Instead, she's finding her own way to do what she's most interested in.

And Sophie's right. That is amazing, isn't it?

A Typical Unschooling Morning with My Girls

By about 8:30 am each day, we've done all the less interesting work. It's out of the way. Gone. Now we can get on to the more exciting part of our day.

We chat about what everybody wants to do. What plans do people have? Plans? Of course, there are some things on our timetable that are planned, such as music lessons. Someone might want to go to town for some other purpose. And then we all have our own projects that we are working on. Yes, we always have so many things we want to do. We have to make some decisions about how we are going to spend this particular day.

I spend the mornings with my younger girls, Sophie (14) and Gemma-Rose (11) doing what they want to do. There are certain things the girls *have* to do every morning. When I say 'have to do' I mean that they choose to do them. These are such things as piano practices. They choose to practice the piano because they know that if they don't, they won't improve their skills, and they want to learn to play like their older sisters. That's not a problem. They each just need to put aside about half an hour every morning to do that. Their practice time is in the morning because the older girls get the use of the piano in the afternoon. Practising in their allotted and agreed upon time: that's just being considerate.

Every morning, there are certain things that the girls insist I do. They like me to read to them. If I don't read to them regularly, books don't get finished, and that can be frustrating. So I have some commitments as well. Sophie has some extra commitments of her own. She has set herself the goal of finishing some coding courses. She realised that she wouldn't make much progress if she didn't work on these on a regular basis. So she's been trying to do a little bit each day to work towards the certificates of each course. She has finished a few courses recently and has moved on to some other ones.

300

So I don't think unschooling is necessarily about drifting through life from one thing to another as it occurs to us. We need to put work into certain things regularly. I'd never finish any of my novels if I didn't intentionally work on them. It's the same with the girls. They wouldn't finish their projects either.

But there's still plenty of time in our days for having fun, living in the moment, and taking advantage of whatever comes along. Even though we all have things we're working on, we don't live life to a schedule. It's an adventure. Our time's our own. We can choose what we want to do. If we want to start the day with reading, we can. If we have music lessons, we're free to drive to town for them. And we can go shopping while we're out. Or we can go to the park and visit the lake. We don't have to hurry home because we don't have workbooks that are waiting for us. (We're not going to get 'behind'.) We can walk around the lake. We can go for a run. We can just sit and chat and have coffee. These are all very good learning experiences in themselves. So some days we stay home, and other days we go off and have our adventures elsewhere.

Would you like to hear about a particular unschooling day?

The house was tidy and organised for the day. We'd said our prayers together. And then I asked, "What do you want to do today?"

"Can we go to the post office?" asked Gemma-Rose. "I want to post my letters."

My eleven-year-old daughter has been writing a lot of letters recently. She wrote them all in cursive handwriting, her latest interest. There was a time when I doubted Gemma-Rose would ever learn to do 'running writing'. Several years ago, I tried to teach her, but she dug in her heels and refused to cooperate. But a couple of weeks ago, I found my two youngest daughters sitting side by side writing together.

"Gemma-Rose was admiring my handwriting," explained Sophie. "She wanted me to show her how to do cursive writing."

Once Gemma-Rose had decided she wanted to learn, it took four days for her to conquer this new skill. She filled up her notebook with handwriting, and I had to buy her a new one. She's filling that one up too. And she's writing lots of letters.

So at 9 am, on that particular morning, Sophie, Gemma-Rose and I put on our coats and headed out the door. Nora, our dog, came with us. It was rather cold and, as we began the walk to our village post office, I searched my coat pockets for my gloves.

By the time we were on the return journey, after posting our letters and visiting a couple of shops, the day had warmed up a little. My gloves were back in my pocket, and I was enjoying the feel of the sun on my skin. As we strolled along, I looked at the girls and the dog, the gum trees rising high above the houses, and the sun in the clear blue sky, and I felt so thankful. I imagined school children working at their desks, and structured homeschoolers sitting around their tables with their work spread out in front of them. And what were we doing? We were outside enjoying the pleasures of an early spring morning.

When we got home, we filled the kettle and then made some coffee and hot chocolate. While I sipped my drink, I checked my emails. And then we spent a bit of time chatting together, just relaxing. I didn't think, "Look, we haven't got anything done yet today. It's already 10 o'clock. The day's moving on." I used to think like that. I'd worry about filling up the day as efficiently as possible. I'd watch the clock and want to cram in as much learning as I could. I'd get to the point where I'd wonder if we'd done enough. How much is enough? Could we finish for the day?

All the experiences we'd had that morning were very valuable. It's important to take time to be a family and to enjoy the outdoors. I knew we'd get on with the 'real work' – the things we have to do – in time. So once we'd had our coffee, the girls did get on with their piano practices which did have to be done. And then they wanted me to read to them...

Before we knew it, it was lunchtime. I guess that was a typical morning.

Part XVI: Term Times and Holidays

The Changing Seasons of the Unschooling Year

I saw a friend the other day who asked, "When are you finishing your school work for the year?"

I grinned wickedly and replied, "Finishing? We haven't even started. We haven't done anything for a long time."

I shouldn't joke. People will think unschoolers are lazy and do nothing. I should take the time to explain properly exactly what we do. For, of course, we do lots of things. We're always learning. The girls are just not doing 'school work' in the same way most other people are.

Anyway, my friend's question made me think about Christmas. I guess at this time of the year most people are busy tying up the term's loose ends, so they're free to focus on Christmas preparations. They're looking forward to the holidays.

So are we 'finishing up' for Christmas like most other homeschoolers?

Well, we're not busy completing planned school work in preparation for a holiday. But life *is* changing as Christmas approaches. We seem to be slowing down naturally.

Even though learning happens all year round, our learning year isn't the same from January to December. Our days aren't all alike. We adjust our days, taking into account what's going on in our lives.

The season and the weather affect what we do. We don't want to be stuck inside on a beautiful sunny day. That's the perfect time for picnics and nature walks, trips to the beach and outdoor sports. On cold winter days, our thoughts turn to more formal type learning. No one minds working on a computer when the sun isn't beckoning from outside.

And then we have days where we are healthy and full of energy. We run along rabbit trails, taking delight in all the new things we are learning. But sometimes we are sick or overtired, and we need to rest. This is a good time for quiet reading or DVDs or even just sleeping.

There are times when a family member has a particular need which must take priority. When we had babies and toddlers, they always came first.

Unexpected things happen, like bushfires, and we need to go with the flow until life calms down again.

There are some things that do follow the official school terms like outside music lessons. And August is always the month for music exams. The girls spend extra time practising the piano and singing at this time of year. When a concert is approaching, music is again the priority of the day.

April and November are always novel writing months when we all take up the NaNoWriMo (National Novel Writing Month) challenge.

The liturgical year and our own special celebrations affect our life too. If we are busy with a lot of other things, how can we savour and learn from the traditions and different seasons of the Church year? We want to take time to enjoy our special days too, instead of squeezing them in around everything else.

So the learning year flows and ebbs in its natural rhythm. The year isn't all the same. It isn't artificially organised around the official school terms. It just follows life. It is life. And that means different types of learning happen depending on where we are in our year.

So what are we doing at the moment?

It's summer, and the sun is shining. We want to be outside. We are enjoying running through the bush early in the mornings before breakfast. It's Advent, so we're involved with all the traditions and preparations that lead to Christmas. The girls are making gifts. People are singing and playing the piano. There are Christmas concerts and Masses to prepare for. The girls are reading and drawing and watching various DVDs. They are writing

Christmas letters and diary entries. We've been talking and discussing and listening to each other as usual. My husband Andy is a school teacher. In just over a week, he will be home for his long break. We want to spend time with him, resting and relaxing and enjoying. Soon we will be off on lots of outings and picnics.

And then in the New Year, when Andy returns to school, and the weather begins to cool down, life will change once more in a natural way. This learning season will end. Another one will begin.

So back to my friend's question. When are we finishing up for the year? We're not.

We're just changing seasons.

An Unschooling Holiday

This morning, I crept out of bed just before 7 o'clock and met my kindred spirit, Charlotte, in the kitchen. Neither of us likes lying in bed late. But everyone else was still snuggled up under their quilts, enjoying a relaxing start to the day. No need to hurry. We are on holiday. Yes, our third term of the school year has just ended and a holiday atmosphere prevails in our home.

I wonder why holidays mean so much to us even though we are unschoolers. Haven't we vowed not to classify our days as 'school days' or otherwise because we recognise that learning takes place all the time? Don't we enjoy our unschooling days together? All that is true. But we still look forward to holiday time. I was talking about this with the girls the other day.

"Dad will be home for two weeks," said Charlotte. "That makes the holidays special." Andy is a school teacher. "I'm looking forward to spending time doing things with Dad. We can relax in the mornings because he doesn't have to rush out the door."

"Perhaps holidays are special because we learn different things from normal," suggests Sophie. Lots of learning is still going on, but everyone seems to spend more time on individual projects that require minimal assistance. We put our family learning on hold for two weeks.

I love holidays because I can toss the homeschool records book into the basket, knowing I won't have to scrawl a single note about achievements, progress, plans, and learning experiences for two whole weeks. The records book is an unavoidable nuisance to satisfy the authorities. I am free of it for the moment.

I enjoy strewing and sharing and discussing life with my children. But for the next few days, I am leaving them entirely to their own devices. Ordinarily, I make myself available to my children for much of the day: I am willing to read to them, help them with projects, drive them to music and other lessons, and arrange trips to the library. But during the holidays, I can take time for myself. As we no longer have any very little ones, I can blog first thing in the morning if I want to. Or read a book of my own. Or go shopping.

Last night, Gemma-Rose came to say good night. I gave her a huge hug. "I haven't seen you all day. What have you been doing? I've missed you."

And it's true. Although holidays are good, and I enjoy time to myself, I do miss the close contact with my children and our usual routine.

As I cuddled Gemma-Rose, I thought about the term that has just ended and all the things we'd done together. "Didn't we have fun with our cameras when we went bushwalking? And I enjoyed watching *Princess Ida*!"

"I liked learning piano with Imogen," said Gemma-Rose, "and reading together."

"I wonder what will happen next in *White Boots*," I pondered.

My youngest daughter's eyes lit up. "I can't wait for the term to start so we can continue reading."

Yes, I am looking forward to another school term too.

But of course, we have our beach holiday first. Seven whole days with the girls, sharing new experiences together. I can't wait.

I often hear unschoolers say, "We don't have holidays. Our days are the same regardless of whether it is school term or holiday time." I can understand that. Learning goes on every day of the year. Unschooling never stops. But for us, we are looking forward to a change in routine. Because doesn't everyone need a change every now and then? Yes, we all need holidays. Even unschoolers.

What Unschoolers Miss Out On

Have you ever started the school term with loads of enthusiasm and excitement? Perhaps you've thought, "This term is going to be perfect!" Even though the last term wasn't. And the one before that also ended with a fizzle instead of a bang.

I remember many school terms that began with hope and ended with relief.

Oh yes, during the holidays between school terms, I'd make elaborate and what I thought were exciting plans. I'd read books, buy resources, and write loads of notes. On the first day of the term, I could hardly wait to begin. My kids got caught up in my excitement too. For a few days. Or was that a few hours?

It didn't take long for things to go downhill as everyone realised what a big task we had ahead of us. All those outside expectations that dragged us away from what we really wanted to do. We'd start to battle about work: "But you have to do this," I'd say. "It's good for you to do things you don't want to do."

As the weeks went by, I'd say, "Keep going. It's not long until you can do what you like." I was looking forward to doing what I liked too. I also couldn't wait for the school work battles to be over for another term.

I have to admit, we hardly ever lasted the whole term. A week or so before the start of the official school holiday, I'd slam our books shut, toss them back on the shelf, and announce, "I've had enough! Let's end the term early!"

My kids would grin. So would I. We were free! We didn't have to do anything for the next few weeks. No school work. No record keeping. No one could make us learn anything we didn't want to know about.

Here in Australia, the official school year ended a week ago. Last Saturday morning, while most children were probably sleeping in late after a tiring and busy school term, we got out of bed at 4.30 am. Soon after 6 am, we were at our local nature reserve setting up our cameras to film a music video for my daughter Imogen. Despite the term having ended, we continued to 'work'.

On the first day of the holidays, we missed out on an opportunity to sleep late. Did we miss out on anything else? Oh, yes.

We missed out on that huge overwhelming feeling of relief that used to flood through us when the school term ended. We didn't shout, "We're free!"

You see, my children are free all the time. Free to learn what's important to them. Free to choose to learn things they feel that they should know. Free to direct their own learning instead of following someone else's plan. Free to learn whether it's the school term or not.

So on the first day of the long summer holidays, we were working as we made a music video. And we missed out on that overwhelming feeling of relief.

Giving Up My Perfect Start-of-the-Year Plans

On the other side of the world from us, homeschoolers are going back to school.

Parents have browsed catalogues. They've bought curricula, resources, and books. They've drawn up plans. Hope and excitement are in the air.

When I was a fairly new homeschooling mother, I had similar feelings of excitement and anticipation at the start of the new school year. After weeks of preparation, I was ready. I had a stack of fabulous must-have resources. I'd written the perfect plan.

I got up on the first morning of the new school year thinking, "This is going to be a good year! This time, I've got it all worked out." I hoped that the excitement I was feeling wouldn't quickly disappear.

But I soon discovered I didn't have everything worked out perfectly after all. Sometimes we hit a crisis on the very first day of term. Other times we made it to the end of the first week before a melt-down occurred. What was the problem? My children didn't seem to appreciate my well thought out plans or my must-have resources. They wouldn't cooperate.

"But why do we have to do that, Mum?" they moaned.

"Because it's in the plan."

After my children had moaned and groaned some more at these senseless words, I'd add something like, "It's good for you to do things you don't like doing. It will teach you to persevere when the going gets tough. Life isn't all fun and games. Some things you need to know whether you want to learn them or not. Now sit down and do what you're told."

It usually didn't take me very long to cave in and abandon my 'perfect' plan. I couldn't take the stress. Instead, I returned to my default 'plan' of making things up as we went along, following the interests of my children and concentrating on enjoying both my children and the learning adventure. But, although we were much happier homeschooling this way, some worrisome thoughts lingered at the back of my mind:

Was I encouraging my children to be self-centred and lazy by not insisting they complete the work I'd planned for them? Had I given in to them when I should have stood firm? And aren't there some things that every child has to know? Would there be gaps in their education if I didn't make them stick to my plan that covered what I considered the essential areas of knowledge? How would they ever get into university?

And so I made another plan and tried to enforce learning again. And again, I failed. Then I tried again. But one day I broke the cycle. I managed to banish all those anxious thoughts. I was beginning to understand how children learn.

Children are naturally curious and love learning (until adults start to interfere). This self-motivated learning is much more valuable than that which results from an external motivator, such as a determined mother armed with her 'perfect' plan. It's the type of learning that will be retained and enjoyed for its own sake. Children aren't lazy. They will choose to learn about all kinds of things, even those that are very challenging. They will learn everything they need to know, including things mothers consider essential. They can even get into university if that's what they want to do.

There is another reason I gave up forcing my plans upon my children. It can be hard work making a child learn something she just doesn't want to know about. Tears and anger can result as both mother and child get frustrated. To me, such frustration is just not worth it. It gets in the way of good relationships. "Yes, there might be tears today, but your kids will thank you later," someone might say. But what if they don't? I prefer not to take a risk. Instead, I am relying on love.

So I decided to abandon my perfect plans once and for all.

Of course, it's not the start of the new school year here in Australia. Our school year began months ago in February. We are heading towards the end of the third term of the year. There's only one more term until the long summer break.

"It's only a couple of weeks until the holidays," I tell my youngest daughter Gemma-Rose.

She screws up her face and sighs loudly, and then asks, "Why are the school terms so short? It feels like only three weeks since the last holiday."

"You don't want holidays?" I ask.

"I prefer term time. The holidays aren't nearly so interesting."

"We won't have time to do our usual activities, but Dad will be home for a couple of weeks," I say. "We could go on a few outings and picnics."

Gemma-Rose smiles. Maybe holidays aren't so bad after all.

I'm looking forward to the holidays. I'll miss helping the girls with their activities, but I will be able to spend lots of time with my husband. And I'm not going to waste a single moment of that time writing a complicated homeschooling plan for next term.

On the first day of next term, Andy will return to school, and we'll just slide quietly into our usual term-time routine. Charlotte, my high schooler will return to the many activities that absorb her, sharing with me from time to time. My younger girls will happily reclaim both my time and attention. With my mind swirling with ideas, children who have ideas of their own, a world full of interesting things to discover, and a keen love of learning, I just know it will be a good, productive and enjoyable term.

There is a feeling of excitement in the air. It's not a huge, loud, attention-grabbing kind of excitement. It has nothing to do with 'going back to school'. I know it won't suddenly disappear, seizing my hope as it departs.

Instead, this excitement is quiet and gentle. It hovers over every unschooling day. Peace and love accompany it. And it makes me glad I was able to let go of my own 'perfect' plans.

Funny How Things Change

Last Friday I was ready to swing into a new season of our unschooling year. "No more record keeping for this term," I announced to my girls. No more looking out for educational experiences to turn into Evernote notes. No more strewing. No more reading aloud.

No more:

"Would you like to...?"

"Shall we...?"

"This looks interesting..."

"Did you know...?"

Time to take a break, relax, spend more time on my own projects, and look forward to Easter.

But on Monday morning, my youngest daughter, Gemma-Rose asked, "Would you like to read us another chapter of *Return to Billabong*, Mum?"

"Wouldn't you prefer to do something of your own?"

"No. I'd like to listen to you read." So I opened the book to read more of Mary Grant Bruce's novel.

After I'd closed the book, I opened my computer, hoping to edit a bit of my novel. But as usual, it didn't take me long to get distracted. I rediscovered the Evernote Clearly extension, and wanting to try it out, I searched online for a copy of Banjo Paterson's poem *Clancy of the Overflow*.

"Wow! Look at this," I said to my daughter Sophie, showing her the 'clean and easy to read' poem I'd clipped using Clearly. "Isn't this a great way to clip poems before putting them into a notebook?" A notebook? There was nowhere to put the poem because I hadn't created one for this week. I decided to create one, after all.

But it's no good just popping a poem into a notebook. The girls wanted to read *Clancy of the Overflow* before it disappeared into the records. So we read it out loud and enjoyed it immensely.

While I'd been searching for the poem, I'd also discovered a YouTube video of Banjo Paterson reciting his own poem. We watched this next. It was a rather strange animation of a photo. We were tempted to google 'making animations using still photos', but I decided to leave that for another day. Instead, I clipped the video link so we will be able to find it again.

Clancy of the Overflow is related to another novel we're currently reading: *To Love a Sunburnt Country* by Jackie French. Gemma-Rose placed the book on the table in front of me, but I overlooked her hint.

Instead, I said, "Haven't you got anything you'd like to do? How about drawing?" So Gemma-Rose hunted out her sketchbook and pencils. Half an hour later, she said, "Do you think my dragon looks more like a horse?" Minutes later, we were on YouTube watching how-to-draw-dragons videos.

And then Gemma-Rose, taking advantage of the fact we were on YouTube, said, "Shall we watch another episode of *Secrets of a Castle*, Mum?"

We settled down on the sofa together and enjoyed finding out about medieval weapons. When the episode was over, someone said, "I didn't know some of our English words and sayings are related to archery." Of course, we had to do some further research. We found an article explaining the origin of 'picking a quarrel', 'upshot' and 'point-blank'. "Isn't this interesting?" I said as I clipped the information into this week's notebook.

Next, Sophie downloaded her own Clearly extension. "I could use it to collect photography articles," she said. "Did you see the photo I put up on the *365 Project* website?" And then she added: "By the way, I watched a video on the *Beth-a-dilly* blog. I learnt how she edits her photos to get her personal look. Did you know she began working as a professional photographer six months after teaching herself how to use her DSLR camera?" I didn't. I could see Sophie was feeling inspired.

Gemma-Rose then said, "Sophie, you could do your piano practice while I read to Mum." She hunted out *The Far Side of the Loch* by Melissa Wiley while Sophie opened her music book.

But sad to say, I had my head in my computer, and I kept muttering," In a minute... in a minute..." and Gemma-Rose gave up. She left the book on the coffee table and returned to her dragons.

Later, I noticed Gemma-Rose's book. "Do you still want to read to me?" She did.

After the chapter had ended, I said, "Would you like me to read you a chapter of *To Love a Sunburnt Country*?" She nodded, as she ran off to get Sophie so she could listen too.

And so the day ended. It hadn't gone as I'd expected. I didn't drift through the day, doing my own thing. Instead, I was very involved with my girls, as they kept saying:

"Would you like to...?"

"Shall we...?"

"This looks interesting..."

"Did you know...?"

It seems we haven't moved onto the next season in our unschooling year after all, even though the official school term is nearly over. And that's okay. My novel can wait. So can my other projects. I'm still enjoying spending time with my girls.

In days gone by, we'd be hanging out for the end of each term. "That's enough!" I'd declare a week (or two) early. "I've had enough."

"Hurray!" my kids would shout. They'd had enough too.

Funny how things change.

Part XVII: Homeschool Record Keeping

How We Unschool Despite Having to Fulfil Homeschool Registration Requirements

Can we unschool if our kids have to be legally registered as homeschoolers? What if we have to provide evidence that they are learning certain things? Our family is unschooling despite having to fulfil homeschooling requirements. How are we doing this? This is what I'd like to talk about next.

Wouldn't it be wonderful if we didn't have to answer to anyone and could unschool our children with total freedom? I guess some people are fortunate to be able to do this. But we're not.

In our state of Australia, if we want to homeschool, we have to fulfil certain requirements. Our children are supposed to follow the same syllabus as the one used in schools. And we have to prove they've done that. But how can we do that if we're unschoolers? What if my girls aren't at all interested in what they are 'supposed' to be learning? What if they want to do something else?

I can fight the system. Maybe the registration process will become more relaxed if we all protest and work together. Perhaps we won't always have to live under this strict system. It's possible we might gain the freedom to unschool without any restrictions. And I'm hoping this will happen.

But what about now? How can we unschool today without compromising our educational beliefs but still stay within the system? How does our family do that?

It's fortunate that my girls have a wide range of interests. We are all visibly and audibly excited about anything and everything so I think that helps. Usually, I can translate my children's interests into the right educational language and apply it to all the required key learning areas without a lot of trouble. I just need to be good at matching up the right areas of the syllabus to what my girls are doing naturally.

For example, we took a trip to Canberra not so long ago. When we came back, our heads were buzzing with all we'd seen at the various museums we'd visited. We'd heard about Walter Burleigh Griffin, the American architect who designed Canberra. He also bought acreage in Sydney, planning to build a community of knitlock houses which would blend in with the natural environment. Our imaginations were captured. We wanted to know more.

One thing led to another, and later when it came time to update my homeschool records, I realised the girls had shown interest in so many things that just happen to be 'required' learning, without any planning whatsoever. Their natural interest was enough to enable me to tick off a number of outcomes in the syllabus. Of course, Walter Burleigh Griffin might not be mentioned in the syllabus but 'design', 'relationship with places', 'safe living', 'Federal government' and other topics, which we explored, are.

So the girls learn, I record, and life goes on.

But occasionally there are times when the girls show no interest in a required topic at all. What do I do? I could say to my girls, "You have to learn this and that and the other because that's what the education department demands. When you've finished doing the required stuff, you can then go back to following your interests." But I don't.

Doing things only because you are required to isn't real learning. It's just a waste of time. My children wouldn't really be unschooling if we worked in this way. I am not willing to compromise, even if compromising means we'd sail through the registration process without any trouble.

Is there another solution to this problem? I think there is. We need to look at the school syllabus in a new way.

What is a syllabus? Is it a boring list of things someone not very important has decided our kids must learn? Or could it represent a whole range of wonderful learning experiences? *Everything* in this world is potentially interesting. Just because the education department has marked some topics as essential doesn't mean they automatically become boring and irrelevant. It is possible my children still might be interested in something that's in the syllabus. How do I find out? I could do some strewing.

Of course, I don't look at the syllabus through schooly eyes. I look past all the jargon that clutters up each requirement, that turns something potentially interesting into something deadly boring. I try to find something that ignites my own interest, something that makes me feel excited. Because if I'm not interested in what I am about to strew, there is less possibility my children will be interested.

For example, Sophie (13) is supposed to know all about rates and ratios in maths. I took this from the stage statement for the maths syllabus for children her age:

Students are familiar with the concepts of ratios and rates and apply these when solving problems.

I could say, "Sophie, you need to know about ratios. Let's get this out of the way so I can tick it off. Just do this worksheet, and then we can say the topic is done." Or I could try something else. This is what I did the other day:

I did a bit of browsing on the Internet and found a video about scale models. I then said, "Hey, girls, this is so interesting! (I was telling the truth, not trying to trick them.) Do you want to watch this with me?"

The girls picked up on my tone of voice and came running. They were eager to share what I had discovered. Of course, I didn't mention the word syllabus. Why should I have? Why spoil something genuinely interesting by associating it with the word 'required'. This information isn't the exclusive property of the education department. We are entitled to learn about it just because we want to. And many times that's exactly what we end up doing.

So we watched the video and then we started talking about scale model cars, maps, model railways, model villages, dolls' houses. Dolls' houses? I remembered when Andy and I saw Queen Mary's dolls' house at Windsor Castle many years ago. Sophie and Gemma-Rose wanted to hear about it. They picked up on my tone of excitement. I really did enjoy seeing that house. I found the fact that everything is a perfect scale model of something in real life very fascinating. And so did the girls. We found a website about the dolls' house. Then we remembered our visit, a couple of years ago, to the model village, Cockington Green. The discussion continued. Ratios turned out to be a very interesting topic!

But what if my strewing fails? I could say, "I presented my children with the opportunity to learn such and such, but they rejected it." Because all we really have to do is provide our kids with opportunities for learning. No one can force them to learn. They have to cooperate. And if they won't, despite our best efforts, there's not much we can do about it.

Of course, there may be some things on the syllabus we feel are inappropriate for our children. I'd just gently object, saying they do not meet the needs of our girls, or go against our beliefs. There's something in the guidelines that says that our homeschool plans have to take into account the needs and interests of our children. It's useful to know about statements like these hidden away amongst the more frightening official words. We can use them, with confidence, at the right time.

Looking for resources to strew, translating my daughters' learning into the right kind of language, and trying to juggle their needs with those required by the educational authorities is hard work at times. I have to stay a step ahead of my girls, and always have to be on the look-out for things that might interest them. I have to be aware of what's in the syllabus and be creative about how I interpret the official requirements. I must keep up with changes to the guidelines. And I must be confident too. I know my kids, what they're learning, and how they're developing. I just need to convince the official representative from the education department that I know what I'm doing.

Is all the effort worth it? We think so. My girls can happily follow their interests, unaware of all the behind-the-scenes work I'm doing that allows them to learn in the way that works best.

So we can unschool, despite having to fulfil homeschooling requirements. We can still live an amazing unschooling life!

Using a Gentle Approach to Change People's Minds about Unschooling

Sometimes when I'm hopping around the unschooling blogosphere, I stumble across places where I don't feel I belong. As I read the posts, I can feel the high emotions: "No one can tell us what to do with our own children. Society is wrong, and we're going to fight the system."

And although I agree, I don't see myself as a person who's willing to put on my tough boots, arm myself with strong language, and head into battle. This doesn't mean I don't want to do anything about the situation. It just means I prefer trying a gentle approach if I can do this without compromising my children's way of life. For, of course, if I ever do have to choose between my own family and outsiders who want to control what we do, I can be as tough as anyone.

But can a gentle approach be effective in changing people's minds about unschooling? Sometimes just the word 'unschooling' can raise people's hackles. They won't even listen, so there's no point talking. They have misinformed preconceived ideas about what unschooling is. Most times, I can shrug my shoulders and not worry about what other people think of our way of life. I don't need to convince anyone that what we're doing is okay. They have no influence over us. Or do they?

It is very inconvenient, but there are actually some people in this world who can make rules about the way we raise our kids and how we educate them. I'm talking about the educational authorities from our state governments. I understand why they think we need rules. They don't want any kids falling between the cracks and missing out on their right to be educated. The rules were made to protect children. But these rules can seem very unnecessary, especially to anyone who is living an unschooling life.

So how do we deal with what appears to be an unfair registration process? Do we stand up and be very vocal as we fight? As a group, I think we should work towards registration reform. But is there also a less confrontational way we can use as individuals? Can we unschool without compromise, and remain within the system? Is there a way to present our children's learning to the education department, that ensures they are impressed, despite the fact our children are unschoolers? Can we change people's minds gently? I think we can.

We have been unschooling for a very long time. At the same time, we've been legally registered as homeschoolers. Although I'd prefer not to keep homeschooling records, I can't really complain. We have always done what we've liked while flying through our registration visits without any problems.

Whenever our AP (Authorised Person) from the education department visits us, she expects to see evidence of what my children have been learning and how they are progressing. She also wants to know what we plan to do for the next registration period. So how do we provide what is needed when we don't have bookwork or assignments or tests to show our AP? We find a method of record keeping that showcases unschooling. One that effectively captures all the many and varied learning experiences that our children are involved with. We want our AP to look at our records and think, "Wow, this child is doing some amazing things. There is no doubt she is learning."

I used to use an exercise book for record keeping. Each day, I'd scribble down everything my children had done or said or made or watched or listened to. And this method did work. But it required a lot of writing on my part and a lot of reading on the AP's. It wasn't visually exciting. It didn't really bring unschooling alive.

But then I discovered Evernote. This is a digital notetaking and organising system.

Evernote allows me to:

- Make written notes of activities and conversations.
- Add photos of all the wonderful things my girls have been doing.
- Clip articles from the Internet about things we've been doing or discussing.

- Link to the videos my children have made and other people's too.
- Add images of books we've read and DVDs we've watched.
- Add audio files of my children singing and playing the piano.
- Clip Google maps of places we've visited or talked about.
- Add scans of artworks, concert programs, letters and any other relevant paperwork.
- Import emails.

These are just a few examples of the things that I include in our homeschooling records. It seems to me that there's a way to include any learning experience within an Evernote note.

Now there might be other equally effective methods of keeping unschooling records. I'm not suggesting that Evernote is the only system that will work. (Though I do love and recommend it!) We just need to use a method that captures unschooling in such a way that it's immediately obvious that our kids are getting a wonderful education. We want our records to speak for themselves. If they do, we won't have to say anything. We might even choose not to mention the word unschooling. But if we do, our gentle approach just might convince our AP that unschooling is okay.

There's something else that will bring our AP onside, and that's our children themselves. When our kids talk articulately about their interests in a manner way beyond their years, who can fail to be impressed?

And this leads me to another thought: sometimes it's quite okay to avoid criticism by not telling everyone exactly what we're doing. When people ask us how we're homeschooling, we could say what I used to say, "We're doing our own thing," and leave it at that. Somewhere down the track, people are going to notice our unschooling children and how well they're doing. And perhaps when that happens, we can say, "Hey, we've been unschooling all this time. This is the fruit of our approach to education."

The last time we had a registration visit, our AP stopped on our doorstep as she was leaving and waved her arm towards the houses further down the street and said, "No one knows about the amazing things that are happening behind your door!" She'd been very impressed by what she'd seen in our Evernote notebooks.

We said goodbye to our AP and returned inside with huge grins on our faces. We'd done it again. We'd got through another registration visit, fulfilling all the requirements without compromising our unschooling way of life. I hadn't had to fight for our right to do what we liked. All I'd done was keep effective records. My children and my records spoke for themselves.

Sometimes all we need is a gentle approach.

Are You a Curious Unschooler?

Do you ever follow rabbit trails, going from one thing to other until your head is spinning with new knowledge?

My head is constantly spinning. I guess my girls' heads are too. You see, I don't keep my discoveries to myself.

I'm always saying things like:

"Hey, girls, listen to this..."

"Did you know...?"

"Can I tell you about...?"

"Would you like me to read...?"

"What do you think about this?"

"Want to watch this video with me?"

"Wow, you won't believe what I just found out!"

"This is so interesting!"

And usually, hearing the excitement in my voice, my girls look up from whatever they're doing. They want to know more too.

I'm interested in everything. So are my children. I'm glad they are because the world is a fascinating place and I love exploring it with them. It also makes fulfilling homeschool registration requirements very easy. At the end of each day, I always have lots of notes, covering a wide range of topics, to add to my Evernote records book.

I wonder: why am I interested in everything? Why are my children? Is it something to do with our personalities? Or is everyone interested in everything? Or do we all start out being curious people and then some of us change along the way?

Little children want to know about everything. They're full of questions. Sometimes they have so many questions we can't keep up. How do we answer them all? Or maybe we don't. Could we sometimes give kids the impression that we have more important things to do than satisfy their curiosity? Do they learn that asking questions isn't a good thing to do?

I wonder: can we regain our curiosity? Can we pass on a curious attitude to our kids?

Perhaps we all need to slow down and look more carefully at the world around us. I bet we miss loads of opportunities to ask questions and ponder possible answers.

But what type of questions?

The other day, I saw a sign stating that our local area is now a coal mining-free place. It was a new sign erected by our council. Why did it suddenly appear? What exactly does it mean? Surely we have a coal mine close by? I did some googling. Soon I was investigating legal, environmental, health, indigenous, foreign investment, local employment, and other issues. I looked at maps. I watched videos. I read about protests. I looked at photos. I even listened to some indigenous music. And I shared most of what I discovered with my daughters.

Head buzzing, I made dozens of notes in my records book, not only for registration purposes but also for us. My notebooks are bursting with information we want to remember.

The same thing happened when we were out on a picnic some months ago. I'd brought along a packet of muesli bars. As we sat at our table in the nature reserve, munching away, we examined the muesli bar wrappers. "What's lupin, Mum? It's one of the ingredients."

Was lupin a health condition or a rabbit? Or something else? I didn't know. We decided it must be associated with allergies because there was a warning on the wrapper. When we got home, we did some googling and discovered lupin is a pulse. We found out a lot of other things too.

I'm always asking questions and searching for answers. So are my girls. We investigate how things work. We make connections. We ponder solutions to problems. We look at our remarkable world with a sense of awe.

Now I'm thinking about the word 'curious'. Depending on how we use it, it could mean:

marked by a desire to investigate and learn

Or it might mean:

exciting attention as strange, novel, or unexpected

Do curious unschoolers have a desire to investigate? Or are they strange, odd or eccentric people who excite attention? Or could both be true?

Be strange. Be interested in *everything*. Be a curious unschooler!

Part XVIII: Difficult Days

Not every unschooling day is perfect. Sometimes we're tired, or we feel out of sorts. Perhaps unexpected things happen that we have to deal with. How can we think about our kids' education when we're overwhelmed with other things? Maybe we need to adjust our expectations. Go with the flow, and accept what comes our way. And have confidence that our kids are learning even if our circumstances aren't ideal.

Learning from Life

Today I am tired. I don't feel like strewing. I don't feel like discussing or watching or listening. I don't feel excited or enthusiastic. My children feel the same way. We've been living with an out-of-control fire on our doorstep for the last five days, and yes, we are all tired.

Normally, I have loads of learning experiences to record in our homeschool records book at the end of each day, despite our unstructured relaxed lifestyle. The girls are eager to learn. They find plenty to get involved with. I share with them. They share with me. But today, I am sure we will have no learning experiences whatsoever to record. Today's record page will remain blank.

"Just write 'school closed due to bushfire'," suggests my daughter Imogen. The local village school was closed today. We smile. Our 'school' never closes. But the education department doesn't know that. Today our 'school' is closed too. That sounds good for the official records.

Our 'school' never closes? We learn from life and life never stops. The girls like to say that the only way anyone can prevent themselves from learning is to sit inside a cardboard box. And even then, they'll learn that it's very boring sitting there doing nothing.

"There's loads you can write in your records book, Mum," says Charlotte. "We've learnt heaps recently. We know all about bushfires and how to fight them."

"And how to prepare a house for a fire," adds Sophie.

"We know about winds and hot temperatures and evacuation," says Gemma-Rose.

"We've seen fire trucks and watched a water bombing helicopter being filled with water and then seen them in action," says Imogen.

331

"Firefighters visit schools to talk to the kids about bushfire safety," says Charlotte. "We've talked to firefighters on our own street lots of times in the past few days. You could write down that we've had visiting firefighters come to talk to us."

I think of all the tired firefighters who are working a stone's throw away from our home. There's one person on continual duty at a water tanker which we can see from our driveway. He refills the truck water tanks as they reappear out of the bush. While he's waiting for another truck to arrive, he is quite happy to talk to us about the bushfire fighting operation.

"We've seen big earth moving equipment too." The girls haven't finished. "So we all know about making fire breaks. Oh yes, back burning as well."

"And what about those firefighters who are dropped by parachute into the thick of the bush, armed with a shovel so that they can make fire breaks by hand?" These RAFT (Remote Area Firefighting Team) fighters seem so remarkable to us.

"We've looked at maps and watched reports..." My list of learning experiences is getting longer and longer.

Last Friday we evacuated our house for a few hours when conditions seemed very poor. We packed the three cats into their carriers and placed the guinea pig into a box. We loaded the van with a few things we want to save if our house does burn down, and then we headed to town where it's safe. We spent the afternoon in a park by the lake.

"Do you think we could describe our evacuation to town as a field trip?" I ask.

"We gave verbal reports of the fire to other people. We discussed past fires. We talked about how fires begin, and what we can do to minimise the possibility of them starting."

I scribble fast. My page is overflowing. Life has certainly taught us a lot this week. And not all of it is concerned with facts. We've also learnt about courage and community spirit and the extraordinary generosity of family and friends.

But today, we are tired.

"I think it would be quite okay if we all sat and did absolutely nothing for the whole of today," I announce.

Later, I notice someone at a computer, and someone else putting together a jigsaw. One of my daughters is in the middle of a complicated game, and another is reading. I suspect that even while they're doing 'absolutely nothing', they are still doing a whole heap of learning.

The girls are right. There is just no way to prevent learning. It happens. Just like life.

Unschooling in a Crisis

"So what have we got planned for today, Mum?" Sophie asks me.

"Well, nothing really," I reply. "We can't go anywhere because of the bushfire, but I guess I don't have to keep such a close eye on the fire updates. I could read to you, or we could watch a DVD together."

Sophie smiles. Doing something together? That sounds good.

We've been living next to a huge bushfire for eight days now. Life has not been normal for all that time. You could say we've been experiencing a bit of a crisis.

I've hardly done anything with the girls all week. It's hard to concentrate when there's the possibility we might have to evacuate our house at any moment. We're all longing for life to return to normal. We want to watch and listen and discuss and enjoy our days together once more. But despite us not having had much interaction this week, I am sure the girls have learnt just as much, or even more than they usually do.

When life is normal, I do a lot of strewing to enrich my children's environment. But I haven't done any of that for days. Does that worry me? No. It hasn't been necessary. How much more enriched can our life get at the moment? We've had firefighters and fire trucks in our street. Helicopters have flown overhead. We've watched fire reports and discussed our fire survival plan. Life cannot get any more exciting and interesting. So I don't feel bad about not strewing.

I don't even feel bad about spending so much time on my computer, my eyes stuck to the fire updates. My girls haven't sat on the sofa with blank looks on their faces waiting for me to appear and tell them what to do. No, they have found loads of things to do on their own. They're used to directing their own learning. Yes, a lot has been going on despite life being difficult.

I remember another difficult time in our life. That was when our son Thomas died. He lived for only a day and changed our lives forever. That crisis was a lot harder to deal with than a bushfire on our doorstep.

I couldn't think about homeschooling when my heart was breaking. I didn't even try to. For three months, I concentrated on nothing more than my grief. My children played many, many computer games during that time. Well, it was more like one computer game was played many, many times. Our computer resources were rather limited in those days. Even today if I hear the music belonging to that game, I feel tearful. It brings back some painful memories. When my children had to give up their computer seat to an impatiently waiting sibling, they read and played and amused themselves. For weeks and weeks, my children did whatever they wanted without any direction from me. I didn't read to them or take them to the library. We didn't go on any educational type outings. I didn't share anything with them. Or did I?

I actually shared one of life's biggest lessons: the loss of a loved one. They learnt all about death and suffering and later, joy and healing. They learnt what life is all about. They could never have learnt that lesson from a book. It's something, just like a bushfire, you wouldn't want to ask for as a learning experience. But sometimes we don't have a choice. Things happen. And because they do, we all learn.

So it seems to me that there is no reason to worry about our kids' education during a crisis. Just go with the flow, and use the crisis as a learning experience. Yes, life is different. We might want to do more with our children than we can. We may yearn for ordinary days, learning together in our usual way. But learning? That will still happen.

"Hey, girls!" I say. "I've just ordered seasons 2 and 3 of *Five Mile Creek* on DVD." The girls' faces light up. "They'll take about two weeks to arrive."

See, our crisis is almost over. The fire is still burning, but I'm able to look ahead. I'm thinking about strewing again. I've been online shopping instead of checking on the fire. Well, to be honest, I checked on the fire at the same time. I have hope our house will still be here when the postman arrives with our DVDs.

Yes, in two weeks' time, probably even sooner, life should be back to normal.

I can't wait.

Tired and Cranky and Lacking Enthusiasm

I was awake nice and early this morning. Too early. I lay awake at 4 am thinking: *How will I be able to run if I don't get more sleep? How will I get through the day?* But of course, sleep never happens when we most want it. So I got up this morning, a Monday morning, and I didn't experience the usual wonderful start-of-the-week feeling. I didn't think, "Five days to fill! What amazing things will we do?"

Maybe you're looking for an inspiring story. And here I am telling a tired morning story. Sometimes our lives can seem perfect. Unschooling is always a joy. We've got it all worked out. But not today. Today is not a perfect day. Today I am tired, and all my enthusiasm has seeped away. I didn't jump out of bed this morning eager to learn and share with my girls.

By 6.15 am, I was finally ready to go back to sleep, but it was too late. Andy urged me out of bed.

"You'd better get up if you're going for a run."

"It's raining," I assured my husband. "I can hear it pouring down. Just take a look out the window. We can't run in this weather."

"It's not raining," smiled Andy. "Get up!" He's usually a very kind husband.

So the girls and I headed down to the park for our usual run even though I hadn't had the usual amount of sleep. Actually, the run wasn't too bad. I didn't break any records and went so slowly I was in danger of stopping, but I ran.

Imogen and Gemma-Rose wanted to run two more laps than the rest of us, so we left them at the bush tracks and went home in search of breakfast and showers. A long time later, the girls hadn't returned, and I had to send Sophie back to the park to see if they were okay.

"What were you doing?" I asked when they finally appeared.

"We ran some extra laps. We ran 15 laps. That's 9 K."

Now I should have said something that was encouraging such as, "Wow! That's a long way. You must feel good." Instead, I said, "You told me you were only going to run two more laps. You should have been home a long time ago. What about the morning jobs?"

I listened to myself. I recognised the signs. I was tired, and I knew it wouldn't be long before I was both tired and cranky.

The girls hurried to catch up with their chores, but a short while later, someone dropped an empty glass jam jar on the floor. The girls were silent. They looked at me warily. The tension was increasing. We cleaned up the mess, but five minutes later, another jam jar hit the tiles. Someone ran for the broom again. It was at that point I breathed deeply and decided I needed to take action. Otherwise, today was going to be a total disaster.

So what did I do? I threw aside all those wonderful ideas I was going to share with the girls and decided to do nothing more taxing than reading aloud. I find reading aloud good when I am tired. I can disappear into another world and forget all about myself.

So I read and then the girls wanted to read to me. They love sitting in the reader's chair. Then I encouraged them to do something that didn't need my help. I'm so glad they're unschoolers and used to taking the lead. They practised the piano and then explored some online websites, and played some games. And what did I do? I answered some emails. Oh, yes, I did something else. I will admit it. I also visited Facebook a few times.

I think about how I wasted time online this morning, time I could have spent with the girls. And I am not sorry in the least. I know that Facebook saved my children from having to endure an out-of-sorts mother. All those friends out there. I enjoyed reading their posts. I forgot about being tired. Facebook has its time and place.

According to my records book, it hasn't been the greatest of days. Yes, the girls found plenty to do, but it wasn't an exciting learning day. I could get anxious about this, except I know that what we did on this particular day isn't really that important in the grand scheme of things. This day is only one out of many. It will probably fade from our memories, and certainly, no one else will ever know it wasn't a perfect day.

"Go and rest, Mum," my children urged after we'd finished lunch. So that's what I'm doing. In days gone by, I might have struggled on, making not only myself suffer, but everyone around me as well. But today, I'm not going to fight this tiredness. I have limits, and I recognise that.

You know, I think I'm going to survive this day.

I didn't get that wonderful Monday morning feeling today. I didn't awake full of anticipation, eager to begin the week. But that's okay. There's always tomorrow, another day. Isn't that a great thing about life? We can start each day afresh.

I think about tomorrow. A little feeling of anticipation and eagerness is starting to return. If I sleep tonight I might have enough energy to try out those maths puzzles with Sophie, find a poem in that new library book to strew in front of the girls, help the girls find some McCubbin paintings to add to their jigsaw collection, find the paints they need to finish their salt dough models... We might even take a trip to town. Yes, tomorrow could be good. It could be spectacular. I smile. I'm feeling better already.

Part XIX: Concerns

When a Child Has Only One Interest

"It's all very well letting children follow their interests, but my daughter only wants to do one thing. She's not interested in science or maths or writing. All she wants to do is cook and how's that going to satisfy the educational authorities?" a hypothetical mother asks.

What would I do if one of my girls only wanted to cook and wouldn't consider learning anything else? I might try an idea that I picked up at the very first homeschool conference I ever attended.

"Let's pretend your child's one interest is bees." Jane's words spill out quickly, one after another. She has so much to say and only a couple of hours to say it. She chalks the word 'bees' on the centre of the blackboard in large letters. "Bees is just the starting point. Let's see where that can lead us!" Jane does a little thinking out loud as she bounces about in front of us. Soon she is associating bees with maths, science, geography, history, writing, personal health and development, and creative arts. Her excitement and enthusiasm are contagious. We start offering ideas too. Before long, the blackboard is full of words. Jane has drawn a mind map.

"A mother I know," says Jane, "presented a similar bee mind map as her homeschooling plan for her son's registration, and it satisfied the education department. It covered all the key learning areas."

But back to my hypothetical one-interest child. What if I constructed a 'cooking' mind map? I might add such words as these:

maths: fractions, multiplication, division, measuring volumes and masses, temperatures and time, shopping and money

science: chemical reactions, pasteurisation, freezing, dried foods, plants, fruits, vegetables, herbivores, carnivores, omnivores, food chains, food production, farms, organic food, GM foods, genetics, making a vegetable garden, visiting markets and a garden centre

history: foods associated with different periods in history, eating customs, historical TV series

geography: foods of different countries and cultures, cooking shows set in different countries

personal development: nutrition, digestion, care of teeth, issues such as the low fat industry, sugar, obesity, exercise, hygiene and safe food handling, safety in the kitchen, first-aid for burn, foods associated with the liturgical calendar, feast days, saints, family celebrations, cultural celebrations, historical celebrations

creative and practical arts: trying new recipes, famous chefs, cooking shows and filming, presentation and customer service, photographing food, cooking techniques and tools

English: writing, cooking journal or scrapbook, recipe files, a cooking glossary, reading, demonstrating

Now, these ideas are just a start. I've only been thinking for a few minutes. I bet there are many more that I could add.

Once I've constructed my mind map, I wouldn't use it as a homeschool plan that I'd present to my child. Instead, I would use it as a starting point for finding appropriate resources to enrich her environment, to show her some possibilities she might be unaware of.

I might find some books and movies. And I'd search YouTube for appropriate videos. I'd hunt online for interesting articles. I'd make a list of places we could visit. Then there are games and activities.

Once I have a few resources on hand, I'd start strewing them, tempting my one-interest child to spread her wings and set off in new directions.

But of course, my child might not like any of my strewing ideas. She may very well just want to keep on experimenting in the kitchen in her own way. So will all my work go to waste? No! At the very least, I might discover something I'd like to explore. I could always share what I find out if my child is interested in listening.

After Jane tells us how the bee plan satisfied the education department, she adds, "But by the time the mother was ready to put the plan into action, her son was no longer interested in bees, so she didn't actually use it." She laughs. "The boy had satisfied his curiosity and was ready to move onto new things."

Maybe some kids just like to concentrate on one thing at a time. They'll move on to something else when they're ready. Perhaps having only one current interest isn't a problem after all. What do you think?

When Our Excitement for Learning Disappears

I like to get up early. I leave my bed while everyone else is sleeping, feel my way out of our darkened bedroom, fall over the three hungry cats gathered hopefully at my door, and head to the kitchen to fill the kettle. Animals fed, a mug of tea in my hand, I settle on the family room sofa to read or pray or check the mail.

That's what I did this morning. Half an hour into my quiet time, my daughter Sophie appeared. We sat side by side, rubbing cats' chins, as we chatted.

"You seemed a bit out of sorts this week," I observed. "You didn't feel like your usual self?"

"I feel like I'm drifting."

I know how Sophie feels. I've been feeling the same way. I move from one unsatisfying thing to the other. I wonder what I'm supposed to be doing. Where's all my excitement gone?

I could worry about being stuck in this stagnant state, but I've come to the conclusion that quiet times are a normal part of life. It's probably unrealistic to expect to fly through every day in a constant state of excitement. Think about how tiring that would be. And maybe important work is going on during these seemingly unproductive times, subconsciously, of course. Who knows what is brewing deep within us while all seems quiet on the surface?

I have noticed that quiet times never last forever. One day I wake up and instantly know things have changed. A wonderful new idea will be floating through my mind. I feel full of energy. Before I know it, I'll be chasing knowledge, working on a new project, feeling excited about life once more.

"What do you feel like doing?" I asked Sophie.

"I can't think of anything I really want to do."

344

I could have said, "There's plenty of interesting things you could be doing. Choose something! Don't waste your time." But is that necessary? I think Sophie will find her own way to her next interesting thing without me pressuring her. She probably needs space to rest and read and do nothing in particular. Of course, I could still make a suggestion or two, do some strewing, offer her some new ideas to think about. Something might spark her imagination, set her flying off again on new adventures.

"Now the weather is cool we could go for some more bush walks," I said. "I've been meaning to get the wildflower identification book out. I'd like to know the names of a few more flowers. What do you think?"

We agreed that an outing would be very enjoyable. We could get outside and enjoy nature, take our cameras and capture some photos, and have a picnic. It sounds like just what we need.

Perhaps children, like mothers, need quiet times. Life doesn't always have to be full on. School schedules might suggest learning happens at a constant rate, but I bet it doesn't. I'm talking about the visible kind of learning because, of course, we never quite know what's going on inside a person. We can never measure all that is being processed unobserved.

Do you know what I'm going to do now? I'm off to find that wildflower book. And perhaps I'll take a game or two down from the shelf. We have some CDs we haven't played for a while. And maybe I could strew a painting on the wall.

Regaining Her Enthusiasm for Learning

My daughter Sophie felt like she was just drifting along. She'd lost her enthusiasm for learning. And then one day, she woke up and things had changed.

Sophie and I went to town together for some mother-daughter time. After we'd done a little shopping, I said, "Would you like to have morning tea in a café? Shall we go somewhere where they serve tea in teapots?"

A waitress delivered our order to our table: two white pots of English Breakfast tea, two white and lemon china cups resting on matching saucers, and a plate piled high with apple crumble and a mountain of cream. We smiled.

As Sophie tipped a steaming stream of tea into her cup, words burst from her: "I love my life!"

"Because we're having morning tea together?"

"It's not just that. It's everything. Life is full of interesting things to do!"

"You're not drifting along anymore?" I asked.

"Oh, no!"

"So what have you been enjoying doing?"

"I've been redesigning my blogs and doing those HTML coding lessons. I've been cooking and sewing. I reorganised my bedroom so I can find all of my writing and craft things. I've written some notes for a new novel. I can't wait until next month when Camp NaNoWriMo (National Novel Writing Month) starts! Then there's drawing. I've been learning how to draw realistic people. I enjoyed some history videos. And I've been exercising."

"So you're back on track?"

Sophie's whole face was aglow. "Oh, yes!"

"So how did you get your enthusiasm back?" I asked.

"Well, I got fed up of feeling bored and decided to do something about it."

"You didn't need me to push you along?"

Sophie sipped her tea and then said, "No, when I was ready, I found all sorts of new things to do."

Yes, I didn't need to get anxious. All I had to do was be patient and give Sophie enough time to rediscover her enthusiasm by herself. Of course, that doesn't mean I did nothing to help her. Oh no! While I was waiting, I did some strewing. I kept my eyes open for things that might tempt her. I shared my own interests and activities. But I didn't apply any pressure.

After I'd written my story *Preparing our Kids for an Unknown Future: Can We Do It?* I said, "Hey, Sophie, I found lots of Jane Fonda exercise workouts on YouTube. I wonder what other exercise videos are available."

When she was ready, Sophie searched YouTube and found the *Fitness Blender* channel. On the days we haven't gone running, she's been star jumping and stretching and using hand weights. She's been exercising even on days when the rest of us have decided to rest.

After I'd bought a new template for my blog, I said, "Hey, Sophie, what do you think of this design?" Then I added, "There are loads of other blog templates available."

When she was ready, Sophie googled free blog templates. Soon she was knee deep in HTML codes as she redesigned her own blog.

"Hey, Sophie," I said, "do you remember those HTML coding lessons we were doing a while ago?"

When she was ready, Sophie signed into her account and once more began learning about HTML. "I'd love to write the code for a blog template of my own, wouldn't you?" she asked me. I would!

I hunted out a few books with patterns for attractive sewing projects. "If you'd like to set up my sewing machine on your desk in your room..."

I bought a few extra ingredients and placed them in the pantry. "I've put some new recipes in the Evernote notebook..."

"I've also put some history and science links in the strewing notebook."

"If you'd like me to drive you to town so you can buy some new notebooks..."

"I found some interesting drawing videos on YouTube..."

I'd like to tell you Sophie followed my good example after I said, "Hey, Sophie, come and look at my reorganised room. I've sorted out all my writing and art stuff. Now I can find everything easily." But that wouldn't be true. My room is a mess. That idea was entirely her own!

What if My Child is Ordinary?

Occasionally, I receive an email that goes something like this:

Sue,

I've been reading your blog and enjoying your stories about your daughters. They are doing some amazing things. I can see that unschooling is working for you. But will it work for my family? You see, I have ordinary children. They're not musical like yours. They don't write. They don't draw. In fact, they don't seem to have any particular talents.

Will all unschoolers do amazing things? If you do some googling, you'll find many stories of young unschoolers doing extraordinary things. You might think that every unschooler has a guaranteed, amazing future. But what if it doesn't turn out that way for your kids? Will you think you have failed? Will you wonder if you did something wrong?

I have a few unschooled children who are hoping to do amazing things. In particular, my daughters Imogen and Sophie have big dreams. Imogen is a passionate singer and pianist and writer. Sophie would like to use her passions of photography and videography to share her love of fitness and health via YouTube and books and exercise programs. My daughters are working on these dreams. And who knows? One day maybe someone *will* look at them and say, "Unschoolers do amazing things!"

But I don't think unschooling necessarily means that our kids are going to become famous singers or young entrepreneurs or international sports stars or bestseller authors or big-name fashion designers with their own line of clothing. Some unschoolers are going to have more ordinary looking lives. However, they are still going to do amazing things as they make their mark on the world. They're just going to do it in a quiet way.

Not all my children are doing visibly extraordinary things. For example, my eldest son has an 'average' type job. He isn't making big waves. But this doesn't mean he isn't amazing. No, I think he is a very special person indeed. I say to him, "Go out there and make a difference!" And he does. He uses the talents he has been given to change the lives of all the people he comes into contact with.

I think it's important that we tell our less showy kids that they are amazing, that they have talents, that they're making a difference to the world. Sometimes they might compare themselves to other people who are getting more attention than them. Do they feel they're rather ordinary? Perhaps they think they aren't doing anything of importance. We might need to remind them that they are indeed unique people with a unique mission.

Sometimes parents might not feel very amazing either. We look around and compare ourselves to others, especially to those who are working in a similar field to us and say, "There are far more talented and successful people out there than me. Why should I bother?" We give up. But we shouldn't because, like our kids, we are unique human beings. Each of us has special talents. We each have a voice, unlike anyone else's, and we should use it. How else are we going to change the world? And how else are we going to encourage our kids to do the same?

So I'm always saying to my family, "Go out there and make a difference!" It doesn't matter if they are cantoring the psalm on Sundays, performing on a stage, teaching a classroom of children, listening to someone, or even washing the dishes, I say those words. I remind them that we can do everything in such a way that our efforts make a difference to the people around us and to the world we live in.

But what if we're still not convinced that our child is special. If we're having trouble seeing how extraordinary our children are, perhaps we're not looking at them in the right way. Could it be that we haven't yet let go of our own ideas and expectations?

Should we worry if our children appear to be ordinary? Oh no, because they're not!

Fearing Our Kids Will Fail

Sophie and Gemma-Rose announce their intention to enter a 10 K race. They're excited because they love running. They're willing to train hard. Which they do. Until Sophie's training is interrupted. She has her wisdom teeth removed by an oral surgeon. And for three weeks, she doesn't have the health or the energy to slip on her running shoes and head off to the bush tracks to exercise. Then just when she should be starting to feel better, her recovery is delayed by a gum infection. And a sore foot: maybe Sophie's orthotics need adjusting.

It's only a week before the big race, and Sophie has hardly run at all.

"Perhaps you shouldn't enter the 10 K race," I say. "You haven't run very far since your surgery. Your foot is hurting. And you said you haven't been sleeping well. Perhaps it would be sensible not to push yourself too far. How about running in the 5 K race instead?"

But Sophie ignores my words. "I'll be fine, Mum. This is something I want to do."

So I step back. I don't say another word. But I'm worried. What if Sophie can't run the distance? What if she fails?

Race day arrives. The girls line up with the other runners. They are smiling with anticipation. This is going to be hard work, but it's what they want to do.

The atmosphere is electric. Hundreds of people all sharing the same passion are gathering together. They stretch. They swing their arms. They smile. The clock ticks down. The race starter fires the gun. The girls fly by me and my camera, surrounded by runners of all ages and sizes. Soon they are out of sight.

I stand on the sidelines taking photos. Time passes. I catch a glimpse of both girls. Then a while later, I see them again. I look at my watch. Knowing my girls' best running times, I expect them to head over the finish line very soon. So that's where I go. "I want to be there when the girls finish the race," I tell Andy. Despite walking as fast as I can, I only just make it. As I'm taking up my position, Gemma-Rose sprints past me: "Gemma-Rose Elvis is coming over the line." I can hear the announcer with his loudspeaker. "Hey, isn't that a cool name?"

It is. But even cooler is Gemma-Rose's time. She's run the best 10 K of her life. But where's Sophie? Is she going to finish the race? Can she last the distance? I don't have to wonder for very long. Sophie flies over the line too.

And then she sinks to the ground. I'm a bit alarmed. Is she okay?

"I can't believe it, Mum" Sophie pants. "That's my best time ever. I looked at my pace at the 5 K mark, and I got worried. I thought I was running too quickly. I didn't know if I could keep up the pace until the end." But she did.

The girls grinned for days after that race. They'd both set themselves a challenge, worked hard and achieved great times. The best thing though wasn't the medals they brought home. It was the joy that flowed out of them. The joy that comes from doing something you love.

I'm so glad I stepped back and didn't persist with my negative words. Actually, I wish I hadn't said anything in the first place. How much better it would have been if I'd trusted Sophie's judgement completely.

I think about what would have happened if Sophie had listened to me and had decided not to enter the 10 K race after all. She wouldn't have come home grinning knowing she'd done her very best. My fears would have got in the way of both her achievement and her joy.

Why do I fear for my kids? Do I remember my own experiences of failing? Do the words of disappointed people still echo in my head? "I thought you said you could do that. What happened? You'll have to try harder if you want to succeed." Do I once again hear the laughs of my peers: "Did you see that girl who couldn't even swim the width of the pool? She stood up in the middle of the race!" Perhaps I decided it was better not even to try.

Sophie's achievement reminds me that our kids know themselves better than we do. We should encourage rather than squash them. Let them try. Because what's the worst that can happen?

"What would you have done if you'd run out of energy partway through the race?" I ask Sophie. "What if you hadn't been able to finish?"

"Oh, I would have finished," smiles Sophie. "Even if I'd had to walk over the line, I'd have completed the race."

But what if she hadn't? Would it have mattered? Is failing really such a big deal? No, of course not. We shouldn't fear failure.

What we should fear is not being willing to try.

When a Child Rejects Our Help

Charlotte and I chat as we walk back from the village shops.

"How's your university work going?" I ask.

Charlotte tells me about her latest assignment, a collaborative project. She describes the other members of her team. They come from diverse backgrounds and are of different ages. Charlotte at 17 is the youngest student. I ask Charlotte if she feels at a disadvantage because of her age. She says she doesn't. She feels confident and capable and is more than holding her own.

"So you're getting on okay?" I ask. Charlotte nods. She's having no problems at all studying at university level. It seems like Charlotte gave herself a good education. She prepared herself well for tertiary study.

Charlotte gave herself a good education? Yes, I hardly saw my daughter during her mid-teenage years. She knew what she wanted to do. She was in total control of her days. Charlotte only came to me when she needed some extra resources or on those rare occasions when she hit a problem that she couldn't sort out for herself. I wasn't really involved with her education in the couple of years before she started university.

Some people might think that stepping back and allowing a teenager so much freedom is a bit of a risk. But I didn't have much choice because this is the way Charlotte works. A few times I expressed a desire to get more involved with her life: "Do you need any help, Charlotte? Can I do anything with you?" And she very politely rebuffed me. She said she was quite happy working by herself. She worked better that way.

There were a few times when I worried I wasn't doing enough, so I tried to get closer, to get more involved with what Charlotte was doing. The result? Tension sprang up between us. So I decided it was better to leave Charlotte alone. But I thought I could at least ask her what she was doing. That sounded reasonable to me. But somehow, whenever I questioned my daughter, I got the feeling she thought I was interrogating her. Didn't I trust her? I did. So I stepped back. I let Charlotte do things her own way.

Did my confidence in Charlotte pay off? Yes, it did. She gave herself a good education and was able to go on and study at tertiary level without a problem.

Yes, Charlotte had no problems, but I have to admit that I had one. At odd moments, I wondered: was I still needed? My very independent daughter often seemed like she could cope very well without me. Perhaps I should have been happy about this because don't we want our children to become people who are capable of looking after themselves? We want them to be self-directed learners. But part of me couldn't cope when my offers of help were politely declined. I wanted to be a bigger part of my daughter's life.

Several years ago, Charlotte had to have her wisdom teeth removed at our local hospital. When it was time for my daughter to be wheeled away for surgery, the nurse said to me, "Do you want to come with us? You can stay while we do the prep."

I looked at Charlotte and said, "Do you want me to come with you?" and she smiled and said, "I'll be okay, Mum. You go and get some coffee. I'll see you when it's all over." Yes, once again, my very independent daughter didn't need me.

A couple of hours later, I was back in the waiting room, eager to hear how the surgery had gone.

The waiting room door opened. A nurse appeared. She beckoned me. "Charlotte needs her mum." I followed the nurse along the corridor and into the recovery room. As soon as Charlotte saw me, she gave me a watery smile. She withdrew a shaky hand from under the blanket and reached for mine. She held onto it very tightly as if I were her lifeline.

And I discovered that, despite her independent nature, Charlotte does need me. Not to do anything for her. Just to be her mother. To surround her with my love. To be her safe refuge when life gets difficult.

Our unschooling kids are very capable. Sometimes we might not feel needed. But we are. We play an essential role by encouraging their independence and not holding them back. We need to trust them.

Wrapped in our love, our children will get where they want to go.

Part XX: Criticism and Fears

How do we deal with other people's negative comments? What if someone criticises us for unschooling? Do their words cause our suppressed fears to rise to the surface? Perhaps other people are right. Unschooling might not be such a great idea after all. And if we do start to worry, will our kids pick up on our fears? Do we have to be careful about what we say?

How to Deal with Criticism and Our Fears

Some time ago, I was on YouTube watching a few unschooling videos. I saw one made by an unschooler who looked to be about ten years old. She was talking about her experience of unschooling and what she liked about it. She also explained why she hates school. There was a note: *Please be nice in the comments. If you don't have anything nice to say, please keep it to yourself.* Well, viewers didn't keep their comments to themselves: there are hundreds of comments on that video and more are added each week even though the video is a few years old. Few of them are positive.

Here's a sample of the comments:

Unschooling is a lazy way of life. People assumed that the girl couldn't be bothered to go to school and learn.

Learning can't take place outside of school. Most people couldn't understand why anybody would want to learn if nobody is forcing them.

Everyone else has to go to school, so why shouldn't you go to school too. Nobody has the right to stay home and be happy. There are some things we have just got to do. And going to school is one of them.

If you don't go to school, you won't get an education. If you don't finish school and get your leaving certificate you can't go to university. If you don't go to university, you won't end up with a degree. If you don't get a degree, you won't get a good job. If you don't get a good job, you won't have food...

When I saw all the negative comments, my heart skipped a beat. Would I be able to deal with such criticism? When we open ourselves up, when we are honest and put ourselves out there in the public eye, there is always a danger that people will come along and criticise us and our opinions.

Why do people react in such a negative way? Why do they feel they need, not only to express their opinion but to do it in a very unkind way? Do most people not have effective communication skills? Or do they have a lack of compassion and not care how their words affect other people? Perhaps they are just lazy in the way they express themselves.

My teenage daughter Sophie thinks that people hide behind their computer screens. They know they are never going to meet the people who they're criticising so they think they can say whatever they want. They can't see the other person's reaction so they don't have to face the fact that their words might result in a lot of hurt.

A lot of the video commenters weren't willing to listen to other people's opinions. They weren't open to new ideas. They didn't want to hear what the young unschooler had to say. All they were interested in was leaving some hurtful words.

I wonder if the majority of those people were satisfied with their own education. Do they really remember all they learnt at school? Is the knowledge that they learnt at school relevant to their lives? Were they happy at school? Did they really make the best friends of their lives during this time? I'm not sure that everybody who left a comment had a positive time at school, but they don't want to think about alternatives. They'd rather justify what they experienced.

For example, when we learn things that we have no need of people will say, "It's good for the brain to learn this or that even if we never use it. It's good discipline to learn things that we don't want to know about. You never know when that knowledge might come in handy." Except I think by the time it does come in handy, we will probably have forgotten it and we will have to go and learn it all over again.

If people were unhappy at school, then they won't say they want something better for their children. Instead, they say that they survived the school system and they are okay so their kids will survive it too. School will make them tough.

Yes, people, even when they know their experiences weren't good, justify them. Perhaps they don't want to think about a better way of doing things. It could just be easier to do what everybody else is doing. Thinking about new ideas might be too challenging. What if we decide we are wrong? We might have to change, not only our way of thinking but also what we're doing.

Even if we don't make any unschooling videos and post them on YouTube, we still might have to face criticism for choosing to live this way of life. So how do we deal with our critics? What strategies can we use, not only to protect ourselves from hurtful remarks but also to open the way for a fruitful discussion?

Maybe we need to be very knowledgeable about what we believe: what is unschooling? How does it work? Why do we want to do it? We have to be confident about what we're saying.

Of course, we have to recognise when it is a waste of time to respond to criticism. Some people are just not interested in engaging in a profitable discussion. But sometimes we do want to share what we're doing. Perhaps if our family and close friends understand unschooling, they might support us. So what can we say when someone says something negative about unschooling?

Whatever we say, we have to adopt a non-confrontational manner so that we don't get people offside before they start listening to us. We shouldn't let our emotions rule our words. If people have been unkind to us, we don't have to be unkind in return. We don't have to treat others as they are treating us.

Could we find some common ground, something we might agree with to get started? With carefully chosen words, we might be able to make connections with people who disagree with us. We can open the way for a possible conversation.

"Yes, unschooling does seem neglectful, doesn't it? I used to think it was too until I read..."

"Yes, it's not acceptable for children to be undisciplined and selfish. Maybe the family you're describing isn't really unschooling. Have you heard about unparenting?"

"Yes, it sounds like kids won't learn if they're not forced to, doesn't it? I used to think that too. Would you like to hear what my kids chose to do this week?"

Sometimes our efforts are rewarded. Sometimes they're not. But at least we've tried.

However good we are at explaining unschooling in a non-confrontational way, there are always going to be people who will refuse to be convinced. The only way to cope with this is to be confident about what we're doing. Even if no one agrees with us, we're going to do it anyway. We're not going to let anybody change our minds about how we want to unschool our children.

This is easy to say, but it can be very difficult in practice. We might think that we're secure in our opinions, but then, for example, we might see a YouTube video with a lot of negative comments. We could think, "I'm in the minority. Perhaps everyone else is right." Deep down, we don't really believe they are, but still, we waver. We don't immediately dismiss the comments. Why do we do this? Maybe we are still being influenced by our own experiences of school. Traditional thoughts about education rise to the top of our minds even if we don't want them to. We might have been trying to squash them, and then when we see a lot of critical comments about unschooling, our fears return. We start to go around the circle again, examining everything all over again.

Fears belong to the parent. They have nothing to do with the child. Whether we fear or not, a child is going to learn everything she needs to know, and she is going to be motivated to get where she wants to go. We have to find a way to believe this. We have to trust the learning process and our child. We have to gain confidence. But how do we do this?

We could find out more unschooling. Look at the evidence for it. Think about the questions that arise from negative criticism. Are they really true? Do they make sense? Perhaps we can turn things around: we can think about things in the opposite direction. Does school guarantee success? What is success? Do school kids ever fail to get into university? Are all school kids happy with where they end up? Are we satisfied with our education? Thinking about our own school experiences can be very helpful. Were we happy at school? Was everything that we learnt useful? Do we remember everything we learnt? Did we ever yearn for more time to spend on our interests? When we finished our formal education, did we ever sigh with relief and say, "I'm never going to learn anything ever again"? I remember saying this. Of course, what I meant was, "Nobody is ever going to make me learn anything ever again!"

Just because certain beliefs about education have been in existence for a long time doesn't make them right. I think many people recognise this. For example, they know that the school system is far from perfect. But they still send their children there. Thinking about this, leads to the thought: how can it be wrong to opt out of an imperfect system and do something that we feel is better for our children? Surely we're not the ones who can be criticised?

Ultimately, other people's opinions about our way of life shouldn't matter. We have to do what we feel is best for our family. That might mean we have to do without people's approval. This can be very difficult because we all like knowing that people think we're doing a great job. We like to hear praise and affirming comments from those around us, especially people that we love. Unfortunately, sometimes we have to choose. Do we do what other people would like us to do to get their approval? Or do we do what we feel is best for our family and go our own way? Of course, we don't have to feel entirely alone. We can always join up with an online community or a local unschooling community (if we're fortunate to have one!). We can find our tribe.

One last point: if we're doing things in a different way to most other people, we have to be careful what we share. Or we could just develop a thick skin. Remember the hundreds of comments on that unschooling video? There were lots of grammatical and spelling errors in them. But only the mistakes that were made by unschoolers were commented on. It seems that unschoolers have to be perfect.

Thinking Critically About Unschooling

Maybe we want to know more about unschooling. So where should we look for information? What sources can we trust?

We could start with the Internet, which is a wonderful resource. But before we dive in, it's good to be aware of one problem: there are just as many people out there on the Internet who criticise unschooling as praise it. Actually, there are probably more critics. And they've got very loud voices. Unschooling does suffer from a negative image. This is one of the reasons why I'm so passionate about writing and speaking about unschooling. Let's set the story straight. Unschooling is not what some people think it is.

So when you go looking for answers to questions, it can be a good idea to find out more about the authors of particular articles or the presenters of videos. Are they unschoolers? Have they any experience with unschooling? Are they criticising unschooling but have never actually tried it themselves? Because I think until you try unschooling, nobody really understands it properly.

So some people criticise unschooling, but they've never tried it themselves. For some reason, they don't like the sound of it, and they're going to warn people off. And then there are other people who may have tried unschooling, but it didn't work for them. But maybe it didn't work out because they didn't give it a fair go. Building up trust between children and parents doesn't happen overnight. It takes time for people to let go, to get used to a new way of doing things, to live life differently.

It could also be that some parents weren't really prepared to hand over control. Maybe they had their own ideas about what unschooling should be, and so the experience was a failure, and now they want to warn other people about it.

Or maybe some people met some unschoolers and want to warn others because they didn't like what they saw: "I know a family who unschools and their children are wild." Perhaps those children aren't really unschoolers. Their parents might think they're unschooling when in fact they are unparenting. Or those children might not be wild at all. Perhaps someone is just judging them.

So it can be tricky getting the right information from the Internet.

Sometimes emotional writing can distract us from the facts. We can get carried along by the author's feelings. We can feel her anger or horror or indignation. We begin to wonder: perhaps she's right to warn us about unschooling. Similarly, we can be affected by feelings of love and joy. Perhaps unschooling will fulfil our need of these emotions. We want to agree with the author. We don't look very closely at the facts.

And then there's authoritative language. When someone speaks with authority telling us what we should think and do, we might be tempted to believe they are experts. We wonder if we should listen.

But in all these situations, what are the facts? Where's the evidence for the arguments? Is there enough evidence to avoid unschooling? Or are we reassured and so are willing to give unschooling a go?

Of course, I have a problem with unschooling critics. But I do value critical thinking. A couple of my unschoolers did a critical thinking course at university. I observed from the sidelines. It was an interesting and valuable experience. Being able to think critically about any subject helps us to navigate our way through a vast sea of opinions.

I've only touched on the subject of thinking critically about unschooling, but maybe my words can be used as a starting point.

So what do you think? Will you get carried away by my emotional words of joy and peace? Will you give unschooling a go? I hope so!

Having the Confidence to Ignore the Opinions of Other People

Gemma-Rose is eight years old, and she still can't tell the time. Well, that's not quite true. If I put my watch in front of her and say, "What's the time?" she'll screw up her face and look unhappy for a while, and then eventually she'll give me the correct answer. But her calculating will be accompanied by a lot of huffing and puffing, and the answer won't arrive instantly.

Now this situation might shock some people. Can't all school kids of her age use an analogue watch? Perhaps it confirms some people's negative opinion of homeschooling or unschooling in particular.

I remember an interview I once watched on TV. A current affairs reporter, Matthew, was interviewing a homeschooling family. Both parents, together with their ten-year-old daughter, were in the studio. It must have been quite some time ago when homeschooling wasn't so widespread because this interview was still considered newsworthy enough to be shown on a prime time current affairs show.

It was obvious from the very first question that Matthew was anti-homeschooling.

"So you're teaching your daughter yourselves. And how is it going? Is she learning?" Without pausing for answers, he fired the next question at the daughter: "What's 8 x 9?"

The girl barely had time to think, and no time to answer, before another problem came hurtling towards her.

"So your daughter doesn't know what 8 x 9 is, or how to add up a few simple numbers. Doesn't that worry you? Don't you think you're disadvantaging her by taking her away from good schools?"

The parents tried to defend themselves and explain their educational philosophy, but the interviewer kept cutting into their answers. All he seemed to want to do was prove that homeschooling is a ridiculous idea. It doesn't work. Any parents who remove their children from school are being selfish and irresponsible. And he based his opinion on the girl's inability to answer what he considered to be a few straightforward maths problems.

I think of that girl sitting under the studio lights with cameras pointing at her, listening to the questions of an aggressive stranger. Is it any wonder she couldn't come up with the right answers? And even if she didn't know what 8 x 9 is, does that prove homeschooling doesn't result in learning, that it's a failure? Probably she knew a great deal about other things, things the interviewer didn't think (or want) to question her about.

But back to Gemma-Rose. She can write a novel. She can read Shakespeare and discuss a play intelligently. She can discuss history with her siblings. She reads book after book after book. She knows how to work out her times tables even if she can't recite them quickly. She is familiar with Gilbert and Sullivan, many ballets, lots of poems and paintings and pieces of classical music. She has excellent computer skills. She can make an animated movie and design a computer game. She draws and plays the piano and sings and runs like the wind. I could go on and on. Does it really matter that she can't tell the time?

Can't tell the time?

"Gemma-Rose, can you tell the time?" I ask her.

"Of course I can," she replies rather indignantly.

"What do you use to tell the time?"

"My computer."

Gemma-Rose tells the time using the digital clock on her computer. And now I realise something. She doesn't use her analogue watch. It seems to have disappeared into our home's black hole. We don't have an analogue clock on the wall. Everything in our house is digital. Gemma-Rose doesn't need to know analogue time. She has no use for it. She remembers the principles that I explained to her a while ago, but she has never had a chance to practise them.

So what do I do?

I could find some online interactive activities involving analogue time for her to play with.

I could buy an analogue clock and put it on the kitchen wall where she'll see it every day. I'm sure she'll soon start to look at it and wonder and work things out for herself.

Or I could do nothing. She'll learn analogue time properly one day if she ever finds she needs it.

I think if I choose the last option, I will warn her: "Gemma-Rose, please do not go anywhere near a TV or newspaper reporter. Refuse to answer any questions."

I think of those poor bewildered parents who were interviewed on TV, and I remember how angry I felt. They were two people doing their best for their child, and they were portrayed as fools. Did their confidence take a battering that day? Did their trust in their daughter's ability to learn evaporate because of the aggressive opinion of a stranger? I hope not. Other people's words and opinions shouldn't have so much power over us. But we are human.

My daughter Gemma-Rose who is eight years old (going on nine) still hasn't conquered analogue time. I am announcing it to the world. Will anyone judge unschooling on that statement? Will they compare my daughter's abilities with those of other children? Or will they think, like me, "She will learn everything she needs to know when she needs to know it"?

Yes, I have confidence in my children's ability to learn. And I think Gemma-Rose is doing just fine.

My Teenagers' Unschooling Days

On a typical day, my daughter Sophie (16) gets out of bed soon after 5 am. By 6.10 am, she's heading out the door with sister Imogen who drives her to work. A few minutes later, Gemma-Rose (14) and I also leave the house. We're on our way to the bush tracks at the end of our road for our morning run.

This is how my unschooling teenagers' typical days begin.

A typical day doesn't stay typical for very long. As my girls grow and develop and learn, what they do each day changes. But at any one moment in time, I can say: this is what my children are doing right now. These are their current typical unschooling days.

At the moment, Sophie's part-time job dominates her days. Long empty days, waiting to be filled with whatever she likes, are a thing of the past. I feel rather sad about this. However, Sophie accepts this new situation. Actually, she has chosen it. You see, she has plans. She hopes the skills she's learning and the money she earns from her job will allow her to continue following her passions. In her free time, Sophie works on those passions: she takes photos, cooks, reads, writes, goes to the gym and makes vlogs.

Sophie works in a cafe/post office/ general store from 7 am until 2 pm. Then she catches a bus and a train, and almost an hour and a half later, she arrives at a local town. I meet Sophie at the train station, and we swap news as I'm driving towards the gym. Once there, I hand Sophie her gym bag and then she disappears inside the building to do her workout. While Sophie is exercising, I visit the shopping centre where I buy a coffee, and then I sit at a table in the food court, pull out my iPad and do some work.

"Tell me about your workout," I say as we're driving home. Sophie tells me about the latest program she's using.

Then she says, "I was listening to a podcast about strength training on the bus. Do you want to know what I found out?" I do. For the rest of our journey home, Sophie and I chat about one of her passions: fitness and health.

Gemma-Rose's typical days are totally different from Sophie's. On a typical stay-at-home day, after our morning run, she will help me with the chores. Then we spend some time together. "What shall we do today?" we ask each other. "Shall we watch another episode of *Back in Time for Dinner*? How about reading another chapter of *Great Expectations*? I found some articles about *The Secrets of Your Food*. Do you want to read them? I've put some links to some things that sound interesting in this term's Evernote notebook. Would you like to take a look? Or do you have plans of your own?"

So I spend most mornings with my teenage daughter doing things we both enjoy. We might have a Shakespeare period or a Jane Austen one. Maybe a video will lead us on some interesting science adventures. Or our attention might be captured by a local event or something that's happening further afield. Usually, we're immersed in some topic or other until our curiosity is satisfied. Then we move on to something new.

Lunch time arrives. I ask Gemma-Rose how she plans to spend her afternoon. "I'm going to walk the dog and then do some drawing," she says. Gemma-Rose also plans to practise the piano, work on her novel and cook the dinner.

While Gemma-Rose is occupied, I get involved with my work and interests. I blog or make a podcast or work on one of my books. At about 3 pm, I drive into town to meet Sophie's train. And that's when my day overlaps with hers.

And when Sophie and I arrive home from town, Sophie's day overlaps with Gemma-Rose's.

After Sophie and I walk through the door, someone fills the kettle. Soon we're sipping tea and swapping news of our days. Then Gemma-Rose announces it's dinner time and we head for the table.

Dinner, good conversation, dishes.

One of our dogs barks. She has heard a noise at the door. It's Andy home from work. He's late. There always seems to be one more thing he needs to do for one more person at school before he can set off for home. That's just life, so we don't complain. But we don't wait dinner for Andy either. Unless, of course, we get one of those delightful text messages: "I've finished early. See you for dinner!"

Andy eats his dinner. We again swap news.

Then it's time for a movie or a computer game or a book. Unless it's choir practice night.

Sophie heads to bed first. She has to be up first. I say goodnight next. I don't know what time Gemma-Rose goes to bed. She decides how much sleep she needs. She always appears bright and early for our morning run, so I suppose she has got it all worked out perfectly.

It's 6 am. Sophie is packing her bag and getting ready to leave for work. I'm filling water bottles. Gemma-Rose appears with her running shoes. Imogen is looking for the car keys. Charlotte is still in bed!

And so begins another typical unschooling day.

Part XXI: School

What Do I Think of School?

It's no secret that, as a child, I hated school. It seemed like a waste of time. I had to learn things I wasn't interested in just to pass exams, and when I'd achieved that, I instantly let all that knowledge seep out of my brain. I was kept so busy that I had no time to discover who I am and what talents I have.

More importantly, I didn't like school because of the social side. I was a fringe dweller, someone trying to survive in the harsh school environment that favoured cool kids. I felt different. Not unique and interesting different but unpopular and strange different.

Every year at school, we had to give a speech. One year we had to talk about why school days are the best days of our lives. I remember thinking that if school days are the best days I'm ever going to experience, then the rest of my life is going to be awful. Of course, it isn't. The first day of the rest of my life was when I started living properly. School life is not real life.

I don't want my children to endure the heartbreak and waste of time that I experienced as a child. I'd like them to enjoy their younger child and teenage years without the pressure of having to meet other people's very unimportant expectations. They need to love learning for its own sake. I want my children to know they are uniquely different, and that is good. It's absolutely fine. They have talents and skills they should develop and use. They, like everyone, have a special mission in life. So my children don't go to school.

I feel very blessed that we can keep our children at home. I feel doubly blessed that we are unschoolers living a free life away from other people's timetables and expectations. When we drive past a school, and we see the children all lined up ready to enter the classroom for a day of lessons, I'm very thankful we are outside in the real world, able to do whatever we like.

Yes, there's a lot wrong with the school system. Children shouldn't have to sit at their desks for so many hours a day when the sun is shining, and the world is beckoning. They shouldn't be segregated into particular age groups. They should be able to choose what they learn. And there should be no such thing as exams. I could say more, but you get the idea. And anyway, I don't really want to say more. You see, my husband Andy is a school teacher.

How can Andy go off to school each day and teach in a system that we don't really believe in? He does it because not all children are as fortunate as ours. Schools will always be needed. Not all parents want to homeschool. Not all parents even want their kids at home outside of school hours. Unbelievable as it may seem, school is a refuge for some kids.

My husband is a good teacher. He cares about his students and does all he can for them within the school system. Can one good teacher make a difference in a child's life? We have to believe he can otherwise why try? And I do think one person can influence a life. How many times do we look back and think of one particular person and remember a significant action or word? Those memories can spur us on. They change the way we think about the world.

Even though I know the school system is in desperate need of reform, I don't get visibly angry about it. I don't write articles that ask people to rise up and demand change. I don't do this because my mission isn't to get involved in school reform. There are other people with different skills from mine who are doing that. I have something else I feel I am called to do.

I want to share experiences and information that might help families who want to live outside the school system, who wouldn't use schools even if they were reformed. I want to reassure parents who are unsure about unschooling that children can learn, not only without school but also without the control that comes with structured homeschooling. We can live a free life of love and joy. And our kids will thrive and grow and become the people they are meant to be. Most of all, I want to write about unconditional love.

So what do I think of school? I'm glad my school days are over. I'm grateful my kids don't have to go to school. I also recognise that some people want to send their kids to school. Everyone should be free to make their own choices.

I'd like to add that even if our children or we have had horrific school experiences, it's not the end of the story. School doesn't have the last word. Our lives are what we make of them. After school comes real life. And that can be a huge unschooling adventure!

What if a Child Wants to Go to School?

We're standing on the banks of the river. The sun is rising. I aim my camera towards the orange and red and purples of the early morning sun.

Hallelujah, Hallelujah, Hallelujah, Hallelujah

The words of Leonard Cohen's song float over the water.

I lower my camera and swing it towards my daughter Imogen.

And I think, "Can there be anything more joyful than watching the sun rise over a slowly flowing river while listening to a daughter singing *Hallelujah*?"

There have been times in my life when I thought joy had disappeared forever. Long black days. Days when I was stuck at the bottom of a pit of misery. When the sun didn't rise. But the sun is certainly rising today. The joy I feel eclipses the former pain.

I take hundreds of photos. I capture the sky, Imogen singing, Sophie filming Imogen, Gemma-Rose operating the music, and Charlotte taking clips of everything we're doing so that she can make a behind-the-scenes music video.

Later, when my girls and I have finished filming Imogen's music video, we gather around a picnic table. It's time for breakfast. We chat while we eat.

"Aren't we fortunate?" I say. "While most other people are getting ready for work or school, we're sitting here in the nature reserve. We saw the sun rising. We made a music video. We live such a good life!"

"I'm so glad we don't go to school," says Sophie.

"Why would anyone want to go to school?" asks Gemma-Rose. She looks confused.

Yes, the thought that anyone would want to swap an amazing unschooling life for school seems rather unbelievable to my girls. But it does happen. Or so I've heard.

We ponder Gemma-Rose's question. We think about possible reasons a child might announce that she'd like to go to school.

"A child could be lonely and would like to have more friends."

"Could she feel odd or different? Does she want to be like her age peers so that she feels she belongs?"

"Could a child be curious about school? Maybe his friends go to school, and he wants to try it as well."

There are other possible reasons:

Could a child be worried that she's not learning enough at home? Perhaps she compares herself to her school friends. She realises that they know more about some things than she does. They earn grades that 'prove' they know a lot. (Or at least have memorised the required facts.) Perhaps she feels stupid when talking to her school friends. (They might think she's stupid too.) She doesn't realise that she knows much more about other things than they do.

Perhaps a child doesn't value the things he does know because he feels that the people around him don't value them. Could his family and friends be passing on the message that the formal subjects such as maths and English are more important than his passions?

Maybe the child wants to go to university. Do people wonder how she's going to get there? Do they express their concerns? Does she start to get anxious about the next stage of her life as well?

"Should kids be allowed to go to school?" I ask my girls.

"Yes."

But maybe that's not the real answer. Or the right question. Before enrolling a child in school, could we find out what a child hopes to gain by going to school? What needs will the school experience fulfil? Perhaps these needs can be met in a different way.

We might identify a child's needs by listening carefully.

And then we could explore questions like these:

- Do we provide a stimulating and interesting home life?
- Do we have confidence in our kids?
- Do we encourage and support them? Do we show them we value what they're doing and are willing to help them achieve their goals in any way we can?
- Do we pass on our worries about such things as university?
- Do we want to spend time with our kids? Do we listen and talk? Are we willing to be our children's friends?
- Do our kids need extra opportunities to socialise? Could we help them find suitable groups to join? Are we willing to include our child's friends in our lives?
- Do we revel in our differentness? Is being different celebrated? Does each child know she is accepted and valued for herself?

"None of us wants to go to school," I say, "so we don't really know the reasons a child might want to go there."

Yes, we're just pondering. All we know about is the joy of living an unschooling way of life.

There *is* something else I'm aware of.

I'm sitting here on a weekday morning, chatting to my kids about school instead of hurrying to get them there on time.

For that, I am truly grateful.

Part XXII: Some Last Thoughts

Does the World Need Unschooling?

Maybe after reading my stories, you've decided that unschooling does work. It's a viable option. Unschooling is good for our children. It's good for our families. Maybe you don't need another reason for adopting this way of life. But can I give you one anyway?

Could the world need unschooling?

I think we are all born with the desire to do something meaningful with our lives. We want to make a difference. Just look at young children playing. They dress up as superheroes. They flap their capes and jump from chairs ready to save the world. Parents smile indulgently. Kids are cute. It's a delightful stage of life.

Of course, things change. School days arrive. Life gets serious. There's no time to imagine and dream and make plans to save the world. The capes and masks and tights are left in the dress up box. They're no longer needed. Their owners are growing up. They have their minds on other things. They've learnt that they're not going to be superheroes after all. They have discovered that they have to fulfil other people's expectations. That's going to keep them very busy.

But what would happen if we didn't keep kids busy by making them do what we feel is important? What if we gave them time to find out what they are good at, what they enjoy doing, and what they could achieve? Would they set themselves goals? Would they choose to work hard doing things that are important to them, things they believe in?

Would they still think they can save the world?

Of course, superheroes come in all shapes and sizes. They don't have to look like Mr Incredible or Superwoman. It's not about appearance or even our superhero powers. Anyone can be a superhero. All we need is passion. To have a purpose in life. And then to work hard at it.

Why don't we encourage our kids to follow their passions? To dream big? To go where they want to go? Perhaps we think we know better than them.

Maybe we make kids do things our way because we want them to have a secure future. We think it's prudent to follow the safe and sensible path. But maybe safe and sensible isn't what they need. The amount of money we earn isn't everything. A purpose in life is much more important. This purpose will motivate and push kids to become the people they are designed to be. If we let them, they will rise to the occasion. They will be passionate and enthusiastic about who they are and where they are going. They will experience joy. And who knows where they will end up? Perhaps the things kids choose to do will end up changing the world.

Yes, the world needs people who are passionate, who can think for themselves, who are willing to go out there and work hard at something they believe is important so that they can make a difference.

We can choose safe and secure, which might threaten our kids' happiness and motivation to work hard. Or we could step back and trust. Don't let our fears interfere with our child's mission in life.

Let them, in their own way, make a difference because that's what the world requires.

The world needs unschooling.

Is it Time to Unschool?

You've read my unschooling stories. What do you think? If you're not already unschooling, are you ready to set out on this adventure? Or do you still feel uncomfortable with some of the ideas I've presented? Maybe, despite my reassuring words, unschooling sounds a bit frightening. Perhaps even after reading my book, you feel unprepared for the next huge step.

You could be thinking, "I should read one more book or one more blog before I decide. Ask a few more questions. Think about it for a bit longer."

Yes, we can learn a lot by sharing other people's experiences. But after a while, this isn't enough. If we really want to understand what unschooling is all about, we have to actually start unschooling.

But what if things don't go smoothly? Maybe your kids won't be as eager to learn as you hope. Or they might want to spend their time doing things you don't value. Perhaps you'll get impatient. You might not want to be accepting. Will you end up saying, "This isn't how I imagined unschooling!"?

Life won't instantly become perfect just because you decide to unschool. (Life will never be perfect!) It takes time to let go of old thoughts and put new ones into action. Yes, you might hit a few problems. Just don't give up. Instead, keep trying. Keep learning. Remember what's important and why you wanted to unschool in the first place. Love and forgive and trust. If you go slowly and push through, you'll get there.

And it will be worth it.

Do something important for your family. Be brave. Let go and unschool. If you do, you'll arrive somewhere amazing!

Is it Time to Radically Unschool?

Right back at the beginning of this book, I spoke briefly about radical unschooling, which is an extension of unschooling. Radical unschoolers let unschooling spill over into all aspects of their lives, not just the educational part.

Radical unschooling might sound even more frightening than the regular kind of unschooling. Is it really okay to let kids make their own decisions about every area of their lives? What if they make the wrong choices? What if they become wild? Will everyone think that we are irresponsible parents?

Radical unschooling has a very negative image. If you do some googling, it won't take you long to find lots of stories about kids who won't wash and who eat nothing but junk food. Perhaps they're reluctant to help with the chores. They might spend all night playing computer games or making lots of noise with their friends while parents want to sleep. By the sounds of it, these kids lead very self-centred lives. The stories might convince you that giving kids so much freedom is wrong.

But I don't think these stories are necessarily radical unschooling ones. They sound more like unparenting stories to me. No, in my experience, radical unschooling doesn't look like this at all.

Radical unschooling is a life of unconditional love:

Live radically.

Love unconditionally.

When we love unconditionally, we become connected with our kids. We respect and trust them. They respect and trust us. We listen to each other and discuss anything and everything. The lines of communication are open. And although kids could do whatever they like, they choose to use their freedom to do what is good and right. (Of course, no one is perfect.)

So radical unschooling doesn't result in wild kids who care about nobody but themselves. Instead, radical unschooling is all about connecting family members together with strong bonds of love so that they can learn from each other, support and encourage and help one another, and enjoy being together. Radical unschooling is really all about families helping each other become the people we are meant to be.

Would you like to hear more? I hope so because I'm passionate about radical unschooling! I want to say, "Unschooling is very good indeed, but radical unschooling is even better. Take the next step. Don't be scared."

If you have enjoyed this book, I hope you'll want to read my second unschooling book: *Radical Unschool Love*. It's the next instalment of our unschooling story.

Notes

Why Unschooling Isn't a Method of Homeschooling

Quote from *Unschooling 101* by Bridget Bentz Sizer

Sandra Dodd's website: *Sandra Dodd*

Igniting a Child's Love of Learning

Books by Suzie Andres:

Homeschooling with Gentleness

A Little Way of Homeschooling: Thirteen Families Discover Catholic Unschooling

Does Unschooling Work? / What Do Children Need to Learn? / Making Children Learning What They Don't Want to Know / Preparing Our Kids for an Unknown Future

Quotes by John Holt

Books by John Holt

How Children Learn

How Children Fail

Learning All the Time

Teach Your Own

Encouraging Our Kids to Become Independent Learners

Leonie's blog post: *Nurturing Independence*

Leonie's blog: *Living Without School*

Helping a Child Discover Her Talents

Quote from the TEDx talk *Life is Your Talents Discovered* by Sir Ken Robinson

Where You Can Find Us

My blog: *Stories of an Unschooling Family*

My podcast: *Stories of an Unschooling Family*

My YouTube channel: *Sue Elvis*

My Instagram account: stories_ofan_unschoolingfamily

My second unschooling book:

Radical Unschool Love

My children's novels:

The Angels of Abbey Creek

The Angels of Gum Tree Road

Imogen's novel: *The Crystal Tree*

Imogen's website: *Write. Rewrite. Read*

Imogen's Instagram Account: write.rewrite.read

Imogen's music on YouTube: *Imogen Elvis*

Acknowledgements

Thank you to my daughters Imogen and Charlotte for your help designing the cover and formatting this book.

Thank you to my beta readers Jacqueline, Anna and Imogen. Your suggestions and sharp typo-spotting eyes are appreciated.

Thank you to Hayley for transcribing many of my videos and podcasts so that I could turn them into stories for this book.

And a huge thank you to my family Andy, Felicity, Duncan, Callum, Imogen, Charlotte, Thomas, Sophie and Gemma-Rose for letting me write your stories. Without you, there would be no book.

Sue Elvis is a long time unschooling mother who lives with her husband Andy and some of their eight children somewhere south of Sydney, Australia.

Sue enjoys running through the beautiful Australian bush with her children and her dogs, Nora and Quinn. While she is racing up and down the hills, she thinks up new ways to spread the word about unschooling.

When she's not having fantastic learning adventures with her family, Sue can found at her computer tapping out books and blog posts, recording podcasts, and uploading videos to YouTube.

Made in United States
Orlando, FL
29 April 2024